Rick Steves'
PARIS

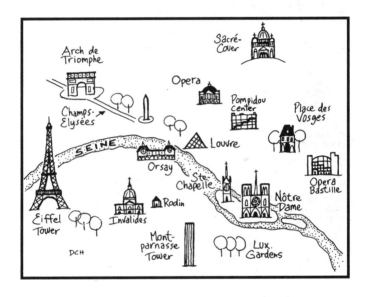

by Rick Steves, Steve Smith
and Gene Openshaw

John Muir Publications
Santa Fe, New Mexico

Other JMP travel guidebooks by Rick Steves
Europe 101: History and Art for the Traveler (with Gene Openshaw)
Rick Steves' Europe Through the Back Door
Rick Steves' Mona Winks (with Gene Openshaw)
Rick Steves' Best of Europe
Rick Steves' France, Belgium & the Netherlands (with Steve Smith)
Rick Steves' Germany, Austria & Switzerland
Rick Steves' Great Britain & Ireland
Rick Steves' Italy
Rick Steves' London (with Gene Openshaw)
Rick Steves' Postcards from Europe
Rick Steves' Russia & the Baltics (with Ian Watson)
Rick Steves' Scandinavia
Rick Steves' Spain & Portugal
Asia Through the Back Door (with Bob Effertz)
Rick Steves' Phrase Books: German, Italian, French,
     Spanish/Portuguese, and French/Italian/German

John Muir Publications, P.O. Box 613, Santa Fe, NM 87504
Copyright © 1999 by Europe Through the Back Door
Cover copyright © 1999 by John Muir Publications
All rights reserved.

Printed in the United States of America. Third printing April 1999.

Portions of this book were originally published in *Rick Steves' Mona Winks*
© 1998, 1996, 1993, 1988 by Rick Steves and Gene Openshaw and in *Rick Steves'*
France, Belgium & the Netherlands © 1999, 1998, 1997, 1996, 1995 by Rick Steves
and Steve Smith.

ISBN 1-56261-468-1
ISSN 1522-3299

For the latest on Rick's lectures, guidebooks, tours, and public television series,
contact Europe Through the Back Door, Box 2009, Edmonds, WA 98020,
tel. 425/771-8303, fax 425/771-0833, Web site: www.ricksteves.com, or e-mail:
rick@ricksteves.com.

Europe Through the Back Door Editor: Risa Laib
John Muir Publications Editors: Dianna Delling, Krista Lyons-Gould
Production: Janine Lehmann
Cover and Interior Design: Janine Lehmann
Typesetting: Kathleen Sparkes
Maps: David C. Hoerlein
Photography: Rick Steves, unless otherwise noted
Printer: Publishers Press
Front cover photo: Tour Eiffel; Paris, France; copyright © Blaine Harrington III

Distributed to the book trade by Publishers Group West,
Berkeley, California

Although the author and publisher have made every effort to provide accurate,
up-to-date information, they accept no responsibility for loss, injury, loose stools,
or inconvenience sustained by any person using this book.

CONTENTS
paris

NUMBERS INDICATE ARRONDISSEMENTS (DISTRICTS)

1/2 MILE

INTRODUCTION

Paris—the City of Light—has been a beacon of culture for centuries. As a world capital for art, fashion, food, literature, and ideas, it stands as a symbol of all of the fine things that human civilization can offer. Come prepared to celebrate rather than judge the cultural differences, to capture the romance and joie de vivre that Paris exudes.

Paris offers sweeping boulevards, sleepy parks, world-class art galleries, chatty crêpe stands, Napoleon's body, sleek shopping malls, the Eiffel Tower, and people-watching from outdoor cafés. Climb the Notre-Dame and Eiffel Tower, cruise the Seine and the Champs-Élysées, and master the Louvre and Orsay museums. Save some after-dark energy for one of the world's most romantic cities.

Sip decaf with Deconstructionists in a street-side café. Step into an Impressionist painting in a tree-lined park. Endure a rude waiter in the same restaurants that once insulted other visitors, from van Gogh and Picasso to Hemingway and Gershwin to Milan Kundera and Woody Allen.

This Information Is Accurate and Up-to-Date

This book is updated every year. Most publishers of guidebooks that cover a city from top to bottom can afford an update only every two or three years. Since this book is selective, covering only the places we think make the top week or 10 days in and around Paris, we can update it each summer. Even with an annual update, things change. But if you're traveling with the current edition of this book, we guarantee you're using the most up-to-date information available. This book will help you have an inexpensive, hassle-free trip. Use this year's edition. Saving a few bucks by traveling on old information is not smart. If you're packing an old book, you'll learn the seriousness of your mistake . . . in Paris. Your trip costs at least $10 per waking hour. Your time is valuable. This guidebook saves lots of time.

Welcome to Our Paris City Guide

This book is organized in the following way:

Paris Orientation includes tourist information, public transportation, and easy-to-read maps. The "Planning Your Time" section offers a suggested schedule with thoughts on how to best use your limited time.

Sights provides a succinct overview of Paris' most important sights, arranged by neighborhood, with ratings: ▲▲▲—Don't miss; ▲▲—Try hard to see; ▲—Worthwhile if you can make it; No rating—Worth knowing about.

The **Walks** cover five of Paris' most enjoyable neighborhoods: Historic Core of Paris (Notre-Dame and Sainte-Chapelle), Champs-Élysées, Marais, rue Cler (near Eiffel Tower), and Montmartre.

The **Self-Guided Museum Tours** take you through Paris' seven most interesting museums: Louvre, Orsay, L'Orangerie, Rodin, Cluny, Napoleon's Tomb, and Versailles.

Day Trips recommends nearby sights, ranging from châteaus to Monet's Giverny to Disneyland Paris.

Sleeping in Paris is a guide to our favorite budget hotels in three cozy neighborhoods, with orientation tips geared to make you feel at home.

Eating in Paris offers good-value restaurants ranging from inexpensive eateries to splurges, arranged by neighborhood, with a special section on Grand Cafés.

Paris with Children includes our top 10 recommendations to keep your kids (and you) happy in Paris.

Shopping in Paris helps you shop painlessly and enjoyably, without letting it overwhelm your vacation or ruin your budget.

Paris at Night is a guide to entertainment and evening fun, with music, bus tours, and river cruises, plus information on how to easily translate *Pariscope* magazine, the weekly entertainment guide.

Transportation Connections covers connections by train and plane, with detailed information on Paris' two airports and six train stations, laying the groundwork for your smooth arrival and departure.

The **Appendix** includes a Paris history, climate chart, telephone tips, French survival phrases, and a handy almanac of resources.

Throughout the book, when you see a ✪ in a listing, it means that the sight is covered in much more depth in one of our walks or self-guided tours—a page number will tell you just where to look to find more information.

Browse through this book and choose your favorite sights. Then have a great trip! You'll become your own guide with our self-guided walks and museum tours. Traveling like a temporary local, you'll get the absolute most out of every mile, minute, and dollar. You won't waste time on mediocre sights because, unlike other guidebooks, we cover only the best. Since lousy, expensive hotels are a major financial pitfall, we've worked hard to assemble the best accommodations values. And, as you explore the city we know and love, we're happy you'll be meeting some of our favorite Parisian people.

Trip Costs

Five components make up your trip costs: airfare, surface transportation, room and board, sightseeing/entertainment, and shopping/miscellany.

Airfare: Don't try to sort through the mess. Find and use a good travel agent. A basic round-trip U.S.A.–Paris flight costs $700 to $1,100, depending on where you fly from and when.

Surface Transportation: For a typical one-week visit, allow about $50 for Métro tickets and a couple of day trips. Add an additional $100 if you opt for taxi rides to and from the airport (or save money by taking a shuttle express, airport bus, or the RER).

Room and Board: You can thrive in Paris on $70 a day per person for room and board. A $70-a-day budget allows $10 for lunch, $20 for dinner, and $40 for lodging (based on two people splitting the cost of a $80 double room that includes breakfast). That's doable. Students and tightwads do it on $40 ($20 per bed, $15–20 for meals and snacks). But budget sleeping and eating require aggressive utilization of the skills and information covered in this book (and in much greater depth in *Rick Steves' Europe Through the Back Door*).

Sightseeing and Entertainment: We recommend getting the Paris Museum Pass, which covers most sights in Paris. (For more information, see Sights chapter.) You'll pay about $30 for a three-day pass and $45 for a five-day pass. Without a museum pass, figure $6 to $8 per major sight (e.g., Louvre is $8, Rodin is $6), $4 for minor ones (climbing church towers), and $25 for bus tours and splurge experiences (concerts in Sainte-Chapelle). An overall average of $15 a day works for most. Don't skimp here. After all, this category directly powers most of the experiences all the other expenses are designed to make possible.

Shopping and Miscellany: Figure $3 per ice-cream cone, coffee, or soft drink. Shopping can vary in cost from nearly nothing to a small fortune. Good budget travelers find that this category has little to do with assembling a trip full of lifelong and wonderful memories.

Exchange Rate

We've priced things in this book in the local currency:

> 5.5 French francs (F) = about $1.

To easily convert French prices into dollars, divide by five. (Say 120F = $24, even though it's actually $22.)

Prices, Times, and Discounts

The prices in this book, as well as the hours and telephone numbers, are accurate as of late 1998. Europe is always changing, and we know you'll understand that this, like any other guidebook, starts to yellow even before it's printed.

In Europe—and in this book—you'll be using the 24-hour clock. After 12 noon, keep going—13:00, 14:00, and so on. For anything over 12, subtract 12 and add p.m. (for example, 14:00 is 2:00 p.m.).

This book lists peak-season hours for sightseeing attractions. Off-season, expect generally shorter hours and more lunchtime breaks.

While discounts for sights and transportation are not listed in this book, seniors (60 and over), students (with International Student Identification Cards), and youths (under 18) often get big discounts—but only by asking.

When to Go

Late spring and fall are best for weather but most crowded. Summers are generally hot and dry; look for the rare room with air-conditioning if you wilt in the heat. Hotels are easy in the summer, and while many French businesses close in August, the traveler hardly notices. Paris makes a great winter getaway. Airfares are cheap and the city feels lively but not particularly touristy. The only problem—weather—is fixed by dressing correctly. Expect cold and rain but no snow.

Red Tape and Business Hours

You need a passport but no visa or shots to travel in France. On Monday many businesses are closed until 14:00, and often all day. Many small markets, *boulangeries* (bakeries), and the like are open Sunday morning until 12:00.

PTT (Postal, Telegraph, and Telephone) offices' hours vary, though most are open weekdays from 8:00 to 19:00 and Saturdays from 8:00 to 12:00. Stamps are also sold at the *tabac* (tobacco shop).

Banking

Bring your ATM, credit, or debit card, along with traveler's checks in dollars.

The best and easiest way to get cash in French francs is to use the omnipresent French bank machines (always open, lower fees, quick processing); you'll need a four-digit PIN (numbers only, no letters) with your Visa or MasterCard. Some ATM bankcards will work at some banks, though Visa and MasterCard are more reliable. Before you go, verify with your bank that your card will work. Bring two different cards or two copies of the same card; demagnetization seems to be a common problem. "Cash machine" in French is *distributeur automatique des billets*, or D.A.B. (day-ah-bay).

Regular banks have the best rates for cashing traveler's checks. For a large exchange, it pays to compare rates and fees. The Bank of France (Banque de France) usually offers the best rates. Banking hours vary, though most are open Tuesday through Friday 9:00 to 16:30. Some branches open Saturday morning, and many close on Monday.

Post offices, train stations, and tourist offices usually change money if you can't get to a bank. Post offices (which take cash or American Express checks) give a good rate, have longer hours, and charge no fee.

Just like at home, credit (or debit) cards work easily at larger hotels, restaurants, and shops. Smaller businesses prefer payment in local currency. Smart travelers function with hard local cash.

Don't be petty about changing money. The greatest avoidable money-changing expense is having to waste time every few days returning to a bank. Change 10 days' or two weeks' worth of money, get big bills, stuff it in your money belt, and travel!

The Language Barrier

You've no doubt heard that the French are "mean and cold and refuse to speak English." This is an out-of-date preconception left over from the de Gaulle days. The French are as friendly as any other people. Parisians are no more disagreeable than New Yorkers. And, without any doubt, the French speak more English than Americans speak French. Be reasonable in your expectations: Small-town French postal clerks are every bit as speedy, cheery, and multilingual as ours are back home.

With an understanding of French culture, you're less likely to misinterpret the French people. The French take great pride in their culture, clinging to their belief in cultural superiority despite the fact that they're no longer a world superpower. Let's face it, it's tough to keep on smiling when you've been crushed by a Big Mac, lashed by Levis, and drowned in instant coffee. To the French,

America must seem a lot like Ross Perot in a good mood. The French are cold only if you decide to see them that way. Look for friendliness and give them the benefit of the doubt. The cultural fine points, not rugged Yankee individualism, are respected here.

Communication difficulties in France are exaggerated. To hurdle the language barrier, bring a small English/French dictionary, a phrase book (look for ours), a menu reader, and a good supply of patience. If you learn only six phrases, learn and use these: *bonjour* (good day), *pardon* (pardon me), *s'il vous plaît* (please), *merci* (thank you), *au revoir* (good-bye), and *Comment trouvez-vous mon haleine?* (how's my breath?). The French place great importance on politeness.

The French are language perfectionists—they take their language (and other languages) seriously. Often, they speak more English than they let on. This isn't a tourist-baiting tactic but timidity on their part to speak another language less than fluently. Start any conversation with "*Bonjour, Madame/Monsieur. Parlez-vous anglais?*" and hope they speak more English than you speak French. In transactions, a small notepad and pen minimize misunderstandings about prices—have vendors write down the price.

Travel Smart

Reread this book as you travel. Buy a phone card and use it for reservations and confirmations. Enjoy the friendliness of the local people. Ask questions. Most locals are eager to point you in their idea of the right direction. Wear your money belt and see simplicity as a virtue. Those who expect to travel smart, do. Plan ahead for banking, laundry, post office chores, and picnics. Mix intense and relaxed periods. Every trip (and every traveler) needs at least a few slack days. Pace yourself. Assume you will return.

As you read through this book, note the days when sights are closed. Sundays have pros and cons, as they do for travelers in the U.S.A. (special events and weekly markets, limited hours, shops and banks closed, limited public transportation, no rush hours). Saturdays are virtually weekdays (with most places open until lunchtime). Popular places are even more popular on weekends and inundated on three-day weekends (most common in May).

French Tourist Offices in the U.S.A.

France's national tourist offices in the U.S.A. are a wealth of information. Before your trip, request any specific information you may want (such as city maps and schedules of upcoming festivals).

French Tourist Offices: 444 Madison Ave., 16th floor, New York, NY 10022; 676 N. Michigan Ave. Suite 600, Chicago, IL 60611; and 9454 Wilshire Blvd., Suite #715, Beverly Hills,

CA 90212. Their information number (in Washington, D.C.) is 202/659-7779, and their Web site is www.francetourism.com. For the latest on Paris, visit http://www.pariscope.Fr.

Recommended Guidebooks

For most travelers, this book is all you need. But if you'd like more information, you may want to buy an additional guidebook. The Michelin Green Guide which is somewhat scholarly, and the more readable *Paris Access* guide are both well-researched. If you'll be traveling elsewhere in France, consider *Rick Steves' France, Belgium & the Netherlands.*

Rick Steves' Books and Videos

Rick Steves' Europe Through the Back Door 1999 (John Muir Publications, 1999) gives you budget travel tips on minimizing jet lag, packing light, planning your itinerary, traveling by car or train, finding budget beds without reservations, changing money, avoiding rip-offs, outsmarting thieves, hurdling the language barrier, staying healthy, taking great photographs, using your bidet, and lots more. The book also includes chapters on 37 of Rick's favorite "Back Doors."

Rick Steves' Country Guides are a series of eight guidebooks covering Europe; France, Belgium, and the Netherlands; Great Britain and Ireland; Italy; Spain and Portugal; Germany, Austria, and Switzerland; Scandinavia; and Russia and the Baltics. All but the last two are updated annually and come out in January.

Rick Steves' City Guides include this book and *Rick Steves' London*. With the sleek Eurostar train, London is now just three hours from Paris. Consider combining the two cities (and books) for a great visit.

Europe 101: History and Art for the Traveler (co-written with Gene Openshaw, John Muir Publications, 1996) gives you the story of Europe's people, history, and art. Written for smart people who were sleeping in their history and art classes before they knew they were going to Europe, *101* carbonates Europe's sights.

Rick Steves' Mona Winks (also co-written with Gene Openshaw, John Muir Publications, 1998) gives you fun, easy-to-follow self-guided tours of Europe's top 20 museums. All of the *Mona Winks* chapters on Paris are included in this Paris guidebook. But if you'd like similar coverage for the great museums in London, Amsterdam, Venice, Florence, and Rome, *Mona*'s for you.

The *Rick Steves' French Phrase Book & Dictionary* (John Muir Publications, 1999) gives you the words and survival phrases you'll need while traveling in Paris.

Of the 52 shows in my television series, *Travels in Europe with Rick Steves*, two cover Paris and six half-hour shows cover other parts of France. These may re-air on your local public television station or the Travel Channel. They're also available as information-packed videotapes, along with my two-hour slide show lecture on France (call 425/771-8303 for our free newsletter/catalog).

Rick Steves' Postcards from Europe (John Muir Publications, 1999), my new autobiographical book, packs 25 years of travel anecdotes and insights into the ultimate 3,000-mile European adventure. Through my guidebooks, I share my favorite European discoveries with you. *Postcards* introduces you to my favorite European friends.

Maps

The maps in this book, drawn by Dave Hoerlein, are concise and simple. Dave, who is well-traveled in Paris, designed these maps to help you orient quickly and get to where you want to go painlessly. Once in Paris, simply pick up the free Paris map at your hotel and you're ready to travel.

Transportation

Transportation concerns within Paris are limited to the subway, buses, and taxis, all covered extensively in the Orientation chapter. If you have a car, stow it. You don't want to drive in Paris. For all the specifics on transportation throughout France by train or car, see *Rick Steves' France, Belgium & the Netherlands 1999*.

Telephones and Mail

Make local and long distance calls from the public phones on the street. An efficient card-operated system has replaced coin-operated public phones in Paris. Phone cards are a breeze to use. Buy a phone card (*une télécarte*), available at any post office, train station, and most newsstands and tobacco shops (*tabac* in France). There are two denominations of phone cards in France: *une petite* costs 42F; *une grande* is 98F. When you use the card, simply take the phone off the hook, insert the card, and wait for a dial tone. The price of the call (local or international) is automatically deducted. Buy a card at the beginning of your trip and use it for hotel reservations, calling tourist information offices, and phoning home.

France's newest phone card (KOSMOS) is not inserted into the phone, but allows you to dial from the comfort of your hotel (or anywhere) and charge the call to the card for lower rates than with a *télécarte*. It's simple to use, instructions are provided in English, and the card is sold wherever *télécartes* are sold. And while the per-minute rates are cheaper than a *télécarte*, it's slower to use, so local calls are more quickly made with a *télécarte* from a phone booth.

U.S.A. Direct services are no longer a good value. While it's psychologically comforting to dial an AT&T, MCI, or Sprint access number and get an operator in Atlanta, this will now double your per minute costs for calls from Paris to the U.S.A. The cheapest way to phone home is to use your French phone card and call directly from a phone booth. You can make a very quick call for as little as 50 cents.

France has a dial-direct 10-digit telephone system. There are no area codes. To call to or from anywhere in France, including Paris, you dial the 10 numbers directly. All Paris numbers start with 01. If you encounter any old eight-digit numbers, add that prefix.

To dial out of France, you must start your call with its international code: 00. To call France from another country, start with the international access code of the country you're calling from (00 for most European countries and 011 from America), then dial France's country code (33), then drop the lead 0 of the 10-digit local number and dial the remaining 9 digits. For example, the number of our favorite hotel in Paris is 01 47 05 49 15. To call it from home, dial 011-33-1 47 05 49 15. For a listing of international access codes and country codes, see the Appendix. Paris time is six/nine hours ahead of the east/west coast of the U.S.A.

Mail: To arrange for mail delivery, reserve a few hotels along your route in advance and give their addresses to friends, or use American Express Company's mail services (available to anyone who has at least one Amex traveler's check). Allow 10 days for a letter to arrive. Phoning is so easy that we've dispensed with mail stops altogether.

Sleeping

A comfortable hotel in Paris costs less than half what a comparable hotel in the U.S.A. or London costs. It's a great hotel city. Still, you should reserve in advance to secure the best hotel for you. We like places that are clean, small, central, traditional, inexpensive, friendly, and not listed in other guidebooks. Most places we list have at least five of these seven virtues.

Paris Hotels

In this book, the price for a double room will normally range from $40 (very simple, toilet and shower down the hall) to $150 (maximum plumbing and more), with most clustering around $75. A triple and a double are often the same room, with a small double bed and a sliver single, so a third person sleeps very cheaply. Most

Sleep Code

To give maximum information with a minimum of space, we use these codes to describe accommodations listed in this book. Prices listed are per room, not per person.

S = Single room (or price for one person in a double)

D = Double or Twin (French double beds can be very small)

T = Triple (generally a double bed with a single)

Q = Quad (usually two double beds)

b = Private bathroom with toilet and shower or tub

t = Private toilet only (the shower is down the hall)

s = Private shower or tub only (the toilet is down the hall)

CC = Accepts credit cards (**V** = Visa, **M** = MasterCard, **A**= American Express). If CC isn't mentioned, assume you'll have to pay cash.

* = French hotel rating system, ranging from zero to four stars.

According to this code, a couple staying at a "Db-275F, CC:V" hotel would pay a total of 275 French francs (or about $50) for a double room with a private bathroom. The hotel accepts Visa or French cash in payment.

hotels have a few singles, triples, and quads. While groups sleep cheap, traveling alone can be expensive—a single room usually costs about the same as a double.

French receptionists are often reluctant to mention the cheaper rooms. Study the room price list posted at the desk. Understand it. You'll save about $15 on the average if you get a room with a "shower down the hall" rather than in your room. Ask for a room *sans douche* (without shower) rather than *avec douche* (with shower). A room with a bathtub (*salle de bain*) costs $5 to $10 more than a room with a shower. A double bed (*grand lit*) is $5 to $10 cheaper than twins (*deux petits lits*). Hotels are inclined to give you a room with a tub (which the French prefer). If you prefer a double bed and a shower, you need to ask for it—and you'll save up to $20. If you'll take twins or a double, ask for a *chambre pour deux* (room for two) to avoid being needlessly turned away.

The French have a simple hotel rating system (zero through four stars) depending on the amenities offered. We like the one- or two-star hotels. More than two stars gets you expensive and unnecessary amenities. Unclassified hotels (no stars) can be bargains or depressing dumps. You'll almost always have the option of breakfast at your hotel, which is pleasant and convenient, but—at 25F to 50F—often double the price of the corner café. While hotels hope you'll spring for their breakfast, this is optional unless otherwise noted.

Rooms are safe. Still, keep cameras and money out of sight. Towels aren't routinely replaced every day; drip-dry and conserve. If that French Lincoln-log pillow isn't your idea of comfort, American-style pillows (and extra blankets) are usually in the closet or available on request. To get a pillow, ask for "*Un oreiller, s'il vous plaît*" (un oar-ray-yay, see-voo-play).

Making Reservations

Reserve ahead for Paris, the sooner the better. May, June, September, and October are the busiest months. We've taken great pains to list telephone numbers with long-distance instructions (see Telephones and Mail, above, and the Appendix). Use the telephone and convenient telephone cards. Most hotels listed are accustomed to English-only speakers. A hotel receptionist will trust you and hold a room until 16:00 without a deposit, though some will ask for a credit-card number. Honor (or cancel by phone) your reservations. Long distance is cheap and easy from public phone booths. Don't let these people down—we promised you'd call and cancel if for some reason you won't show up. Don't needlessly confirm rooms through the tourist office; they'll take a commission.

To reserve from home, call, fax, e-mail, or write the hotel. E-mail is preferred when possible. Phone and fax costs are reasonable, and simple English is usually fine. To fax, use the fax form in the Appendix. If you're writing, add the zip code and confirm the need and method for a deposit. A two-night stay in August would be "2 nights, 16/8/99 to 18/8/99"—European hotel jargon uses your day of departure. You'll often receive a letter back requesting one night's deposit. A credit card will usually be accepted as a deposit, though you may need to send a signed traveler's check or a bank draft in the local currency. If your credit card is the deposit, you can pay with your card or cash when you arrive. If you don't show up, you'll be billed for one night. Reconfirm your reservations a day in advance for safety.

Hostels and Foyers

Parisian hostels charge about $18 per bed. Some require a hostel membership; the best don't. Get a hostel card before you go if you need one. Travelers of any age are welcome if they don't mind dorm-style accommodations and meeting other travelers. Travelers without a hostel card can generally spend the night for a small extra "one-night membership" fee. Cheap meals are sometimes available, and kitchen facilities are usually provided for do-it-yourselfers.

Apartments
It's easy, though not necessarily cheaper, to rent a furnished apartment in Paris. Consider this option if you're either traveling with a family or staying two weeks or longer. For listings, see the end of the Sleeping chapter.

Eating in France
The French eat long and well. Relaxed lunches, three-hour dinners, and endless hours sitting in outdoor cafés are the norm. They have a legislated 35-hour workweek and a self-imposed 36-hour eat-week. The French spend much of their five annual weeks of paid vacation at la table. Local cafés, cuisine, and wines become a highlight of any French adventure—sightseeing for your palate. Even if the rest of you is sleeping in cheap hotels, let your taste-buds travel first-class in Paris. (They can go coach in England.) You can eat well without going broke, but choose carefully—you're just as likely to blow a small fortune on a mediocre meal as you are to dine wonderfully for $15.

Restaurants
You can order *à la carte* like the locals do, or get the no-brainer menu, which is a fixed-price meal offering three or four courses—and generally a good value. The fixed-price menu gives you your choice of soup, appetizer, or salad; your choice of three or four main courses (*plats*) with vegetables; plus a cheese course and/or a choice of desserts. Service is included, but wine or drinks are generally extra.

In France an entrée is the first course and *le plat* is the main course. *Le plat* or *le plat du jour* (plate of the day) is the main course with vegetables (usually 50–70F). For a light, healthy, fast, and inexpensive option in a pricey restaurant, the various salads are 40F to 50F well spent. Soft drinks and beer cost 8 to 20F ($1.50 to $4), and a bottle or carafe of house wine—which is invariably good enough for Rick and Gene, if not always Steve—costs 30F to 70F ($6 to $14). Service is always included. To get a waiter's or waitress' attention, simply say, "*S'il vous plaît*" (please). To alienate the same person, snap your fingers and say "*garçon*."

Café Culture
French cafés (or *brasseries*) provide reasonable light meals and a refuge from museum and church overload. They are carefully positioned viewpoints from which to watch the river of local life flow

by. It's easier for the novice to sit and feel comfortable in a café when you know the system.

Check the price list first. Prices, which must be posted prominently, vary wildly between cafés. Cafés charge different prices for the same drink depending upon where you want to be seated. Prices are posted: *comptoir* (counter/bar) and the more expensive *salle* (seated).

Your waiter probably won't overwhelm you with friendliness. Notice how hard they work. They almost never stop. Cozying up to clients (French or foreign) is probably the last thing on their minds.

The standard menu items are the Croque Monsieur (grilled cheese sandwich) and Croque Madame (Monsieur with a fried egg on top). The *salade compose* (com-po-zay) is a hearty chef's salad. Sandwiches are least expensive but plain unless you buy them at the *boulangerie* (bakery). To get more than a piece of ham (*jambon*) on a baguette, order a sandwich *jambon-crudité* (crew-dee-tay), which means garnished with lettuce, tomatoes, cucumbers, and so on. Omelettes come lonely on a plate with a basket of bread. The *plat du jour* (daily special) is your fast, hearty 50 to 60F hot plate. Regardless of what you order, bread is free; to get more, just hold up your bread basket and ask, "*Encore, s'il vous plaît.*"

To order coffee, here is the lingo:
- *un express* (uh nex-press) = shot of espresso
- *une noisette* (oon nwah-zette) = shot of espresso with a shot of milk
- *café au lait* (kah-fay oh lay) = coffee with milk. Also called *un grand crème* (uh grahn krem = big) or *un petit crème* (uh puh-tee krem = average).
- *un café longue* (uh kah-fay lone-guh) = cup of coffee, closest to American-style
- *un décaffine* (uh day-kah-fee-nay) = decaf, and can modify any of the above drinks

Note: By law the waiter must give you a glass of tap water with your coffee if you request it; ask for "*un verre d'eau*" (uh vayre dough).

House wine at the bar is cheap (5–10F per glass, cheapest by the *pichet*, or pitcher), and the local beer is cheaper on tap (*une pression*) than in the bottle (*bouteille*). While prices include service, tip, and tax, it's polite to round up for a drink or meal well served (e.g., if your bill was 24F, leave 25F).

Breakfast

Petit déjeuner (peh-tee day-zhu-nay) is typically *café au lait* (espresso with hot milk), hot chocolate, or tea; a roll with butter and

marmalade; and a croissant. Don't expect much variety for breakfast, but the bread is fresh and the coffee is great. While available
at your hotel (25–50F), breakfasts are cheaper at the corner café.
It's entirely acceptable to buy a croissant or roll at a nearby bakery
and eat it with your cup of coffee (no refills) at a café. Some hotels
offer a *petit-déjeuner* buffet (about 50F) with cereals, yogurt,
cheeses, fruit, and breads. If the morning egg urge gets the best of
you, drop into a café and order *une omelette* or *oeufs sur le plat* (fried
eggs). You could also buy or bring plastic bowls and spoons from
home, buy a box of French cereal and a small box of milk, and eat
in your room before heading out for coffee. We carry fruit and a
package of Vache Qui Rit (Laughing Cow) cheese to supplement
the morning jelly.

Lunch

For lunch—*déjeuner* (day-zhuh-nay)—we picnic or munch a take-
away *boulangerie* sandwich.

French picnics can be first-class affairs and adventures in high
cuisine. Be daring. Try the smelly cheeses, ugly pâtés, sissy
quiches, and minuscule yogurts. Local shopkeepers are accustomed
to selling small quantities of produce. Try the tasty salads to go
and ask for *une fourchette en plastique* (a plastic fork).

Gather supplies early; you'll probably visit several small stores
to assemble a complete meal, and many close at noon. Look for a
boulangerie (bakery), a *crémerie* (cheeses), a *charcuterie* (deli items,
meats, and pâtés), an *épicerie* or *alimentation* (small grocery with veg-
gies, drinks, and so on), and a *pâtisserie* (delicious pastries). For the
best picnic-shopping in Paris, try the rue Cler neighborhood; take
the Rue Cler Walk (see page 68), and shop as you go.

Local *supermarchés* offer less color and cost, more efficiency,
and adequate quality. Department stores often have supermarkets
in the basement.

If not picnicking, look for food stands and bakeries selling
take-out sandwiches and drinks, or *crêperies* or *brasseries* for fast and
easy sit-down restaurant food. *Brasseries* are cafés serving basic fare
such as omelets, chicken, and fries, as well as simple sandwiches
and hearty salads. Look for their *plat du jour* (daily special). Many
French restaurants offer good value, three- to five-course menus at
lunch only. The same menu is often 40F more at dinner. For more
tips, see Café Culture, above.

Dinner

For *dîner* (dee-nay), choose restaurants filled with locals, not places
with big neon signs boasting, "We Speak English." Consider your
hotelier's opinion. If the menu (*la carte*) isn't posted outside, move

along. Also look for set-price menus and restaurants serving regional specialities. Ask the waiter for help deciphering *la carte*. Go with his or her recommendations and anything *de la maison* (of the house). Galloping gourmets should bring a menu translator; the Marling Menu Master is excellent. Remember, if you ask for a menu, you'll get a meal (*la carte* is the list of what's cooking), and if you ask for an entrée, you'll get a first course (soup, salad, or appetizer). The wines are often listed in a separate *carte des vins*. Tipping (*pourboire*) is unnecessary, though if you enjoyed the service, it's polite to leave a few francs.

Drinks
In stores, unrefrigerated soft drinks and beer are one-third the price of cold drinks. Milk and boxed fruit juice are the cheapest drinks. Avoid buying drinks to go at streetside stands; you'll find them far cheaper in a shop. Try to keep a water bottle with you. Water quenches your thirst better and cheaper than anything you'll find in a store or café. We drink tap water throughout France.

The French often order bottled water with their meal (*eau minérale*, oh mee-nay-rahl). If you'd prefer a free pitcher of tap water, ask for *une carafe d'eau*. Otherwise, you may unwittingly buy bottled water. When ordering a beer at a café or restaurant, ask for *une pression* or *un demi* (draft beer), which is cheaper than bottled. When ordering table wine at a café or restaurant, ask for a pitcher (*un pichet*, pee-shay), again cheaper than a bottle. If all you want is a glass of wine, ask for *un verre de vin*. You could drink away your children's inheritance if you're not careful. The most famous wines are the most expensive, while lesser-known taste-alikes remain a bargain. If you like brandy, try a *marc* (regional brandy, e.g., *marc de Bourgogne*) or Armagnac, cognac's cheaper twin brother. Pastis, the standard *apéritif*, is a sweet anise or licorice drink which comes on the rocks with a glass of water. Cut it to taste with lots of water. France's best beer is Alsatian; try Krônenburg or the heavier Pelfort. *Une panache* (pan-a-shay) is a very refreshing French shandy (7-Up and beer). For a fun, bright, non-alcoholic drink, order *un diabolo menthe* (7-Up with mint syrup). The ice cubes melted after the last Yankee tour group left.

Stranger in a Strange Land
We travel all the way to Europe to enjoy differences—to become temporary locals. You'll experience frustrations. Certain truths that we find "God-given" or "self-evident," like cold beer, ice in drinks, bottomless cups of coffee, hot showers, body odor smelling bad, and bigger being better, are suddenly not so true. One of the benefits of travel is the eye-opening realization that there are logical,

civil, and even better alternatives. Paris is an understandably proud city. To enjoy its people you need to celebrate the differences. A willingness to go local ensures that you'll enjoy a full dose of European hospitality.

Back Door Manners

While updating our guidebooks, we hear over and over again that our readers are considerate and fun to have as guests. Thank you for traveling as temporary locals who are sensitive to the culture. It's fun to follow you in our travels.

France Tours by Rick Steves and Steve Smith

At Europe Through the Back Door, we organize and lead tours covering Paris and the highlights of France. These depart each year from April through October, are limited to 24 people per group, have two guides, and big buses with lots of empty seats. For details on how to travel with us, call 425/771-8303 for a free newsletter.

Send Us a Postcard, Drop Us a Line

If you enjoy a successful trip with the help of this book and would like to share your discoveries, please fill out and send the survey at the end of this book to us at Europe Through the Back Door, Box 2009, Edmonds, WA 98020. We personally read and value all feedback. Thanks in advance—it helps a lot.

For our latest travel information, tap into our Web site: www.ricksteves.com. Our e-mail address is rick@ricksteves.com. Anyone is welcome to request a free issue of our *Back Door* quarterly newsletter.

Judging from all the positive feedback and happy postcards we receive from our traveling readers, it's safe to assume you're on your way to a great vacation—independent, inexpensive, and with the finesse of an experienced traveler.

From this point, "we" (your co-authors) will shed our respective egos and become "I."

Thanks, and bon voyage!

BACK DOOR TRAVEL PHILOSOPHY
As Taught in *Rick Steves' Europe Through the Back Door*

Travel is intensified living—maximum thrills per minute and one of the last great sources of legal adventure. Travel is freedom. It's recess, and we need it.

Experiencing the real Europe requires catching it by surprise, going casual . . . "Through the Back Door."

Affording travel is a matter of priorities. (Make do with the old car.) You can travel—simply, safely, and comfortably—anywhere in Europe for $60 a day plus transportation costs. In many ways, spending more money only builds a thicker wall between you and what you came to see. Europe is a cultural carnival and, time after time, you'll find that its best acts are free and the best seats are the cheap ones.

A tight budget forces you to travel close to the ground, meeting and communicating with the people, not relying on service with a purchased smile. Never sacrifice sleep, nutrition, safety, or cleanliness in the name of budget. Simply enjoy the local-style alternatives to expensive hotels and restaurants.

Extroverts have more fun. If your trip is low on magic moments, kick yourself and make things happen. If you don't enjoy a place, maybe you don't know enough about it. Seek the truth. Recognize tourist traps. Give a culture the benefit of your open mind. See things as different but not better or worse. Any culture has much to share.

Of course, travel, like the world, is a series of hills and valleys. Be fanatically positive and militantly optimistic. If something's not to your liking, change your liking. Travel is addicting. It can make you a happier American, as well as a citizen of the world. Our Earth is home to nearly 6 billion equally important people. It's humbling to travel and find that people don't envy Americans. They like us, but with all due respect, they wouldn't trade passports.

Globetrotting destroys ethnocentricity. It helps you understand and appreciate different cultures. Travel changes people. It broadens perspectives and teaches new ways to measure quality of life. Many travelers toss aside their hometown blinders. Their prized souvenirs are the strands of different cultures they decide to knit into their own character. The world is a cultural yarn shop. And Back Door Travelers are weaving the ultimate tapestry. Come on, join in!

ORIENTATION

Many people fall in love with Paris. Some see the essentials and flee, overwhelmed by the huge city. With the proper approach and a good orientation, you'll fall head over heels for Europe's capital city.

This orientation to the City of Lights will illuminate your trip. The day plans—for visits of one to seven days—will help you prioritize the many sights. You'll tap into Paris' information sources for current events. Most important, you'll learn to navigate Paris by Métro, bus, taxi, or foot. For most travelers, the key to the city is a Métro ticket.

Planning Your Time

Paris in One, Two, or Three Days
If you have only one day, just do Day One; for two days, do the first two days.

Day 1
Morning: Follow Historic Paris walk, featuring Île de la Cité, Notre-Dame, Latin Quarter, and Sainte-Chapelle.
Afternoon: Tour Louvre Museum.
Evening: Cruise Seine River or take illuminated Paris by Night bus tour.

Day 2
Morning: Follow Champs-Élysées Walk, from Arc de Triomphe down the grand Champs-Élysées boulevard to Tuileries Gardens.
Mid-day: Tour Orsay Museum.
Afternoon: Catch RER from Orsay to Versailles. To avoid crowds, see the park first and the palace late.
Evening: Enjoy Trocadero scene and twilight ride up Eiffel Tower.

Day 3
Morning: Follow Marais Walk.
Afternoon: Tour Rodin Museum, then Napoleon's Tomb and military museums at Les Invalides.
Evening: Take Montmartre Walk, featuring Sacré-Coeur.

Paris in Four to Seven Days Without Going In-Seine

Day 1
Morning: Follow Historic Paris walk, featuring Île de la Cité, Notre-Dame, Latin Quarter, and Sainte-Chapelle.
Afternoon: Café-sitting and shopping.
Evening: Seine River cruise or illuminated Paris by Night bus tour.

Day 2
Morning: Tour Louvre Museum.
Afternoon: Follow Champs-Élysées Walk, from Arc de Triomphe down the grand Champs-Élysées boulevard to Tuileries Gardens.
Evening: Take Montmartre Walk, featuring Sacré-Coeur.

Day 3
Morning: Take Rue Cler Walk.
Mid-Day: Tour Orsay Museum.
Afternoon: Catch RER from Orsay to Versailles. To avoid crowds, see the park first and the palace late.

Day 4
Morning: Follow Marais Walk.
Afternoon: Tour Rodin Museum, then Napoleon's Tomb.
Evening: Enjoy Trocadero scene; twilight ride up Eiffel Tower.

Day 5, 6, and 7
Choose from:
Shopping and cafés
Montmartre and Sacré-Coeur (by day)
Picasso, Cluny, Marmottan, or L'Orangerie Museums
　(L'Orangerie open only May–August in 1999)
Day trip to Chartres
Day trip to Vaux-le-Vicomte and Fontainebleau
Day trip to Disneyland Paris
Evening: Night bus or boat tour (whichever you have yet to do)

Paris: A Verbal Map

Paris is split in half by the Seine River, divided into 20 *arrondissements* (proud and independent governmental jurisdictions), and

Daily Reminder

Mondays: These museums—Orsay, Rodin, Marmottan, and Versailles—are closed today; the Louvre is more crowded because of this. Many small stores don't open until 14:00. Some restaurants close on Mondays. It's discount night at most cinemas.

Tuesdays: These museums—Louvre, Picasso, and Cluny—are closed today. Versailles and the Orsay can be jammed. (L'Orangerie is closed on Tuesdays during its brief 1999 May–August season; otherwise it's closed entirely for renovation.)

Wednesdays: All museums are open. The weekly *Pariscope* magazine comes out today.

Thursdays: All museums are open.

Fridays: All museums are open. Afternoon trains and roads leaving Paris are crowded; TGV reservation fees are higher.

Saturdays: Candlelight visits of Vaux-le-Vicomte (May-October); otherwise avoid weekend crowds at area châteaus. Paris department stores are busy.

Sundays: Some museums are two-thirds-price all day (Louvre, Orsay, Cluny, Picasso). The fountains run at Versailles. The Marais is the place to window shop and café hop; many of Paris' stores are closed on Sunday, but as this is the Jewish Quarter, it hops. Organ concerts at St. Sulpice and possibly at other churches. Free evening concert at the American Church (18:00).

circled by a ring-road freeway (the *périphérique*). You'll find Paris easier to negotiate if you know which side of the river you're on, which *arrondissement* you're in, and which subway (Métro) stop you're closest to.

If you're north of the river (the top half of any city map), you're on the Right Bank (*rive droite*). If you're south of it, you're on the Left Bank (*rive gauche*).

Arrondissements are numbered, starting at Notre-Dame (ground zero) and moving in a clockwise spiral out to the ring road. The last two digits in a Parisian zip code are the *arrondissement* number, and the notation for the Métro stop is "Mo." In Parisian jargon, Napoleon's tomb is on *la rive gauche* (the Left

Bank) in the 7ème (7th *arrondissement*), zip code 75007, Mo: Invalides. Paris Métro stops are used as a standard aid in giving directions, even for those not using the Métro. As you're tracking down addresses, these definitions will help: place (square), rue (road), and pont (bridge).

Arrival in Paris

For a comprehensive rundown on Paris' six train stations and two airports, see the Transportation Connections chapter, which starts on page 197.

Tourist Information

Avoid the Paris tourist offices—long lines, short information, and a 5F charge for maps. This book, the *Pariscope* magazine (described below), and one of the freebie maps available at any hotel are all you need. The main TI is at 127 avenue des Champs-Élysées (daily 9:00–20:00), but the TIs at the Louvre, Eiffel Tower, and train stations Gare de Lyon and Gare de Montparnasse are handier (daily 8:00–20:00). For a complete list of museum hours and scheduled English museum tours, pick up the free *Musées, Monuments Historiques, et Expositions* booklet from any museum.

   Pariscope: The *Pariscope* weekly magazine (or one of its clones, 3F at any newsstand) lists museum hours, art exhibits, concerts, music festivals, plays, movies, and nightclubs. See Tour of *Pariscope* on page 192.

   Maps: While Paris is littered with free maps, they don't show all the streets. You may want the huge Michelin #10 map of Paris. For an extended stay, we prefer the pocket-size and street-indexed *Paris Practique* (40F).

   Bookstores: There are many English-language bookstores in Paris where you can pick up guidebooks (for nearly double their American price). A few are: Shakespeare & Company (daily 12:00–24:00, lots of used travel books, 37 rue de la Boucherie, across the river from Notre-Dame), W. H. Smith (248 rue de Rivoli, Mo: Concorde, tel. 01 44 77 88 99), and Brentanos (37 avenue de L'Opéra, Mo: Opéra, tel. 01 42 61 52 50).

   American Church: The American Church is a nerve center for the American èmigrè community. It distributes the *Free Voice*, a free, handy, and insightful monthly English-language newspaper, with useful reviews of concerts, plays, and current events (available at around 200 locations in Paris), and *France—U.S.A. Contacts*, an advertisement paper, full of useful information for those looking for work or long-term housing. The church faces the river between the Eiffel Tower and Orsay Museum (65 quai d'Orsay, Mo: Invalides, tel. 01 47 05 07 99).

PARIS OVERVIEW

TRAIN STATIONS/ GARES:

① **ST-LAZARE** TO NORMANDY

② **NORD** TO LONDON & BRUSSELS VIA EUROSTAR, TO N. EUROPE

③ **L'EST** TO E. FRANCE, S. GERMANY, SWITZERLAND, AUSTRIA

④ **LYON** TO S.E. FRANCE & ITALY

⑤ **D'AUSTERLITZ** TO S.W. FRANCE, LOIRE & SPAIN

⑥ **MONTPARNASSE** TO NORMANDY, BRITTANY, CHARTRES, TGV TO LOIRE & S.W. FRANCE

ARRONDISSEMENTS
(DISTRICTS)

Helpful Hints

Theft Alert: Use your money belt, and never carry a wallet in your back pocket or a purse over your shoulder. Thieves thrive in tourist areas and the Métro (at stations and in subway cars).

Paris Museum Pass: This worthwhile pass, covering most sights in Paris, is available at major Métro stations, tourist offices, or museums. For detailed information, see the Sights chapter on page 27.

Telephone Cards: Pick up the essential France *tèlécarte* at any *tabac* (tobacco shop), post office, or tourist office (*une petite*

carte is 42F; *une grande* is 98F). Smart travelers check things by telephone. Most public phones use these cards. For a list of useful phone numbers, see the Appendix.

Toilets: Carry small change for pay toilets, or walk into any outdoor café like you own the place and find the toilet in the back. Remember, the toilets in museums are free and generally the best you'll find. Modern super-sanitary street booths provide both relief and a memory.

Getting Around Paris

By Métro: Europe's best subway is divided into two systems—the Métro (puddle-jumping everywhere in Paris) and the RER (which makes giant speedy leaps around town and connects suburban destinations). You'll be using the Métro for almost all your trips.

In Paris you're never more than a 10-minute walk from a Métro station. One ticket takes you anywhere in the system with unlimited transfers. Save 40 percent by buying a *carnet* (car-nay) of 10 tickets for 52F at any Métro station (a single ticket is 8F). Métro tickets work on city buses, though one ticket cannot be used as a transfer between subway and bus.

The Mobilis ticket (30F) allows unlimited travel for a single day on all bus and Métro lines. If you're staying longer, the *Carte d'Orange* pass gives you free run of the bus and Métro system for one week (75F and a photo, ask for the *Carte d'Orange Coupon Vert*) or a month (254F, ask for the *Carte d'Orange Coupon Orange*). These pass prices cover only central Paris; you can pay more for passes covering regional destinations (e.g., Versailles). The weekly pass begins Monday and ends Sunday, and the monthly pass begins the first day of the month and ends the last day of that month, so mid-week or mid-month purchases are generally not worthwhile. All passes can be purchased at any Métro station (most have photo booths).

To get to your destination, determine which "Mo" stop is closest to it and which line or lines will get you there. The lines have numbers, but they're best known by their direction or end-of-the-line stop. (For example, the "La Defense/Château de Vincennes" line runs between La Defense in the west and Vincennes in the east.)

Once in the Métro station, you'll see blue-and-white signs directing you to the train going in your direction (e.g., direction: La Defense). Insert your ticket in the automatic turnstile, pass through, reclaim and keep your ticket until you exit the system (fare inspectors accept no excuses from anyone). Transfers are free and can be made wherever lines cross. When you transfer, look for the orange *correspondence* (connections) signs when you exit your first train, then follow the proper direction sign.

Tips for the Métro and RER

Key Words

direction (dee-rek-see-ohn): direction

correspondance (kor-res-pohn-dahns): transfer

sortie (sor-tee): exit

carnet (kar-nay): cheap set of 10 tickets

Pardon, madame/monsieur (par-dohn, mah-dahm/mes-yur): Excuse me, lady/bud.

Je descend (juh day-sahn): I'm getting off.

Donnez-moi mon porte-monnaie!: Give me back my wallet!

Etiquette

• When waiting at the platform, get out of the way of those exiting their train. Board only once everyone is off.

• Avoid using the hinged seats when the car is jammed; they take up valuable standing space.

• When in a crowded train, try not to block the exit. If blocking the door when the train stops, step out of the car and to the side, let others off, then get back on.

• Don't talk loudly in the cars. Listen to how quietly Parisians can communicate and follow their lead.

• On escalators, stand on the right, pass on the left.

Before you *sortie* (exit), check the helpful *plan du quartier* (map of the neighborhood) to get your bearings, locate your destination, and decide which *sortie* you want. At stops with several *sorties*, you can save lots of walking by choosing the best exit.

Thieves spend their days in the Métro. Be on guard. For example, a pocket picked as you pass through a turnstile leaves you on the wrong side and the thief strolling away. Any jostle or commotion (especially when boarding or leaving trains) is likely the sign of a thief or team of thieves in action. Paris is most dangerous late at night.

Paris has a huge homeless population and over 12 percent unemployment; expect a warm Métro welcome by panhandlers, musicians, and those selling magazines produced by the homeless community.

By RER: The RER (*Réseau Express Régionale*, air-ay-air) is the suburban train system, indicated by thick lines on your subway map and identified by letters A, B, C, and so on. The RER works like the Métro, but is much speedier because it makes only a few stops within the city. One Métro ticket is all you need for RER rides within Paris. You can transfer between the Métro and RER systems with the same ticket. Unlike the Métro, you need to insert your ticket in a turnstile to exit the RER system. To travel outside the city (to Versailles or the airport, for example) you'll need to buy a separate, more expensive ticket at the station window before boarding, and make sure your stop is served by checking the signs over the train platform (not all trains serve all stops).

By City Bus: The trickier bus system is worth figuring out. Métro tickets are good on both bus and Métro, though you can't use the same ticket to transfer between the two systems. One ticket gets you anywhere in central Paris, but if you leave the city center (shown as section 1 on the diagram on board the bus), you must validate a second ticket. While the Métro shuts down about 00:30, some buses continue much later. Schedules are posted at bus stops. Handy bus system maps (*plan des autobus*) are available in any Métro station and are provided in your *Paris Practique* map book if you invest.

Big system maps, posted at each bus and Métro stop, display the routes. Individual route diagrams show the exact route of the lines serving that stop. Major stops are painted on the side of each bus. Enter through the front doors. Punch your Métro ticket in the machine behind the driver, or pay the higher cash fare. Get off the bus using the rear door. Even if you're not certain you've fig- ured it out, do some joyriding (outside of rush hour). Lines #24, #63, and #69 are Paris' most scenic routes and make a great intro- duction to the city. Bus #69 is particularly handy, running between the Eiffel Tower, rue Cler (recommended hotels), Orsay, Louvre, Marais (recommended hotels), and Père Lachaise Cemetery. The most handy bus routes are listed for each hotel area recommended (see Sleeping on page 162).

By Taxi: Parisian taxis are almost reasonable. A 10-minute ride costs about 50F (versus about 5F to get anywhere in town on the Métro). You can try waving one down, but it's easier to ask for the nearest taxi stand (*Où est une station de taxi?*; oo ay oon stah- see-ohn duh taxi) or ask your hotel to call for you. Higher rates are charged from 22:00 to 06:30, all day Sunday, and to either airport. If you call from your hotel, the meter starts as soon as the call is received. Taxis are tough to find on Friday and Saturday night, especially after the Métro closes (around 00:30).

By Foot: Be careful out there! Parisian drivers are notorious for ignoring pedestrians. Never assume you have the right of way, even in a crosswalk. When crossing a street, keep your pace constant and don't stop suddenly. Parisian drivers carefully calculate your speed and will miss you, providing you don't alter your route or pace.

Organized Tours of Paris

Bus Tours: Paris Vision offers handy bus tours of Paris, day and night (advertised in hotel lobbies); their "Illuminated Paris" tour is explained in Entertainment (p. 192). Paris also has a "hop-on, hop-off" bus service called **Open Deck Tours**. You can buy a two-day ticket for 170F (from the driver) and use the bus to connect the major sights (running commentary, two buses per hour). You'll see these bright yellow topless double-decker buses all over town.

Boat Tours: Several companies offer one-hour boat cruises on the Seine. The **Bateaux-Mouches** boats depart every 30 minutes (from 10:00–23:00, best at night) from the pont de l'Alma, the pont Neuf, and Eiffel Tower (40F, 20F–under age 14, tel. 01 42 25 96 10). Offered from June-September only, the **Bateau-Bus** is a river bus that connects five stops along the river: Eiffel Tower, Orsay, Louvre, Notre-Dame, and place de la Concorde (departures every 45 minutes from about 10:00–19:00; pick up a brochure at any TI).

Walking Tours: Use the walking tours in this book and be your own guide. Paris Walking Tours offers a variety of walks nearly daily for 60F (tel. 01 48 09 21 40, fax 01 42 43 75 51, Web site: http://ourworld.compuserve.com/homepages/ParisWalking). Or, consider hiring a Parisian as your personal guide. Arnaud Servignat (tel. 01 42 57 03 35, fax 01 42 62 68 62, e-mail: arnoud.saigon @wanadoo.fr) and Marianne Siegler (tel. 01 42 52 32 51) are licensed local guides who freelance for individuals and families ($150/4 hrs, $250/day).

PARIS
SIGHTS

These sights are arranged by neighborhood for handy sightseeing. When you see a ✪ in a listing, it means the sight is covered in much more depth in one of our walks or self-guided tours.

The Paris Museum Pass: All of the sights listed in this chapter are covered by a Paris Museum Pass, except for the Eiffel Tower, Montparnasse Tower, Marmottan Museum, and the ladies of Pigalle.

In Paris there are two classes of sightseers: those with a museum pass and those without. Serious sightseers save time (by skipping lines) and money by getting this pass. Sold at museums, main Métro stations, and tourist offices, it pays for itself in two admissions and gets you into sights with no lining up (one day–80F, three consecutive days–160F, five consecutive days–240F).

Included sights (and admission prices without the pass) you're likely to visit: Louvre (45F), Orsay (39F), Sainte-Chapelle (32F), Arc de Triomphe (35F), Napoleon's Tomb (37F), Carnavalet Museum (35F), Conciergerie (28F), Sewer Tour (32F), Cluny Museum (30F), Notre-Dame towers (30F) and crypt (32F), L'Orangerie (30F), Picasso Museum (30F), Rodin Museum (28F), and the elevator to the top of the Grand Arche de La Defense (40F). Outside Paris, the pass covers the Palace of Versailles (45F) and its Grand Trianon (25F) and the Château Chantilly (35F). Tally it up—but remember, an advantage of the pass is that you skip to the front of all lines—saving hours of waiting in the summer (though everyone must pass through the slow-moving metal detector lines). If buying a pass at a museum with a long line, skip to the front and find the sales window. And with the pass, you'll pop painlessly into sights that you're walking by (even for a few minutes) that might otherwise not be worth the expense (e.g., Notre-Dame crypt, Conciergerie, Victor Hugo's House). The free museum and monuments directory that comes with your pass lists the latest hours, phone numbers, and specifics on what kids pay. The cut-off age for free entry varies from 5 to 18. Most major, serious art museums let young people up to 18 in for free. For some reason, anyone over age five has to pay to tour the sewers.

Museum Tips: The Louvre and many other museums are closed on Tuesday. The Orsay, Rodin Museum, and Versailles are closed Monday. Most museums offer reduced prices and shorter hours on Sunday. Many sights stop admitting people 30 to 60 minutes before they close, and many begin closing rooms 45 minutes before the actual closing time. For the fewest crowds, visit very early, at lunch, or very late. Most museums have slightly shorter hours October through March. French holidays can really mess up your sightseeing plans (Jan. 1, May 1, May 8, July 14, Nov. 1, Nov. 11, and Dec. 25). The best Impressionist art museums are the Orsay, Marmottan, and L'Orangerie (all described below, and also see our self-guided tours of the Orsay and L'Orangerie).

Paris Museums near the Tuileries Gardens

The newly renovated Tuileries Gardens were once the private property of kings and queens. Paris' grandest public park links the museums: Louvre, L'Orangerie, Jeu de Paume, and the Orsay.

▲▲▲**Louvre**—This is Europe's oldest, biggest, greatest, and possibly most crowded museum. It's packed with Greek and Roman masterpieces, medieval jewels, Michelangelo statues, and paintings by the greatest artists from the Renaissance to the Romantics (mid-1800s).

Cost: 45F, 26F after 15:00 and on Sunday; those under 18 enter free.

Hours: Wednesday–Monday 9:00–18:00, closed Tuesday, all wings open Wednesday until 21:45, Richelieu Wing (only) until 22:00 on Monday. Closed January 1, Easter, May 1, November 1, and Christmas Day. Tel. 01 40 20 53 17 or 01 40 20 51 51 for recorded information.

Location: At "Palais Royal/Musée du Louvre" Métro stop. The old "Louvre" Métro stop called "Louvre Rivoli" no longer goes to the Louvre. ✪ See Louvre Tour on page 79.

▲**L'Orangerie**—This small, quiet, and often-overlooked museum is open only May–August in 1999. It houses Monet's water lilies, many famous Renoirs, and a scattering of other great Impressionist works. The two breezy round rooms of water lilies are two of the most enjoyable rooms in Paris (30F, Wednesday–Monday 9:45–17:15, closed Tuesday, located in Tuileries Garden near place de la Concorde, Mo: Concorde, tel. 01 42 97 48 16). ✪ See L'Orangerie Tour on page 123.

PARIS, TUILERIES GARDENS

Jeu de Paume—This one-time home to the Impressionist art collection (now located in the Musée d'Orsay) hosts rotating exhibits of top contemporary artists (38F, Tuesday 12:00–21:30, Wednesday–Friday 12:00–19:00, weekends 10:00–19:00, closed Monday, on place de la Concorde, just inside Tuileries Garden on rue de Rivoli side, Mo: Concorde).

▲▲▲**Orsay Museum**—This is Paris' 19th-century art museum (actually, art from 1848–1914), including Europe's greatest collection of Impressionist works.

Cost: 39F, 27F for the young and old, under 18 free. English language tours usually run daily except Sunday at 11:30, cost 38F, take 90 minutes, and are also available on audiotape. Tel. 01 40 49 48 48.

Hours: Tuesday–Saturday 10:00–18:00, Thursday until 21:45, Sunday 9:00–18:00, closed Mondays. From June 20 to September 20, the museum opens at 9:00. Last entrance is 45 minutes before closing.

Location: Directly at the RER-C stop called Musée d'Orsay; the nearest Métro stop is "Solferino," three blocks south of the Orsay. From the Louvre, it's a 10-minute walk downstream to the Orsay.

★ See Orsay Tour on page 97.

Historic Core of Paris:
Notre-Dame, Sainte-Chapelle, and More

✪ All of these sights are covered in detail in the Historic Paris Walk on page 39. Only the essentials are listed here.

▲▲**Notre-Dame Cathedral**—The 700-year-old cathedral is packed with history and tourists. Study its sculpture and windows, take in a Mass, eavesdrop on guides, and walk all around the outside. (Free, daily 8:00–18:45; treasury–15F, daily 9:30–17:30; ask about the free English tours, normally Wednesday and Thursday at noon and Saturdays at 14:30; Mo: Cité, Hôtel de Ville, or St. Michel.) Sunday Masses are at 8:00, 8:45, 10:00, 11:30, 12:30, and 18:30. Clean 2.70F toilets in front of the church near Charlemagne's statue. ✪ See page 39.

Church Tower: Climb to the top for a great gargoyle's-eye view of the city. You get 400 steps for only 30F (entrance on outside, north tower open 9:30–17:30, closed at lunch and earlier off-season).

Crypt: The archaeological crypt is a worthwhile 15-minute stop with your museum pass (32F, 50F with Notre-Dame's tower, daily 10:00–18:00, closes at 17:00 October-April; enter 100 yards in front of church). You'll see Roman ruins, trace the street plan of the medieval village, and see diagrams of how the earliest Paris grew and grew, all thoughtfully explained in English.

Behind the Notre-Dame, squeeze through the tourist buses, cross the street, and enter the iron gate into the park at the tip of the island.

▲▲**Deportation Memorial (Mémorial de la Déportation)**—This memorial to the 200,000 French victims of the Nazi concentration camps draws you into their experience. (Free, Monday–Friday 8:30–21:45, weekends and holidays from 9:00, sometimes closes from 12:00–14:00, shorter hours off-season, east tip of the island near Île St. Louis, behind Notre-Dame, Mo: Cité.) ✪ See page 45.

Île St. Louis— This island behind Notre-Dame is known for its good restaurants (see Eating), great Bertillon ice cream (31 rue Saint Louis en l'Île), and interesting shops (along rue Saint Louis en l'Île). ✪ See page 45.

Cité "Métropolitain" Stop and Flower Market—On place Louis Lepine, between Notre-Dame and Sainte-Chapelle, you'll find a turn-of-the-century subway entrance and a flower market (that chirps with a bird market on Sunday).

▲▲▲**Sainte-Chapelle**—The triumph of Gothic church architecture is a cathedral of glass like no other. It was speedily built from 1242 to 1248 by St. Louis IX to house the supposed Crown of Thorns (32F, daily 9:30–18:30, off-season 10:00–16:30, Mo: Cité, call 01 48 01 91 35 for concert information). ✪ See page 50.

▲**Conciergerie**—Marie-Antoinette was imprisoned here, along with 2,600 others on their way to the guillotine (28F, daily 9:30– 18:30, 10:00–17:00 in winter, good English descriptions). ✪ See page 54.

▲**Samaritaine Department Store Viewpoint**— For a great, free viewpoint, take the elevator to the 9th floor and walk to the 11th-floor rooftop panorama (daily 9:30–19:00, reasonably priced café on 10th-floor terrace, supermarket in basement, Mo: Pont Neuf, tel. 01 40 41 20 20). ✪ See page 190.

Southwest Paris: Eiffel Tower Neighborhood

▲▲▲**Eiffel Tower**—Crowded and expensive but worth the trouble. Go early (by 9:30) or late in the day (after 18:00) to avoid most crowds; weekends are worst. Pilier Nord (the north pillar) has the biggest elevator and, therefore, the fastest moving line.

The Tower is 1,000 feet tall (six inches taller in hot weather), covers 2.5 acres, and requires 50 tons of paint. Its 7,000 tons of metal are spread out so well at the base that it's no heavier per square inch than a linebacker on tiptoes. Visitors to Paris may find Mona Lisa to be less than expected, but the Eiffel Tower rarely disappoints, even in an era of skyscrapers.

Built a hundred years after the French Revolution (and in the midst of an Industrial one), the Tower served no function but to impress. Bridge-builder Gustave Eiffel won the contest for the 1889 Centennial World's Fair by beating out such rival proposals as a giant guillotine. To a generation hooked on technology, the Tower was the marvel of the age, a symbol of progress and of man's ingenuity. To others it was a cloned-sheep monstrosity. The writer Maupassant routinely ate lunch in the Tower just so he wouldn't have to look at it.

Delicate and graceful when seen from afar, it's massive—even a bit scary—from close up. You don't appreciate the size until you walk toward it—like a mountain, it seems so close but takes forever to reach. There are three observation platforms, at 200, 400, and 900 feet; the higher you go, the more you pay. Each requires a separate elevator (and a line), so plan on at least 90 minutes if you want to go to the top and back. The view from the 400-foot-high second level is plenty.

Begin at the first floor, read the informative signs (in English) describing the major monuments, see the entertaining free movie on the history of the Tower, and consider a drink overlooking all of Paris at the café or at the reasonable restaurant Altitude 95 (decent 100F meals until 20:00 and Paris' best view bar). Take the elevator to the second floor for even greater views. As you ascend through the metal beams, imagine being a worker, perched high

——— EIFFEL TOWER NEIGHBORHOOD ———

above nothing, riveting this giant erector set together. On top, all of Paris lies before you, with a panorama guide. On a good day, you can see 40 miles.

Cost and Hours: It costs 20F to go to the first level, 40F to the second, and 57F to go all the way for the 1,000-foot view (not covered by museum pass). On a budget? You can climb the stairs to the second level for only 12F (summers daily 9:00–24:00, off-season 9:30–23:00, tel. 01 44 11 23 23, Mo: Trocadero, RER: Champs de Mars).

The best place to view the Tower is from Trocadero square to the north (a 10-minute walk across the river, and a happening scene at night). Consider arriving at the Trocadero Métro stop and then walking toward the Tower. The big J-number panel, emblazoned across the Tower, clicks down the days (j for *jour*) until the new millenium. Another great viewpoint is the long, grassy field of Champ de Mars to the south (after about 21:00 the *gendarmes* look the other way as Parisians stretch out or picnic on the grass). However impressive it may be by day, it's an awesome thing to see at twilight, when the Tower becomes engorged with light, and virile Paris lies back and lets night be on top.

▲**Paris Sewer Tour (Egouts)**—This quick and easy visit takes you along a few hundred yards of underground water tunnel lined with interesting displays, well-described in English, explaining the evolution of the world's longest sewer system. (If you lined up

Paris' sewers they would reach beyond Istanbul.) Don't miss the slide show, fine WCs just beyond the gift shop, and the occasional tours in English (32F, Saturday–Wednesday 11:00–17:00, closed Thursday and Friday, where the pont de l'Alma hits the Left Bank, tel. 01 47 05 10 29).

▲▲**Les Invalides: Napoleon's Tomb and Army Museum**— The emperor lies majestically dead inside several coffins under a grand dome—a goose-bumping pilgrimage for historians. Napoleon is surrounded by the tombs of other French war heroes and Europe's greatest military museum in the Hôtel des Invalides. Follow signs to the "crypt," where you'll find Roman Empire–style reliefs listing the accomplishments of Napoleon's administration. The restored dome glitters with 26 pounds of gold (37F, daily 10:00–18:00, closes off-season at 17:00, tel. 01 44 42 37 67, Mo: La Tour Maubourg or Varennes). ✪ See Napoleon's Tomb tour on page 131.

▲▲**Rodin Museum**—This user-friendly museum is filled with passionate works by the greatest sculptor since Michelangelo. See *The Kiss, The Thinker, The Gates of Hell*, and many more. Don't miss the room full of work by Rodin's student and mistress, Camille Claudel. (28F, 18F on Sunday, 5F for gardens only, which may be Paris' best deal as many works are well-displayed in the beautiful gardens; Tuesday–Sunday 9:30–17:45, closed Monday and at 17:00 off-season, 77 rue de Varennes, tel. 01 44 18 61 10, Mo: Varennes, near Napoleon's Tomb.) Good self-serve cafeteria and idyllic picnic spots in family-friendly back garden. ✪ See Rodin Museum tour on page 126.

▲▲**Marmottan**—In this private, intimate, less-visited museum you'll find more than 100 paintings by Claude Monet (thanks to his son Michel), including the *Impressions of a Sunrise* painting that gave the movement its start—and name (40F, Tuesday–Sunday 10:00–17:30, closed Monday, not covered by museum pass, 2 rue Louis Boilly, Mo: La Muette, follow the museum signs six blocks through a park to the museum, tel. 01 42 24 07 02). Combine this fine museum with a stroll down one of Paris' most pleasant shopping streets, the rue de Passy (from La Muette Métro stop).

Southeast Paris: Latin Quarter

✪ The Historic Paris Walk, on page 39, dips into the Latin Quarter.

▲**Latin Quarter**—This Left Bank neighborhood, just opposite Notre-Dame, is the Latin Quarter. This was a center of Roman Paris. But its touristic fame relates to the Latin Quarter's intriguing artsy, bohemian character. This was perhaps Europe's leading university district in the Middle Ages—home, since the 13th century, to the prestigious Sorbonne University. Back then, Latin was the language of higher education. And, since students here came from all over Europe, Latin served as their linguistic common denominator. Locals referred to the quarter by its language: Latin. In modern times this was the center of Paris' café culture. The neighborhood's main boulevards (St. Michel and St. Germain) are lined with cafés—once the haunts of great poets and philosophers, now the hangout of tired tourists. While still youthful and artsy, the area has become a tourist ghetto filled with cheap north African eateries.

▲**Cluny Museum (Musée National du Moyen Age)**—This treasure trove of medieval art fills the old Roman baths, offering close-up looks at stained glass, Notre-Dame carvings, fine goldsmithing and jewelry, and rooms of tapestries—the best of which is the exquisite *Lady with the Unicorn.* In five panels, a delicate-as-medieval-can-be noble lady introduces a delighted unicorn to the senses of taste, hearing, sight, smell, and touch (30F, Wednesday–Monday 9:15–17:45, closed Tuesday, near the corner of boulevards St. Michel and St. Germain, Mo: Cluny, tel. 01 53 73 78 00). ✪ See Cluny Museum Tour on page 135.

St. Germain-des-Prés—A church was first built on this site in A.D. 452. The church you see today was constructed in 1163. The area around the church hops at night with fire-eaters, mimes, and scads of artists (Mo: St. Germain-des-Prés).

▲**St. Sulpice Organ Concert**—For pipe-organ enthusiasts, this is a delight. The Grand-Orgue at St. Sulpice has a rich history, with a line of 12 world-class organists (including Widor and Dupre) going back 300 years. Marcel Dupre started the tradition of opening the loft to visitors after the 10:30 service on Sundays. Daniel Roth continues to welcome guests in three languages while playing five keyboards at once. The 10:30 Sunday Mass is followed by a 20-minute recital at 11:40. If you're lucky, at 12:00 the small unmarked door will open (left of entry as you face the rear) and visitors scamper like sixteenth notes up spiral stairs to a world of 6,000 pipes, where they can watch the master perform the next Mass, friends warming his bench, and a committee scrambling to pull and push the 110 stops (Mo: St. Sulpice or Mabillon).

▲**Luxembourg Gardens**—Paris' most beautiful, interesting, and enjoyable garden/park/recreational area is a great place to watch Parisians at rest and play. (See Paris with Children on page 185.) Challenge the card and chess players to a game (near the tennis courts) or find a free chair near the main pond and take a breather. Notice any pigeons? A poor Ernest Hemingway used to hand-hunt (read: strangle) them here. The grand neoclassical-domed Panthéon (now a mausoleum housing the tombs of several great Frenchmen) is a block away and is only worth entering if you have a museum pass. The park is open until dusk (Mo: Odéon). If you enjoy the Luxembourg Gardens and want to see more, visit the more elegant Parc Monceau (Mo: Monceau) and the colorful Jardin des Plantes (Mo: Jussieu or Gare d'Austerlitz, RER: Luxembourg).

▲**Montparnasse Tower**—This 59-floor superscraper—it's cheaper and easier to get to the top of this than the Eiffel Tower—offers one of Paris' best views, since the Eiffel Tower is in it and the Montparnasse tower isn't. Buy the photo guide to the city, then go to the rooftop and orient yourself (42F, daily in summer 9:30–23:00, off-season 10:00–22:00, disappointing after dark, entrance on rue l'Arrivé, Mo: Montparnasse). This is efficient when combined with a day trip to Chartres, which begins at the Montparnasse train station.

Northwest Paris:
Champs-Élysées, Arc de Triomphe, and Beyond

✪ Take the Champs-Élysées Walk, on page 57, for a pleasant downhill stroll connecting the sights from the enduring Arc de Triomphe to the historic place de la Concorde.

▲▲**Champs-Élysées**—This famous boulevard is Paris' backbone, with the greatest concentration of traffic. From the Arc de Triomphe down the Champs-Élysées, all of France seems to converge on place de la Concorde, the city's largest square. It was here that the guillotine took the lives of thousands—including King Louis XVI. Back then it was called the place de la Revolution.

Catherine de Medici wanted a place to drive her carriage, so she started draining the swamp that would become the Champs-Élysées. Napoleon put on the final touches, and it's been the place to be seen ever since. The Tour de France bicycle race ends here, as do all parades (French or foe) of any significance. While the boulevard has become a bit hamburgerized, a walk here is a must. Take the Métro to the Arc de Triomphe (Mo: Étoile) and saunter down the Champs-Élysées (Métro stops every few blocks: Étoile, George V, FDR). ✪ See page 57.

▲▲▲**Arc de Triomphe**—Napoleon had the magnificent Arc de Triomphe commissioned to commemorate his victory at the Battle of Austerlitz. There's no triumphal arch bigger (50 meters high, 40 meters wide). And, with 12 converging boulevards, there's no traffic circle more thrilling to experience—either behind the wheel or on foot (take the underpass). An elevator or a spiral staircase leads to a cute museum about the arch and a grand view from the top, even after dark (35F, Tuesday–Saturday 9:00–23:00, Sunday and Monday 9:30–18:00, Mo: Étoile, tel. 01 43 80 31 31). ✪ See page 57.

▲**Grande Arche de La Defense**—The centerpiece of Paris' ambitious skyscraper complex (La Defense) is the Grande Arche. Built to celebrate the 200th anniversary of the 1789 French Revolution, the place is big—38 floors on more than 200 acres. It holds offices for 30,000 people. Notre-Dame Cathedral could fit under its arch. The La Defense complex is an interesting study in 1960s land-use planning. Over 100,000 workers commute here daily, directing lots of business and development away from downtown and allowing central Paris to retain its more elegant feel. This aspect makes sense to most Parisians, regardless of whatever else they feel about this controversial complex. You'll enjoy city views from the Arche elevator (40F includes a film on its construction and art exhibits, daily 9:00–20:00, off-season 9:00–19:00, RER or Mo: La Defense, follow signs to Grande Arche, tel. 01 49 07 27 57).

Northeast Paris: Marais Neighborhood and More

✪ To connect the sights with a fun, fact-filled stroll leading from place de la Bastille to the Pompidou Center, take the Marais Walk on page 64.

▲**Picasso Museum (Hôtel Salé)**—This is the world's largest collection of Pablo Picasso's paintings, sculpture, sketches, and ceramics, and includes his personal collection of Impressionist art. It's well-explained in English and worth ▲▲▲ if you're a fan (30F, Wednesday–Monday 9:30–18:00, closed Tuesday, 5 rue Thorigny, Mo: St. Paul or Chemin Vert, tel. 01 42 71 25 21).

▲**Carnavalet Museum**—The tumultuous history of Paris is well-displayed in this converted Marais mansion. Unfortunately, explanations are in French only, but most displays are somewhat self-explanatory. You'll see paintings of Parisian scenes, French Revolution paraphernalia, old Parisian store signs, a guillotine, a model of 16th-century Île de la Cité (notice the bridge houses), and rooms full of 15th-century Parisian furniture. The medieval rooms and Revolution rooms are the most interesting (35F, Tuesday–Sunday 10:00–17:00, closed Monday, 23 rue de Sévigné, Mo: St Paul, tel. 01 42 72 21 13).

Promenade Plantée Park—This three-mile narrow garden walk, once a train track and now a joy, runs from place de la Bastille (Mo: Bastille) along Avenue Daumesnil to Saint-Mandé (Mo: Michel Bizot). Part of the park is elevated. At times you'll walk along the street till you pick up the next segment. From place de la Bastille, take Avenue Daumesnil (past Opéra building) to the intersection with avenue Ledru Rollin; walk up the stairs and through the gate (free, hours vary with season, open roughly 8:00–20:00).

▲**Père Lachaise Cemetery**—Littered with the tombstones of

many of the city's most illustrious dead, this is your best one-stop look at the fascinating, romantic world of "permanent Parisians." The place is confusing, but maps will direct you to the graves of Chopin, Molière, and even the American rock star Jim Morrison (who died in Paris). In section 92, a series of statues memorializing the war makes the French war experience a bit more real (helpful 10F maps at the flower store near entry, across the street from Métro stop, closes at dusk, Mo: Père Lachaise or bus #69).

▲▲**Pompidou Center**—(Closed for renovation until 2000.) Europe's greatest collection of far-out modern art, the Musée National d'Art Moderne is housed in this colorful exoskeletal building. After so many Madonnas and Children, a piano smashed to bits and glued to the wall is refreshing. It's a social center with lots of people, street theater, and activity inside and out—a perpetual street fair. Ride the escalator for a free city view from the café terrace on top and don't miss the free exhibits on the ground floor (35F, 24F for the young and old, Monday and Wednesday–Friday 12:00–22:00, weekends and most holidays 10:00–22:00, closed Tuesday, Mo: Rambuteau, tel. 01 44 78 12 33). Kids of any age enjoy the fun, colorful fountain (called *Homage to Stravinsky*) next to the Pompidou Center.

North Paris: Montmartre

✪ Connect the sights with the Montmartre Walk on page 73.
▲▲**Sacré-Coeur and Montmartre**—This Byzantine-looking church, while only 130 years old, is impressive. It was built as a "praise the Lord anyway" gesture, after the French were humiliated by the Germans in a brief war in 1871. The church is open daily until 23:00. One block from the church, the place du Tertre was the haunt of Toulouse-Lautrec and the original bohemians. Today it's mobbed by tourists and unoriginal bohemians, but still fun. Wander down rue Lepic to the two remaining windmills (there were once 30). Rue des Saules leads to Paris' only vineyard. Take the Métro to the Anvers stop (one Métro ticket buys your way up the funicular and avoids the stairs) or the closer but less scenic Abbesses stop. A taxi to the top of the hill saves time and sweat.

Pigalle—Paris' red-light district, the infamous "Pig Alley," is at the foot of Butte Montmartre. Ooh la la. More shocking than dangerous. Walk from place Pigalle to place Blanche teasing desperate barkers and fast-talking temptresses. In bars a 1,000F bottle of cheap champagne comes with a friend. Stick to the bigger streets, hang on to your wallet, and exercise good judgment. Cancan can cost a fortune, as can con artists in topless bars.

After dark, countless tour buses line the streets, reminding us that tour guides make big bucks by bringing their groups to touristic nightclubs like the famous Moulin Rouge (Mo: Pigalle or Abbesses).

Disappointments *de* Paris

While Paris can drive you in-Seine with superlatives, here are a few negatives to help you manage your limited time:

La Madeleine is a big stark neoclassical church with a post-card facade and a postbox interior. The famous aristocratic deli behind the church, Fauchon, is elegant, but so are many others handier to your hotel.

Paris' **Panthéon** (nothing like Rome's) is another stark neo-classical edifice filled with mortal remains of great Frenchmen who mean little to the average American tourist.

The old **Opéra Garnier** has a great Chagall-painted ceiling but is in a pedestrian-mean area. Don't go to American Express (behind the Opéra) just to change money. You'll get a better rate at many other banks.

The **Bastille** is Paris' most famous nonsight. The square is there, but confused tourists look everywhere and can't find the famous prison of Revolution fame. The building's gone and the square is good only as a jumping-off point for the Marais Walk (see page 64) or Promenade Plantée Park (see Northeast Paris sights, above).

And the **Latin Quarter** is a frail shadow of its characteristic self. It's more Tunisian, Greek, and Woolworth's than old-time Paris. The café life that turned on Hemingway and endeared boul' Miche and boulevard St. Germain to so many poets is also tram-pled by modern commercialism.

HISTORIC PARIS
WALK

*From Notre-Dame to Sainte-Chapelle
and In Between*

4

paris

Paris has been the capital of Europe for centuries. We'll start
where it did, on the Île de la Cité, with forays onto both the
Left and Right Banks on a walk that laces together the story of
Paris: Roman, medieval, the Revolution, café society, the literary
scene of the '20s, and into the modern world. Allow four hours
to do this three-mile walk justice.

Orientation

All sights that charge admission are covered by the Paris Museum
pass, which for many is a great time- and money-saver.

Notre-Dame: Free, daily 8:00–18:45; treasury–15F, daily
9:30–17:30; Sunday Mass at 8:00, 8:45, 10:00, 11:30, 12:30, and
18:30. Leaflet with church schedule at booth inside entrance. Ask
about free English tours, normally Wednesday and Thurday at
noon and Saturday at 14:30. The tower climb takes 400 steps and
30F—expensive but worth it for the gargoyle's-eye view of the
cathedral, Seine, and city (daily 9:00–17:30, off-season closes earlier and during lunch).

Notre-Dame Archeological Crypt: 32F, 50F with Notre-Dame
Tower, daily 10:00–18:00, closes at 17:00 October–April, entry
100 yards in front of the cathedral.

Deportation Memorial: Free, Monday–Friday 8:30–21:45, weekends and holidays from 9:00, sometimes closes from 12:00–14:00,
shorter hours off-season.

Sainte-Chapelle: 32F, daily 9:30–18:30, off-season 10:00–16:30.

Conciergerie: 28F, daily 9:30–18:30, off-season 10:00–17:00.

NOTRE-DAME

• *Start at the Notre-Dame Cathedral on the island in the River Seine,
the physical and historic bull's-eye of your Paris map. Closest Métro stops*

ÎLE DE LA CITÉ

*are Cité, Hôtel de Ville, and St. Michel, each requiring a short walk.
On the square in front of the cathedral, stand far enough back to take in
the whole facade. Look at the circular window in the center.*

For centuries, the main figure in the Christian "pantheon" has
been the goddess Mary, the mother of Jesus. Common people pray

to her directly in times of trouble, for comfort and to ask her
to convince God to be compassionate with them. The church
is dedicated to "Our Lady"
(Notre Dame), and there she is,
cradling God, right in the heart
of the facade, surrounded by
the halo of the rose window.
Though the church is massive
and imposing, it has always
stood for the grace and compassion of Mary, the "mother
of God."

The people of Paris broke ground in 1163. The cathedral was finished by their great-great-great-great-great-great grandchildren in 1345, a testament to the faith of these people. Look up the 200-foot bell-towers and imagine a tiny medieval community mustering the money and energy to build this. Master masons supervised, but the people did much of the grunt work themselves for free—hauling the huge stones from distant quarries, digging a 30-foot-deep trench to lay the foundations, and treading like rats on a wheel designed to lift the stones up, one by one. This kind of backbreaking, arduous manual labor created the real hunchbacks of Notre-Dame.
• *Walk this way toward the cathedral, and view it from the bronze plaque on the ground marked . . .*

Point Zero

You're standing at the very center of France, from which all distances are measured. The "Cité" started here in the third century B.C. In 52 B.C., the Romans booted out the Parisii tribe, built their government palace at the end of the square behind you, and a Temple of Jupiter where the cathedral sits. Two thousand years of dirt and debris have raised the city's altitude. The archaeological crypt nearby offers a fascinating look at the remains of the earlier city and church below today's street level.

Still facing the church, on your right is a grand equestrian statue of Charlemagne ("Charles the Great"), whose reign marked the birth of modern Europe. Crowned in A.D. 800, he briefly united much of Europe during the Dark Ages. (Maybe more interesting than Chuck the Great are nearby restrooms—the cleanest you'll find in downtown Paris.)

Before renovation, 150 years ago, this square was much smaller, a characteristic medieval shambles facing a run-down church, surrounded by winding streets and countless medieval buildings. The huge church bell-towers rose above this tangle of smaller buildings, inspiring Victor Hugo's story of a deaf, bell-ringing hunchback who could look down on all Paris.
• *Now turn your attention to the church facade. Look at the left doorway and, to the left of the door, find the statue with his head in his hands.*

Notre-Dame Facade

When Christianity began making converts in Roman Paris, this Bishop of Paris was beheaded. But these early Christians were hard to keep down. St. Denis got up, tucked his head under his arm, headed north, paused at a fountain to wash it off, and continued until he found just the right place to meet his maker. The Parisians were convinced of this miracle, Christianity gained ground, and a church soon replaced the pagan temple.

NOTRE DAME FACADE

GREAT VIEW!

← GARGOYLES

MARY IN ROSE WINDOW

28 KINGS OF JUDAH

ST. DENIS (HOLDING HEAD)

PORTAL OF MARY

LAST JUDGMENT

PORTAL OF ST. ANNE

SEINE RIVER

TOWER ENTRANCE   EXIT

ENTER

TO VIEW OF FLYING BUTTRESSES

POINT ZERO

WC →

TO RIGHT BANK

CHARLEMAGNE STATUE →

PLACE DU PARVIS

TO STE CHAPELLE

TO PLACE ST. MICHEL

DCH

By the way, Montmartre (the one hill overlooking Paris) is named for this martyr. Denis eventually died on the edge of town where the church of St. Denis was built (famous in history books as the first Gothic church, but not much to see today).
• *Now look above the central doorway, where you'll find scenes from the Last Judgment.*

Central Portal

It's the end of the world, and Christ sits on the throne of Judgment (just under the arches, holding his hands up). Below him, an angel and a demon weigh souls in the balance. The good people stand to the left, looking up to heaven. The naughty ones to the right are chained up and led off to... a six-hour tour of the Louvre on a hot day. Notice the crazy sculpted demons to the right, at the base of the arch.

• *Above the arches is a row of 28 statues, known as . . .*

The Kings of Judah

In the days of the French Revolution (1789–93), these Biblical kings were mistaken for the hated French kings, and Notre-Dame represented the oppressive Catholic hierarchy. The citizens stormed the church, crying, "Off with their heads!" Plop, they lopped off the crowned heads of these kings with glee, creating a row of St. Denises that wasn't repaired for decades.

But the story doesn't end there. A schoolteacher who lived nearby collected the heads and buried them in his backyard for safekeeping. There they slept until 1977, when they were accidentally unearthed. Today, you can stare into the eyes of the original kings in the Cluny Museum, a few blocks away.

• *Enter the church and find a spot to view the long, high central aisle.*

Notre-Dame Interior

Remove your metaphorical hat and become a simple bareheaded peasant, entering the dim medieval light of the church. Take a minute to let your pupils dilate, to take in the subtle, mysterious light-show God beams through the stained glass windows. Follow the slender columns up to the praying-hands arches of the ceiling and contemplate the heavens. Let's say it's dedication day for this great stone wonder. The priest intones the words of the Mass that echo through the hall: *"Terribilis est locus iste"*—"This place is *terribilis*," meaning awe-inspiring, or even terrifying. It's a huge, dark earthly cavern lit with an unearthly light.

This is Gothic. Taller and filled with light, this was a major improvement over the earlier Romanesque style. Gothic architects needed only a few structural columns topped by pointed arches that crisscross the columns to support the weight of the roof. This let them build higher than ever, freeing up the walls for windows. The church is designed in the shape of a cross, with the altar where the crossbeams intersect.

• *Walk up to the main altar.*

The Altar

This marks the spot where Mass is said and the bread and wine of communion are prepared and distributed. In olden days, there were no chairs. The church can hold up to 10,000 faithful. Join the statue of Joan of Arc (*Jeanne d'Arc*, in the right transept) in gazing up to the rose-shaped window, the only one of the three with its original medieval glass.

This was the holy spot for Romans, Christians . . . and even atheists. When the Revolutionaries stormed the church, they gutted it and turned it into a "Temple for the Cult of Reason." A woman dressed up like the Statue of Liberty held court at the altar as a symbol of the divinity of Man. France today, while nominally Catholic, remains aloof from Vatican dogmatism. Instead of traditional wooden confessional booths, notice the open, glass-walled room where modern sinners seek counseling as much as forgiveness.

Just past the altar are the walls of the choir, where more intimate services can be held in this spacious building. The aisles are lined with chapels, each dedicated to a particular saint. The faithful can pause at their favorite, light a candle as an offering, and meditate in the cool light of the stained glass. (The nearby Treasury, containing lavish robes and golden relic-holders, probably isn't worth the 15F entry fee.)

• *Amble around the ambulatory, spill back outside, and make a U-turn left. Walk along the side of the cathedral that faces the river.*

Notre-Dame Side View

Along the side of the church, you'll notice the flying buttresses. These 50-foot stone "beams" that stick out of the church were the key to the complex architecture of Gothic. The pointed arches we saw inside caused the weight of the roof to push outward rather than downward. The "flying" buttresses support the roof by pushing back inward. Gothic architects were masters at playing architectural forces against each other to build loftier and loftier churches.

Picture Quasimodo running around along the railed balcony at the base of the roof among the gargoyles. These grotesque beasts that stick out from pillars and buttresses represent souls caught between heaven and earth. They also function as rain

spouts when there are no evil spirits to do battle with.

The neo-Gothic 90-meter spire is a product of the 1860 reconstruction of the dilapidated old church. Around its base are apostles and evangelists (the green men) as well as Viollet-le-

Duc, the architect in charge of the work. Notice how the apostles look outward, blessing the city while the architect (at top) looks up the spire, marveling at his fine work.
• *Behind Notre-Dame, squeeze through the tourist buses, cross the street, and enter the iron gate into the park at the tip of the island.*

Deportation Memorial (Mémorial de la Déportation)

This memorial to the 200,000 French victims of the Nazi concentration camps draws you into their experience. As you descend the

steps, the city around you disappears. Surrounded by walls, you have become a prisoner. Your only freedom is your view of the sky and the tiny glimpse of the river below.

    Enter the dark, single-file chamber up ahead. Inside, the circular plaque in the floor reads, "They descended into the mouth of the earth and they did not return."

    A hallway stretches in front of you, lined with 200,000 lighted crystals, one for each French citizen that died. Flickering at the far end is the eternal flame of hope. The tomb of the unknown deportee lies at your feet. Above, the inscription reads, "Dedicated to the living memory of the 200,000 French Deportees sleeping in the night and the fog, exterminated in the Nazi concentration camps." Above the exit as you leave is the message you'll find at all Nazi sights: "Forgive, but never forget."

Île St. Louis

Back on street level, look across the river to the Île St. Louis. If the Île de la Cité is a tug laden with the history of Paris, it's towing this classy little residential dinghy laden only with boutiques, characteristic restaurants, and famous sorbet shops. This island wasn't developed until much later (18th century). What was a swampy mess is now harmonious Parisian architecture.
• *From the tip of the Île de la Cité, cross the bridge to the Left Bank and turn right. Walk along the river, toward the front end of Notre-Dame. Stairs detour down to the riverbank if you need a place to picnic. This side view of the church from across the river is one of Europe's great sights.*

LEFT BANK (RIVE GAUCHE)

The Left Bank of the Seine—"left" if you were floating downstream—still has many of the twisting lanes and narrow buildings of medieval times. The Right Bank is more modern and business-oriented, with wide boulevards and stressed Parisians in suits. Here along the river bank, the "big business" is books, displayed in the green metal stalls on the parapet. These literary entrepreneurs pride themselves in their easygoing business style. With flexible hours and literally no overhead, they run their business as they have since medieval times.

• *When you reach the bridge (pont au Double) that crosses over in front of Notre-Dame, veer to the left, across the street to a small park (square Viviani). Go through the park to the small rough-stone church of St. Julien-le-Pauvre.*

Medieval Paris (1000–1400)

This church dates from the 12th century, and the area around it keeps the same feel. A half-timbered house stands to the right of the entrance. Many buildings in medieval times were built like this, with a wooden frame filled in with a plaster of mud, straw, and dung. Back then, the humble "half-timbered" structure would have been hidden by a veneer of upscale stucco.

Looking along nearby rue Galande, you'll see a few old houses built every which way. In medieval days, people were piled on top of each other, building at all angles, as they scrambled for this prime real estate near the main commercial artery of the day—the Seine. The smell of fish competed with the smell of neighbors in this knot of humanity.

These narrow streets would have been dirt (or mud). Originally the streets sloped from here down into the mucky Seine, until modern quays cleaned that up. Many Latin Quarter lanes were named for their businesses or crafts. The rue de la Bucherie (or "butcher street," just around the corner, in the direction of the river) was where butchers slaughtered livestock. The blood and guts drained into the Seine and out of town.

• *At #37 rue de la Bucherie is . . .*

Shakespeare & Company Bookstore

Along with butchers and fishmongers, the Left Bank has been home to scholars, philosophers and poets since medieval times. This funky bookstore—a reincarnation of the original shop from the 1920s—has picked up the literary torch. In the '20s, it was famous as a meeting place of Paris' literary expatriate elite. Ernest Hemingway, a struggling American writer, strangled and cooked pigeons in the park and borrowed books from here to survive. Fitzgerald, Joyce, and Pound also got their English fix here.

Today it does its best to carry on that literary tradition. Struggling writers are given free accommodations upstairs in tiny, book-lined rooms with views of Notre-Dame. Downstairs, travelers enjoy the best selection of used English books in Paris. Pick up *Free Voice*, published for today's American expatriates, and say hi to George.

• *Return to St. Julien-le-Pauvre, then turn right (west) on rue Galande, which immediately intersects with the busy rue St. Jacques (also called rue du Petit Pont). Way back in Roman times, this was the straight, wide, paved road that brought chariots racing in and out of the city. (Roman-iacs can see remains from the third-century baths, along with a fine medieval collection, at the Cluny Museum, two blocks to the left; see tour on page 135.) Cross rue St. Jacques to the small Gothic church of St. Severin.*

St. Severin

Don't ask me why, but it took a century longer to build this church than Notre-Dame. This is Flamboyant, or "flame-like," Gothic, and you can see the short, prickly spires meant to make this building flicker in the eyes of the faithful. The church gives us a close-up look at gargoyles. This weird, winged species of flying mammal, now extinct, used to swoop down on unwary peasants, occasionally carrying off small children in their beaks. Today, they're most impressive in thunderstorms, when they vomit rain.

The Latin Quarter

While it may look more like the Tunisian Quarter today, this area is the Latin Quarter, named for the language you'd hear on these streets if you walked them in the Middle Ages. The University, one of the leading universities of medieval Europe, was (and still is) nearby.

A thousand years ago the "crude" or vernacular local languages were sophisticated enough to communicate basic human needs, but if you wanted to get philosophical, the language of choice was Latin. The educated elite of Dark Ages Europe was a class that transcended nations and borders. From Sicily to Sweden, they spoke and corresponded in Latin. The most Latin thing about this area now is the beat you may hear coming from some of the subterranean jazz clubs.

Along rue St. Severin you can still see the shadow of the medieval sewer system. (The street slopes into a central channel of bricks.) In the days before plumbing and toilets, when people still went to the river or neighborhood wells for their water, flushing meant throwing it out the window. Certain times of day were flushing times. Maids on the fourth floor would holler *"Garde de l'eau!"* ("look out for the water!") and heave it into the streets, where it would eventually wash down into the Seine.

• *At #22 rue St. Severin, you'll find the skinniest house in Paris, two windows wide. Continue along rue St. Severin to . . .*

Boulevard St. Michel

Busy boulevard St. Michel (or "boul' Miche") is famous as the main artery for bohemian Paris, culminating a block away (to the left) where it intersects with boulevard St. Germain. Although nowadays you're more likely to find pantyhose at 30 percent off, there are still many cafés, boutiques, and bohemian haunts nearby. The Sorbonne—the University of Paris—is also close, if you want to make a detour. Turn left on boulevard St. Michel and go two blocks. It's on the left, set back in a courtyard. For centuries, children of kings and nobles were sent here to become priests, though many returned as heretics, having studied radical new secular ideas as well. Paris still is a world center for new intellectual trends.

• *Cross boulevard St. Michel. Just ahead is a tree-filled square lined with cafés and restaurants.*

Place Saint Andre des Arts

In Paris, most serious thinking goes on in cafés. (For more information, see Les Grands Cafés de Paris on page 181.) For centuries, these have been social watering-holes, where you could buy a warm place to sit and stimulating conversation for the price of a cup of coffee. Every great French writer—from Voltaire and Rousseau to Sartre and Derrida—had a favorite haunt.

Paris honors its writers. If you visit the Pantheon (a few blocks down boulevard St. Michel and to the left), you will find great French writers buried in a setting usually reserved for warriors and politicians.

• *Adjoining this square on the river side is the triangular-shaped place St. Michel, with a Métro stop and a statue of St. Michael killing a devil.*

Place St. Michel

You're standing at the traditional core of the Left Bank's artsy, liberal, hippie, bohemian district of poets, philosophers, and winos. You'll find international eateries, far-out bookshops, street singers, pale girls in black berets, jazz clubs, and—these days—tourists. Small cinemas show avant-garde films, almost always in the *version originale* (V.O.). For colorful wandering and café-sitting, afternoons and evenings are best. In the morning, it feels sleepy. The Latin Quarter stays up late and sleeps in.

In less commercial times, place St. Michel was a gathering point for the city's malcontents and misfits. Here, in 1871, the citizens took the streets from the government troops, set up barricades "Les Miz"-style, and established the Paris Commune. In World War II, the locals rose up against their Nazi oppressors (read the plaques by the St. Michael fountain). And in the spring of 1968, a time of social upheaval all over the world, young students battled riot batons and tear gas, took over the square, and demanded change.

• *From place St. Michel, look across the river and find the spire of Sainte-Chapelle church, with its weathervane angel. Cross the river on the pont St. Michel and continue along boulevard du Palais.*

On your left, you'll see the doorway to Sainte-Chapelle. But first, carry on another 30 meters and turn right at a wide pedestrian street, the rue de Lutece.

CITÉ "METROPOLITAIN" STOP

Of the 141 original turn-of-the-century subway entrances, this is one of 17 survivors now preserved as a national art treasure. (New York's Museum of Modern Art even exhibits one.) The curvy, plant-like iron work is a textbook example of Art Nouveau, the style that rebelled against the Erector-set squareness of the Industrial Age.

The flower market on place Louis Lepine is a pleasant detour. On Sundays this square chirps with a busy bird market. And across the way is the Prefecture de Police, where Inspector Clouseau of Pink Panther fame used to work, and where the local resistance fighters took the first building from the Nazis, leading to the allied liberation of Paris a week later.

• *Pause here to admire the view. Sainte-Chapelle is a pearl in an ugly architectural oyster, part of a complex of buildings that includes the Palace of Justice (to the right of Sainte-Chapelle, behind the iron and bronze gates).*

Return to the entrance of Sainte-Chapelle. You'll need to pass through a metal-detector to get into Sainte-Chapelle. (It's best to leave your Uzi at the hotel.) Walk through the security scanner. Toilets are ahead, on the left. The line into the church may be long. (Museum cardholders can go directly in.) Enter the humble ground floor . . .

SAINTE-CHAPELLE

Sainte-Chapelle, the triumph of Gothic church architecture, is a cathedral of glass like no other. It was speedily built in 1248 for St. Louis IX (France's only canonized king), to house the supposed Crown of Thorns. Its architectural harmony is due to the fact that it was completed under the direction of one architect and in only five years— unheard of in Gothic times. Recall that Notre-Dame took over 200.

The design clearly shows an Old Regime approach to worship. The basement was for staff and more common folks. Royal Christians worshiped upstairs. The paint job, a 19th-century restoration, helps you imagine how grand this small, painted, jewelled chapel was. (Imagine Notre-Dame painted as this is . . .)

• *Climb the spiral staircase to the "Haute Chapelle." Leave the rough stone of the earth, and become enlightened.*

The Stained Glass

Fiat lux. "Let there be light." Christianity, like many religions, intuitively recognized the sun as the source of life on earth. Light shining through stained glass was a symbol of God's grace shining down to earth, and Gothic architects used their new technology to turn dark stone buildings into lanterns of light. For me, the glory of Gothic shines brighter here than in any other church.

There are 15 separate panels of stained glass, with more than 1,100 different scenes, mostly from the Bible. In medieval times, scenes like these helped teach Bible stories to the illiterate. These cover the entire Christian history of the world, from the Creation in Genesis (first window on the left), to the coming of Christ (over the altar), to the end of the world (the rose window at the rear of the church). Each individual scene is interesting, and the whole effect is overwhelming.

Let's look at a single scene. Head toward the altar to the fourth big window on the right. Look at the bottom circle, second from the left. It's a battle scene (the campaign of Holophernes)

SAINTE-CHAPELLE

JESUS'
PASSION SCENES

ALTAR

CAMPAIGN OF
HOLOPHERNES

ST.
LOUIS'
PEEK-A-
BOO
WINDOW

MORE
MOSES

LIFE
OF
MOSES

STAINED GLASS

CAIN
CLUBBING
ABEL

BUTTRESSES

SPIRAL
STAIRCASE

SPIRAL
STAIRCASE

50 FEET

ENTER
BELOW
(INTO LOWER CHAPEL)

DCH

showing three soldiers with swords slaughtering three men. The
background is blue. The men have different colored clothes—red,
blue, green, mauve, and white. Notice some of the details. You can
see the folds in the robes, the hair, and facial features, and look at
the victim in the center—his head is splotched with blood!

Craftsmen made glass (which is, essentially, melted sand), col-
oring it by mixing in metals like cobalt (blue) or copper (green).
Then they'd assemble pieces of different colored glass to make,
say, the soldier in blue with a green shield (upper right). The

pieces were held together by lead. Details like the folds in the robes (see the victim in white, lower left) came by either scratching on the glass, or by baking in imperfections. It was a painstaking process of finding just the right colors, fitting them together to make a scene . . . and then multiplying by 1,100.

Other scenes worth a look:

1) Cain clubbing Abel (first window on the left, second row of circles, far right—Cain is in red).

It takes 13 tourists to build a Gothic church: six columns, six buttresses, and one steeple.

2) The life of Moses (second window, the bottom row of diamond panels). First panel shows baby Moses in a basket, placed by his sister in the squiggly brown river. Next, he's found by pharaoh's daughter. Then, he grows up. And finally, he's a man, a prince of Egypt on his royal throne.

3) In the next window (third on left) you'll see various scenes of Moses. He's often given "horns" because of a medieval mistranslation of the Biblical description of his "aura" of holiness.

4) Over the altar are scenes from Jesus' arrest and crucifixion. Stand at the stairs in front and look over the altar, through the canopy, to find Jesus being whipped (left), Jesus in purple being crowned with thorns (right), Jesus in yellow carrying his cross (a little above), and finally, Jesus on the cross being speared by a soldier (above, left).

(Note: the sun lights up different windows at different times of day. Overcast days give the most even light. On bright sunny days, some sections are glorious while others look like a sheet of lead.)

If you can't read much into the individual windows, you're not alone. The medieval worshiper was a stained glass speed reader, and we're the illiterate ones. (For some tutoring, a little book with color photos is on sale downstairs with the postcards.)

The altar was raised up high (notice the staircase for the priest to the right to better display the relic around which this chapel was built—the Crown of Thorns. This was the crown put on Jesus when the Romans were torturing and humiliating him before his execution. King Louis was convinced he'd found the real McCoy and paid three times as much money for it as was spent on this entire chapel. Today, the supposed crown of thorns is kept in the Notre-Dame Treasury and shown only on Good Friday.

Notice the little private viewing window in the wall to the right of the altar. Louis was both saintly and shy. He liked to be able to go to church without dealing with the rigors of public royal life. Here he could worship still dressed in his jammies.

Lay your camera on the ground and shoot the ceiling. Those pure and simple ribs growing out of the slender columns are the essence of Gothic structure.

Palais de Justice

Back outside, as you walk around the church exterior, look down and notice how much Paris has risen in the 800 years since Sainte-Chapelle was built. You're in a huge complex of buildings that has housed the local government since ancient Roman times. It was the site of the original Gothic palace of the early kings of France. The only surviving medieval parts are the Sainte-Chapelle church and the Conciergerie prison.

Most of the site is now covered by the giant Palais de Justice, home of France's supreme court, built in 1776. "*Liberté, Egalité, Fraternité*" over the doors is a reminder that this was also the head-quarters of the Revolutionary government. Here they doled out justice, condemning many to torture in the Conciergerie prison downstairs, or to have their head removed St. Denis-style by "*Monsieur de Paris*"— the guillotine.

Paris' City Palace in 1650, with Sainte-Chapelle, the Conciergerie, and Pont Neuf (then 30 years old) in the background.

• *Now pass through the big iron gate to the noisy boulevard du Palais and turn left (toward the Right Bank).*

On the corner is the site of the oldest public clock (1334) in the city. While the present clock is Baroque, it somehow still manages to keep accurate time.

Turn left onto quai d'Horologe and walk along the river. The round medieval tower just ahead marks the entrance to the Conciergerie. Even if you don't pay to see the Conciergerie, you can visit the courtyard and lobby. Step past the serious-looking guard into the courtyard.

Conciergerie

The Conciergerie, a former prison and place of torture, is a gloomy place. Kings used it to torture and execute failed assassins. The leaders of the Revolution put it to similar good use. The tower next to the entrance, called "the babbler," was named for the painful sounds that leaked from it.

Look at the stark printing above the doorways. This was a no nonsense revolutionary time. Everything, including lettering, was subjected to the test of reason. No frills or we chop 'em off.

Marie-Antoinette was imprisoned here. During a busy eight-

month period in the Revolution, she was one of 2,600 prisoners kept here on their way to the guillotine.

The interior (requires ticket) with its huge vaulted and pillared rooms, echoes with history, but is pretty barren. You can see Marie-Antoinette's cell, with a collection of Marie-Antoinette mementoes. In another room, a list of those made "a foot shorter at the top" by the guillotine includes ex-King Louis XVI, Charlotte Corday (who murdered Marat in his bathtub), and the

chief Revolutionary who got a taste of his own medicine—Maximilien Robespierre.

• *Back outside, wink at the flak-vested guard (but no jokes about your Uzi), turn left, and continue your walk along the river. Across the river you can see the rooftop observatory of the Samaritaine department store, where we'll end this walk. At the first corner, veer left into a sleepy triangular square called "place Dauphine."*

Place Dauphine

It's amazing to find such coziness in the heart of Paris. The French Supreme Court building looms behind like a giant marble gavel. Enjoy the village-Paris feeling in the park. You may see lawyers on their lunchbreak playing *boules*.

• *Walk through the park to the statue of Henry IV, who in 1607 inaugurated the Pont Neuf. If in need of a romantic little hideaway in the midst of this mega city, take the steps down into the park on the tip of the island and dangle your legs over the prow of this concrete island. From the statue, turn right onto the old bridge. Walk to the little rest nook halfway across.*

Pont Neuf

The Pont Neuf, or "new bridge," is now Paris' oldest. Its 12 arches span the widest part of the river. The fine view includes the park on the tip of the island (note Seine boats), the Orsay Gallery, and the Louvre. These turrets were originally for vendors and street entertainers. In the days of Henry, who originated the promise of "a chicken in every pot," this would have been a lively scene.

• *Directly over the river, the first building you'll hit on the Right Bank is the venerable old department store, Samaritaine. Go through the door, veer left, and catch the elevator to the ninth floor. Climb two sets of stairs to the panorama. (Don't confuse the terrace level with the higher, better panorama. Light meals are served on the terrace. Public WCs on fifth and ninth floors.)*

THE REST OF PARIS

From the circular little crow's nest of the building, ponder the greatest skyline in Europe. Retrace the walk you just made, starting with Notre-Dame and Sainte-Chapelle. Then spin counterclockwise (or run down the stairs to hop on the Métro) and check out the rest of Paris:

The **Pompidou Center**, the wild and colorful rectangular tangle of pipes and tubes, is filled with art that makes this building's exterior look tame (closed for renovation until 2000).

Sacré-Coeur is a neo-Romanesque church topping Montmartre. This is an atmospheric quarter after dark, its streets filled with strolling tourists avoiding strolling artists. ❂ See Montmartre Walk on page 73.

The **Louvre** is the largest building in Paris, largest palace in Europe, and largest museum in the Western world.

Stretching away from the Louvre, the **Tuileries Gardens**, place de la Concorde, and Champs-Élysées lead to the Arc de Triomphe. The gardens are Paris' "Central Park," filled with families at play, cellists in the shade, carousels, pony rides, and the ghost of Maurice Chevalier.

The gardens overlook the grand **place de la Concorde**, marked by an ancient obelisk, where all of France seems to converge. It was "guillotine central" during the Revolution and continues to be a place of much festivity.

Europe's grandest boulevard, the **Champs-Élysées**, runs uphill from place de la Concorde about a mile to the Arc de Triomphe. While pretty hamburgerized, and with rich-and-single aristocrats more rare than ever, the people-watching is still some of Europe's best. ❂ See Champs-Élysées Walk on page 57.

Napoleon began constructing the magnificent **Arc de Triomphe** in 1806 to commemorate his victory at the Battle of

Austerlitz. It was finished in
1836, just in time to be a part
of the Emperor's funeral
parade. Today it commemo-
rates heroes of past wars.
There's no triumphal arch
bigger (50 meters high, 40
meters wide). And, with 12
converging boulevards, there's
no traffic circle more thrilling
to experience—either on foot
or behind the wheel.

Paris, the capital of Europe, is built on an appropriately monumental plan with an axis that stretches from the Louvre, up the
Champs-Élysées, past the Arc de Triomphe, all the way to the
modern arch among the skyscrapers at **La Defense**. (Find the
faint shadow of this arch, just above the Arc de Triomphe.)

The **Orsay Museum**, the train-station-turned-art-museum, is
located just beyond the Louvre on the left bank of the Seine.

The body of Napoleon lies under the gilded dome. This is
surounded by **Les Invalides**, the giant building designed to house
his wounded troops. Today this building houses Europe's greatest
military museum. The Rodin Museum is nearby.

The **Eiffel Tower** is a thousand-foot exclamation point celebrating the 100th anniversary of the French Revolution. Built in
1889 as a temporary engineering stunt, Paris decided to let it be a
rare exception to a downtown building code that allows the skyline
to be broken only by a few prestigious domes and spires.

The 52-story **Montparnasse Tower** looks like the box the
Eiffel Tower came in. It's a city in itself with a work force of 5,000
and an altitude of 700 feet, reminding us that, while tourists look
for hints of Louis and Napoleon, today's work-a-day Paris looks to
the future.

CHAMPS-ÉLYSÉES
WALK

Leaving Paris without strolling the Champs-Élysées is like walking
out of a great restaurant before dessert. This is Paris at its most
Parisian: monumental sidewalks, stylish shops, grand cafés, and
glimmering showrooms. This walk covers about three miles and
takes three hours if done completely. The Arc de Triomphe (open
until 22:00, 23:00 in summer) and Champs-Élysées are best at
night. Métro stops are located every three blocks on the Champs-
Élysées.

Take the Métro to "Charles de Gaulle Étoile"; then follow
access Arc de Triomphe signs to the top of the Champs-Élysées and
face the Arc de Triomphe. Underground WCs are on the left side
of Champs-Élysées, and an underground walkway leading to the
arch is on the right side of the Champs-Élysées.

Begin this walk at the top of the **Arc de Triomphe** (230
steps or elevator—sorry, no discount for walkers; 35F,
Tuesday–Saturday 9:00–23:00, Sunday–Monday 9:30–18:00). A
small museum explains its history; the exhibits are in French, but
there's a good video in English.

Begun in 1806, the arch was intended to honor Napoleon's
soldiers who, in spite of being vastly outnumbered by the Austri-
ans, scored a remarkable victory at the battle of Austerlitz.
Napoleon died during its construction. But it was finished in time
for his funeral procession—carrying his remains from exile in St.
Helena home to Paris—to pass underneath. Today the Arc de
Triomphe is dedicated to the glory of all French armies.

From the rooftop viewpoint, get your bearings with the circular orientation tables. Walk to the back side, opposite the
Champs-Élysées. The avenue Grande Armée leads to the skyscrapers of the La Defense suburb. Notice what a contrast they
make to the regular height of buildings closer to the arch. French

CHAMPS-ÉLYSÉES WALK

President Mitterand had the huge white **Grande Arche de la Defense** built as a centerpiece of this mini-Manhattan (see Sights, Northwest Paris). It's part of the huge axis formed by the arch you're standing on and the Louvre. The wide boulevard lined with grass and trees a little to your left is avenue Foch (named for WWI hero, Foch) and is the best address to have in Paris. (The shah of Iran and Aristotle Onassis had homes here.) The Bois de Boulogne is the big green park at the end of avenue Foch. While the arch was under construction, the surrounding land was a rural forest, looking much like the Bois de Boulogne.

Now scan the cityscape of downtown Paris. Notice the uniform height and symmetry. The beauty of Paris—basically a flat basin with a river running through it—is man-made. The key to this beauty is the relationship between the width of its grand boulevards and the uniformity in the height and design of the buildings. The rude Montparnasse tower (standing like the box the Eiffel Tower came in) served as a wake-up call in the early 1970s to preserve the building height restriction and strengthen urban design standards.

The 12 boulevards that radiate from the Arc de Triomphe were part of Baron Haussmann's master plan for Paris, the creation of a series of major boulevards, intersecting at diagonals with monuments (like the Arc de Triomphe) as centerpieces of those intersections. His plan did not anticipate the automobile—obvious when you watch the traffic scene below. As you gaze down at what appears a chaotic traffic mess, watch how smoothly it really functions. Cars entering the circle have the right of way, those in the circle must yield. Motorcycles are fair game. Pedestrians are used as target practice. Still there are plenty of accidents. Tired of related disputes, insurance companies split the fault and damages of any Arc de Triomphe accidents fifty-fifty.

Look straight down the **Champs-Élysées**. The first street was built at the lower end in the early 1600s by Queen Marie de Medici, a short extension of her Tuileries Gardens. It soon became the place to cruise in your carriage. (It still is today—traffic can be jammed up even at midnight.) One hundred years later it was extended uphill to where you are now.

Like its Roman ancestors, this arch has served as a parade gateway for triumphal armies (French or foe) and important ceremonies. From 1941 to 1944 a large swastika flew from here. Allied troops marched trimphantly under this arch in August 1944.

Descend the arch and stand on the bronze plaque at the **Tomb of the Unknown Soldier** (from WWI). Daily at 18:30 the flame is rekindled and new flowers set in place. On the columns, you'll see lists of battle victories and officers (with a line under the names of those who died in battle).

Walk over to the arch's massive right column (with your back to the Champs-Élysées) to see its most famous sculpture. ***The Departure of the Volunteers***, also called ***La Marseillaise***, is a rousing effort to rally the troops by what looks like an ugly reincarnation of Joan of Arc. On the right side of this column, a scene a little over halfway up the arch shows Naopleon's confident pose as he oversees his victory at Austerlitz.

Walk out to the traffic circle and look down the Champs-Élysées. Plan your walking attack from here. The Louvre is the building at the very end of the avenue through the Tuileries Gardens. Notice where the buildings end and the parkway begins about one-third of the distance to the Louvre. That's the Rond-point intersection, where our walk turns right. As you gaze down the Champs-Élysées, notice how the left sidewalk is more popular with pedestrians. While the left side is most interesting, cross over at least once for the exhilerating view from the center of the avenue's ten lanes. The **tourist information office** is immediately on the right at #127. Le Drugstore (next door) has a small grocery store in the back.

Cross back under the tunnel to the top of the Champs-Élysées. The *nouveau* (new) Champs-Élysées is a revitalized avenue with new street benches, lamps, broader sidewalks, and an army of green-suited workers with small machines designed to keep Paris' most famous avenue spick and span.

Start your descent. The first tiny street you cross, rue de Tilsitt, is part of a shadow ring road—an option for drivers who'd like to avoid the chaos of the arch, complete with stoplights.

On the first block down, stop by Café Vesuvio (#144, reasonable prices) to enjoy fine views of the arch with its rooftop bristling with tourists.

At the Mercedes showroom (#118), you can pick up your new sedan and a leather jacket and purse to match.

Next to the Mercedes showroom is the famous **Lido**, Paris' largest cabaret—check out the photos, video, and prices. These sensational shows pull out every stop for floor customers. Movie-going on the Champs-Élysées is also popular. Check to see if there are films you recognize, then look for the showings (*seances*); if there is a "*v.o.*" next to the time, the film will be in its original version or langauge.

Now cross the boulevard where the elegant avenue George V (home to several four-star hotels and the Crazy Horse Saloon) spills into the Champs-Élysées. **Fouquet's** café-restaurant (under the orange awning) serves the most expensive shot of expresso I found in Paris (27F), but the setting is great. Since the early 1900s Fouquet's has been a favorite of French actors and actresses. The welcome mat of golden plaques honors winners of France's Oscar-like film awards, the Cesars (see Les Grands Cafés de Paris, page 181).

Cross back to the lively side. At #92, a wall plaque marks the place Thomas Jefferson lived while minister to France (1785). The headquarters of Club Med offers an inviting opportunity to sit down and take a quick video trip to the tropics.

Nearby are several **arcades**. My favorite is the Arcade des Champs-Élysées at #76. This refuge of the belle epoque seems out of place today. Wander in. A meal at Batifol's gives you a taste of the old Champs-Élysées (climb three steps for most atmospheric tables; reasonable value; try the *pot-au-feu*).

Farther down *les Champs*, glide down Sephora's ramp at #74 into a vast hall of cosmetics and perfumes. Walk to the back past the nasal pirate's punch of hundreds of people squirting samples. At rue Boetie, map lovers can detour one block to the Institut Geographique National, France's version of the National Geographic Society (9:30-19:00).

Virgin Megastore sells a world of music one block farther down. The Disney store and new Gap stores are reminders of global ecomomics—the French love these stores as much as Americans do. And near the bottom of the Champs-Élysées, Renault and Citroen showrooms glare across the avenue, each offering late night cafés and restaurants. Renault has a neat little antique car museum.

At the Rondpoint the shopping ends and the park begins. This leafy circle is always colorful, lined with flowers or seasonal decorations (thousands of pumpkins at Halloween, hundreds of trees at Christmas).

Now it's decision time. You have three options: 1) You can continue straight (by Métro or foot) to reach place de la Concorde and the Tuileries Gardens. 2) A hard right turn here takes you back to the river and the pont de l'Alma, down Paris' most exclusive shopping street, the avenue Montaigne, where you need an appointment to buy a dress. 3) You can finish the walk with me.

To continue, walk a block past Rondpoint, then turn right on avenue Churchill, and walk between the glass- and steel-domed **Grand and Petit Palais** exhibition halls, built for the 1900 World's

Fair. Today these examples of the "can do" spirit of the turn-of-the-century host a variety of exhibits (details at the TI or in *Pariscope*). The Petit Palais (left side) houses a permanant collection of 19th-century paintings by Delacroix, Cézanne, Monet, and others. The backside of the Grand Palais is the Palais de la Décourverte, an extensive hands-on science museum with everything from a plane-tarium to full-scale dinosaurs (described on page 187). Cross the river on pont Alexandre eyeing the golden dome of Les Invalides. Les Invalides was built by Louis XIV as a veteran's hospital for his battle-weary troops (see Napoleon's Tomb on page 131). This exquisite bridge was built to celebrate a turn-of-the-century treaty between France and Russia. Like the two palaces just passed, it's a fine example of belle epoque exuberance. The barges under the bridge are some of over 2,000 houseboats on the Seine.

At the end of the bridge, turn left and follow the Seine past the Air France bus terminal and Ministry of Foreign Affairs (#37) to the Greek temple-like Assemblée Nationale (at the next bridge). France's 600 members of parliament convene here. Embassies and government offices line the streets behind these buildings.

From here, pont de la Concorde leads to place de la Concorde. The bridge, built of stones from the Bastille Prison (which was demolished by the Revolution in 1789), symbolizes that, with good government, *concorde* (harmony) can come from chaos. Cross the crosswalk, turn left, walk to the center of the bridge, and gaze upriver. Using a clock as a compass, the L'Orangerie is at 10:00 and the tall building with the skinny chimneys (at 11:00) is the architectural caboose of the sprawling Louvre Palace. The park between is the Tuileries Gardens. The Orsay Museum on the right (just this side of the next bridge) is opposite the Tuileries. Leaving the bridge you'll cross a freeway underpass similar to the one at pont de L'Alma, three bridges downstream, where Princess Diana lost her life in the tragic 1997 car accident.

Continue to the **place de la Concorde**, the 21-acre square with the obelisk. Walk to the island in the center. During the Revolution, this was the place de la Revolution. Over 1,300 heads fell here during the Reign of Terror. The guillotine sat here. A bronze plaque on the Arc de Triomphe side of the obelisk memorializes the place where Louis XVI and Marie-Antoinette, among many others, were made a foot shorter at the top. Three worked the guillotine: one managed the blade, one held the blood bucket, and one caught the head, raising it high to the roaring crowd.

Look for **Le Crillon**, Paris' most exclusive hotel, one of the twin buildings that guards the entrance to rue Royale (which leads to the Greek-style Basilique de la Madeleine). Eleven years before the king lost his head on this square, Louis XVI met with Benjamin Franklin in this hotel to sign a treaty recognizing the U.S.A. as an independent country. (For an affordable splurge, consider high tea at Le Crillon; see Les Grands Cafés de Paris on page 181.)

The 2,300-year-old **obelisk** of Luxor now forms the center-piece of place de la Concorde. It was carted here from Egypt in 1829, a gift to the French king. The gold pictures on the obelisk tell the story of its incredible journey.

The obelisk also forms a center point along a line locals call the "royal perspective." From this straight line (Louvre—Obelisk—Arc de Triomphe—Grand Arche de la Defense) you can hang a lot of history. The Louvre symbolized the old regime (divine right rule by kings and queens). The obelisk and place de la Concorde symbolizes the peoples' revolution (cutting off the king's head). The Arc de Triomphe calls to mind the triumph of nationalism (victorious armies carrying national flags under the arch). And the huge modern arch in the distance, surrounded by the headquarters of multinational corporations, heralds a future where business entities are more powerful than nations.

The beautiful **Tuileries Gardens** lead through the iron gates to the Louvre. If high tea at Le Crillon isn't your cup of tea, pull up a chair next to the pond or find one of the cafés in the gardens. If you have energy to burn, tour L'Orangerie (page 123; open only May–August in 1999).

MARAIS WALK

⑥ *paris*

This walk takes you through one of Paris' most characteristic quarters. When in Paris, the natural inclination is to concentrate only on the big sights. But to experience Paris you need to experience a vital neighborhood. This is a good one, containing more pre-Revolutionary buildings than anywhere else in town.

This walk is three miles long. Allow two hours, and add another hour if you visit the Carnavalet Museum.

Ride the Métro to Bastille. At **place de la Bastille**, there are more Revolutionary images in the Métro station murals than on the square. Exit the Métro following signs to rue Saint Antoine (not the signs to rue Saint Antoine du Faubourg). Ascend onto a noisy square dominated by the bronze **Colonne de Juillet** (July Column). Victims of the Revolutions of 1830 and 1848 are buried in a vault 55 meters below this guilded statue of liberty. The actual Bastille, a royal fortress-then-prison that once symbolized old regime tyranny and now symbolizes the Parisian emancipation, is long gone. While only a brick outline of the fortress' round turrets survives (under the traffic where rue Saint Antoine hits the square), the story of the Bastille is indelibly etched on the city's psyche.

For centuries the Bastille was used to defend the city (mostly from its own people). On July 14, 1789, the people of Paris stormed the prison, releasing its seven prisoners and hoping to find arms. They demolished the brick fortress and decorated their pikes with the heads of a few bigwigs. Shedding blood, the leaders of the gang made sure it would be tough to turn back the tides of Revolution. Ever since, the French have celebrated July 14th as their independence day—Bastille Day.

The flashy, glassy-grey, and controversial **Opéra-Bastille** dominates (some say overwhelms) the square. Designed by the Canadian

architect Carlos Ott, this latest
grand Parisian project was opened
with great fanfare by François
Mitterrand on the 200th Bastille
Day, July 14, 1989. (For ticket
information, see Entertainment,
page 194.)

Turn your back to the statue
and, passing the Banque de France
on your right (good rates, long lines, opposite a fine map of the area
on your left), head straight down the busy rue Saint Antoine about
four blocks into the Marais.

The **Marais** neighborhood, still filled with pre-Revolutionary
lanes and buildings, is more characteristic than touristy (unlike the
Latin Quarter). It's medieval Paris. This is how much of the city
looked until, in the mid-1800s, Napoleon III had Baron Haussmann blast out the narrow streets to construct broad boulevards
(wide enough for the guns and marching ranks of the army, too
wide for Revolutionary barricades), creating modern Paris.

Leave rue Saint Antoine at #62 and turn right through two

THE MARAIS WALK

elegant courtyards of **Hôtel de Sully** (62 rue Saint Antoine, open until 19:00, good Marais map on corridor wall). Originally a swamp (*marais*), during the reign of Henry IV it became the hometown of the French aristocracy. In the 17th century, big shots built their private mansions (*hôtels*) like this one—close to Henry's place des Vosges. *Hôtels* that survived the Revolution now house museums, libraries, and national institutions. The aristocrats may be gone, but the Marais—which, until recently, was a dumpy Bohemian quarter—is today a thriving, trendy but real community and a joy to explore.

To get to the **place des Vosges** park, continue through the Hôtel de Sully. The small door on the far right corner of the second courtyard pops you out into one of Paris' finest squares (closes at dusk). Walk to the center, where Louis XIII sits on a horse surrounded by locals enjoying their community park. Children frolic in the sandbox, lovers warm benches, and pigeons guard their fountains, while trees shade this retreat from the glare of the big city. Henry IV built this center-piece of the Marais in 1605. As hoped, this turned the

Marais into Paris' most exclusive neighborhood. **Victor Hugo** lived at #6 and you can visit his house (18F, corner closest the Bastille).

To leave the square, walk behind Louis' horse to the arcade. Follow it left past art galleries and antique shops and onto the boutique-filled rue des Francs Bourgeois (the store at #17 sells used silver, often from famous restaurants, by weight). Browse two blocks off the place des Vosges to the corner of rue de Sévigné, where you'll see the Musée Carnavalet (on right).

The **Carnavalet Museum**, focusing on the history of Paris, is housed inside a Marais mansion with classy courtyards and statues (35F, Tuesday–Sunday 10:00–17:00, closed Monday, 23 rue de Sévigné; for more information, see Sights—Northeast Paris, page 36).

To continue the Marais walk, go another block along rue des Francs Bourgeois (peeking through the gate on the right) and turn left at the post office. (The **Picasso Museum**, described on page 36, is up one block to the right: 30F, Wednesday–Monday 9:30–18:00, closed Tuesday, 5 rue Thorigny.) From rue Pavée, bend right onto rue Rosiers, which runs straight for three blocks through Paris' Jewish Quarter, lively every day except Saturday.

The **Jewish Quarter** is lined with colorful shops and kosher

eateries. Jo Goldenberg's deli-
catessen/restaurant (first corner on left, at #7—scene of a
terrorist bombing in darker
times) is worth poking into.
You'll be tempted by kosher
pizza and plenty of 20F falafel-
to-go (*emporter* = to go) joints.
Rue Rosiers deadends into rue
du Vieille du Temple. Turn right.

Frank Bourgeois is waiting at the corner postcard/print shop.
Turn left on rue des Francs Bourgeois, which leads past the
national archives (peek inside the courtyard) and turns into rue
Rambuteau.

The pipes and glass of the **Pompidou Center** reintroduce
you to our century. Pass that huge building on your left to join the
fray in front of the center (also called the Centre Beaubourg). Survey this popular spot from the top of the sloping square. A tubular
series of escalators leads up the
building (closed for renovation
until 2000).

The Pompidou Center
follows with gusto the 20th-
century architectural axiom
"form follows function." To get
a more spacious and functional
interior, the guts of this
exoskeletal building are draped
on the outside and color-coded: vibrant red for people lifts, cool
blue for air conditioning, eco-green for plumbing, don't-touch-it
yellow for electrical stuff, and white for bones. Enjoy the adjacent
Homage to Stravinsky **fountain**. Jean Tingley designed this new-
wave fountain as a tribute to the composer . . . every fountain rep-
resents one of his hard-to-hum scores.

With your back to the Pompidou Center's escalators, walk
the cobbled pedestrian mall, crossing the busy boulevard
Sebastopol to the ivy-covered pavilions of Les Halles. After 800
years as Paris' down-and-dirty central produce market, this was
replaced by a glitzy but soulless modern shopping center in the
late 1970s. The most endearing layer of the mall is its grassy
rooftop park. The fine Gothic Saint Eustache church overlooking
this contemporary scene has a famous 8,000-pipe organ. The
Louvre and Notre-Dame are just a short walk away. The mall
is served by Paris' busiest Métro hub (the Chatelet-Les Halles
station).

photo: David C. Hoerlein

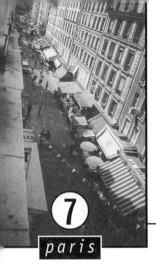

RUE CLER
WALK

The Art of Parisian Living

Paris is changing fast, but a stroll down this street puts you into a thriving traditional Parisian neighborhood.

Shopping for groceries is an integral part of daily life here. Parisians shop almost daily for three good reasons: Refrigerators are small (expensive electricity, tiny kitchens), produce must be fresh, and it's an important social event. Shopping is a chance to hear about the butcher's vacation plans, see photos of the florist's new grandchild, relax over *un café*, and kiss the cheeks of friends (twice for regular acquaintances, three times for friends you haven't seen in a while).

Rue Cler—traffic-free since 1984—offers plenty of space for tiny stores and their shoppers to spill into the street. It's an ideal environment for this ritual to survive and for you to explore. Rue Cler is lined with all the necessary shops—wine, cheese, chocolate, bread, a bank, and a post office. And the shops of this community are run by people who've found their niche . . . boys who grew up on quiche, girls who know a good wine.

If you wish to learn the fine art of living Parisian-style, rue Cler provides an excellent classroom. And, if you wish to assemble the ultimate French picnic, there's no better place. This is the only walking tour in this guidebook you should start hungry. (Do this walk when the market is open and lively: Tuesday–Saturday 8:30–13:00 or 17:00–19:00, Sunday 8:30–12:00, dead on Monday).

1. Bakery: Start your walk where the pedestrian section of rue Cler does, at rue de Grenelle. The corner bakery is typical, with a space in the corner for coffee drinkers and fast-fooders. The almond croissants here are famous among locals. Like locals, we'll buy our baguette later to avoid damaging the slender loaves.

RUE CLER WALK

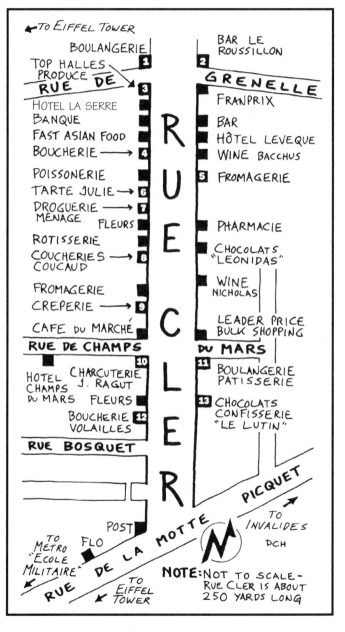

2. Café Roussillon: This café across the street is also typical. Drinks at the bar (*comptoir*) are about half the price of drinks at the tables. The "*tickets restaurant*" and "*cheque déjeuner*" decals on the door advertise that this café accepts lunch checks. In France, an employee lunch subsidy program is an expected perk. Employers issue checks (worth about 30F or $5) for the number of days an employee works in a month. Few workers bring sack lunches. A good lunch is sacred.

3. Top Halles Produce: Fresh produce is trucked in each morning from the huge Rungis market near Orly airport. Rungis' location, outside of town, is handy for small farmers bringing in their goods. Notice the lack of bags. Most locals bring their own.

Parisians shop with their nose. Try it. Insist on quality. Smell the cheap Spanish strawberries. Then smell the French Gariguette. Find the herbs. Is today's delivery in? *Oooh la la*, look at the price of those melons. What's the country of origin? It must be posted. If they're out of season, they come from Guadouloupe. Many people buy only French products.

The Franprix across the street is a small Safeway-type store. Opposite Hôtel Leveque is Asie Traiteur. Fast Asian food to go is popular in Paris. These shops—about as common as bakeries now—are making an impact on Parisian eating habits.

4. Butcher: Next to Asie Traiteur is the Triperie/Boucherie. Look for things you may want to avoid in restaurants: *rognons* (kidneys), *foie* (liver), *coeur de boeuf* (heart of beef). Next door is fish, brought in daily from ports on the English Channel, just 100 miles away. Across the street is a wine shop. Next to that, smell the . . .

5. Fromagerie: A long narrow canopied cheese table brings the *fromagerie* into the street. Wedges, cylinders, balls, and mini-hockey pucks all powdered white, grey, and burnt marshmallow—it's a festival of mold. Most of the street cart is devoted only to the goat cheeses. *Ooh la la* means you're impressed. If you like cheese, show greater excitement with more las. *Ooh la la la la*. My local friend held the stinkiest glob close to her nose, took an orgasmic breath, and exhaled, "Yes, it smells like zee feet of angels." Try it.

Step inside and browse through some of the 400 different types of French cheese. Behind the heavy plastic curtains in the back room are *la meule*, the big 170-pound wheels of cheese (250 gallons of milk go into each wheel). The "hard" cheeses are cut from these. Don't eat the skin of these big ones . . . they roll them on the floor. But the skin on the smaller cheeses—the Brie, the Camembert—is part of the taste. "It completes the package."

At dinner tonight you can take the cheese course just before or as the dessert. On a good cheese plate you have a hard cheese (like Emmenthal), a flowery cheese (maybe Brie or Camembert), a blue, and a goat.

6. Tarte Julie: Perhaps the most tempting store front on rue Cler is Tarte Julie's. The front windows are filled with various pies. The shop's classy old storefront is a work of art that survives from the previous occupant. The inset stones and glass advertise horsemeat: *Boucherie Chevaline*. The decorated front—from the '30s and signed by the artist— would fit in a museum. But it belongs right here. And everyone knows this is a place for a fine tart, not horsemeat.

7. Droguerie Menage and More: This French drugstore sells everything but drugs. It's the classic kitchen/hardware store where you buy corkscrews, brooms, knives, and so on.

Wander on past the flower shop, pharmacy (in France the first diagnosis and prescription is made by the pharmacist—if it's out of his league, he'll recommend a doctor), *rotisserie* (quarter of a roasted chicken, with a salad and a drink to go?), and another wine shop. In France, when invited to dinner, it's bad style to bring a bottle of wine. The host cooks with a particular wine in mind. Bring flowers or chocolates instead.

8. Butcher: At Coucheries Coucaud, sort through pigeons, quail, and rabbit. Hoist a duck and check the feet. They should be rough and calloused—an indication that they weren't stuck in an industrial kennel but ran wild on a farm. While Americans prefer beef, pork, and chicken, the French eat more rabbit, lamb, duck, and horse.

9. Crêperie and More: Across the street you'll find the smallest business on rue Cler, the Crêperie. Savory crêpes come with ingredients we'd put in an omelet (cheese, ham, mushrooms, and so on). They're called *gallettes* and the pancake is made from buckwheat flour. Dessert crêpes are made of wheat flour and come with everything you might enjoy on your ice cream sundae. The Café du Marché, on the corner, is the best place to sit and enjoy the rue Cler action. For a reasonable meal, grab a chair and the waiter will prop the chalky menu listing the "*plat du jour*" (blue plate special) on an empty chair. The shiny sterile Leader Price grocery store (across the street) is a French Costco selling bulk items. Because storage space is so limited in most Parisian apartments, bulk purchases are unlikely to become a big deal here.

10. Charcuterie J. Ragut: Across the street a fine *charcuterie*

sells deli food to go. Because kitchens are so small, these gourmet delis are handy, allowing hosts to concentrate on the main course and buy beautifully prepared side dishes to complete a fine dinner. Notice the system: pay the cashier and return with the receipt to pick up your food.

11. Boulangerie: Locals debate the merits of rue Cler's rival

boulangeries. It's said that a baker cannot be both a good bread man and a good pastry man: "When you do good bread, you have no time to do good pastry." The baker at the rue Grenelle bakery (stop #1) specializes in pastry. The bread suffers. Here, the baker does good bread. He has a man who does the fine little pastries for him.

12. Butcher Shop: Locals know that here, Mom and Pop buy

the veal only "on the foot." Each of the red-and-gold medals, which now hang like a necklace across the ceiling, once hung around the neck of a prize-winning little cow . . . proof of top quality.

The well-dressed butcher is following his father's act. The dad is 87 now. He used to change his apron three times a day . . . so customers expect his son to do the same. The dad lives upstairs but still comes down to see that things are done right.

Over 35 years ago the butcher married the daughter of the couple who ran the fish shop down the street. Their kids have no interest in taking over the butcher shop. Mom and Pop fear it's the end of an era.

13. Le Lutin Gourmand Chocolats Confiseries: Corinne

recently took over the shop from a woman who kept this neighborhood in fine chocolates for 30 years. The wholesalers want you to take the new products, but she keeps the old traditional candies too. "The old ladies, they want the same sweets they had 80 years ago."

Corinne dips and decorates her chocolates in the back where the old-time merchants used to live. Traditionally, in most rue Cler shops, the merchants lived and produced in the back, and sold in the front.

Rue Cler ends at the post office. The École Militaire metro stop is just around the corner. If you bought a rue Cler picnic, you'll find benches and gardens nearby; from the post office, Avenue la Motte Picquet leads to two fine parks: left to Les Invalides or right to the Eiffel Tower. *Bon appétit!*

MONTMARTRE
WALK

⑧

paris

While most tourists make the almost obligatory trek to the top of Paris' touristy Montmartre, eat an overpriced crêpe, and marvel at the view, the neighborhood has a fascinating charm and history missed by most and uncovered with this short walk.

You'll walk about two miles, up and down, on this 90-minute 12-stop tour. To avoid the tourist crowds, arrive by mid-morning. To avoid the climb, catch a taxi (60F from Eiffel Tower to Sacré-Coeur) and begin the tour at the church on top.

Take the Métro to Anvers. Exit the Métro and look up the only real hill in Paris. The peeling and neglected Elysées Montmartre theater at 74 boulevard de Rochechouart is the oldest can-can dance hall in Paris and sets the stage for this area in transition (it's a rowdy rock and roll dancehall today). From artists to Arabs, people have moved to this area for cheap rent. The area still feels neglected, though some urban gentrification is underway as young professionals restore neglected apartments.

Walk two blocks up rue de Steinkerque (the street to the right of Elysées Montmartre) past cheap clothing and souvenir shops to the grassy parkway below the white Sacré-Coeur church. Hike to the church or ride the funicular (costs one Métro ticket, on the right).

1. Sacré-Coeur Church and View: From Paris' highest point (427 feet), the City of Light fans out at your feet. There's the Eiffel Tower, the Montparnasse ("Awful") Tower, and the domed Pantheon, standing on Paris' only other butte.

The Sacré-Coeur ("Sacred Heart") church, with its onion domes and bleached-bone pallor, looks ancient but was built only a century ago by Parisians chastened by German invaders. Otto von Bismark's Prussian army laid siege to Paris for over four months in 1870. Things got so bad for residents that urban hunting for dinner (to cook up cats and dogs) became accepted behavior. The church was erected as a "praise the Lord anyway" gesture after France's humiliation by Germany.

The five-dome Romano-Byzantine basilica took 40 years to build. The church is dedicated to the "sacred heart" of Jesus—which enables Him to understand human needs and feelings. The contrast with the brilliant white exterior and the sooty interior is jarring. Explore the impressive mosaics, especially of Christ with his sacred heart above the altar. Walk around the ambulatory behind the altar. Opposite the ring of stained glass-lit chapels notice the colorful mosaic stations of the cross. Between VII and VIII rub St. Peter's bronze foot and look up to the ceiling.

For a panoramic and unobstructed view of all Paris, climb 262 feet up the tight and claustrophobic spiral stairs to the top of the dome (access is outside church, downstairs to the right, 15F, especially worthwhile if you have kids with excess energy). Skip the crypt (15F). It's just a big empty basement.

• *Leaving the church, turn right and follow the tree-lined street along the top. At rue St. Eleuthere turn right and walk uphill to the church of St. Pierre (at top on right).*

2. Church of St. Pierre: Originally a headquarters for nuns, the church is one of Paris' oldest—some say Dante prayed here. Older still are the four columns inside that may have stood in a temple of Mercury and Mars in Roman times. (Two flank the entrance, and two are behind the altar.) The name "Montmartre" comes from the Roman "Mount of Mars," though later generations—thinking of their beheaded patron St. Denis—preferred a less pagan version, "Mount of Martyrs."

In front of the church, the Café and Caberet La Boheme remind visitors that the community was a haunt of the bohemian crowd in the 19th and early 20th centuries. The artist-filled place du Tertre awaits.

3. Bohemian Montmartre—Place du Tertre: In 1800 a wall separated Paris from this village on the hill. You had to pay a toll to get in. Montmartre was a mining community (the local gypsum was the original plaster of Paris) where the wine flowed cheap and easy. Life here was a working-class festival of cafés, bistros, and dance halls. Painters came here for the ruddy charm, the light, and the low rents. In 1860 Montmartre was annexed into the growing city of Paris. The "bohemian" ambience survived and attracted sophisticated Parisians ready to get down and dirty in the belle epoque of cancan.

MONTMARTRE WALK

❶ SACRE COEUR	
❷ ST. PIERRE	
❸ PLACE DU TERTRE	
❹ DALI MUSEUM	❼ LAPIN AGILE	❿ VAN GOGH'S HOUSE
❺ MONTMARTRE MUSEUM	❽ BATEAU LAVOIR	⓫ MOULIN ROUGE
❻ VINEYARD	❾ MOULIN DE LA GALETTE	⓬ PIG ALLEY

Lined with cafés and filled with artists, hucksters, and tourists, the scene mixes charm and kitsch in ever-changing proportions. The place du Tertre artists, who at times outnumber the tourists, are the great-great-grandkids of the Renoirs, van Goghs, and Picassos who once roamed here—poor, carefree, seeking inspiration, and occasionally cursing a world too selfish to bankroll their dreams (TI on corner, daily 10:00–19:00).

4. Dalí Museum: Too surreal? Escape via the downhill corner
of the square into the tiny place du Calvaire for a great view.

Not surreal enough? Visit the Salvador Dalí Museum (just beyond place du Calvaire). The museum—a beautifully lit black gallery with the right music—offers a walk through statues, etchings, and paintings by Dalí. Don't miss the printed interview on the exit stairs (35F, not covered by museum pass, daily 10:00–18:00, 11 rue Poulbot, well-described in English).

Rue Poulbot leads to rue Norvins, the spine and main tourist drag of the community. Turn left and wander down rue Norvins to the crossroads with rue des Saules. The venerable *boulangerie* on the left (dating from 1900) is one of the last surviving bits of the old-time community. From here we'll side-trip three blocks down the back side of the *mont*, then return to carry on past the *boulangerie*.

Following rue des Saules to the right, notice the dome of Sacré-Coeur rising above the rooftops. Painters such as Maurice Utrillo captured views like this, making the neighborhood famous. Utrillo (1883–1955), the son of a free-spirited single mom, grew up in Montmartre's streets. He fought, broke streetlamps, and haunted the cafés and bars, buying drinks with masterpieces.

5. Montmartre Museum: Follow rue des Saules downhill into the less-touristed backside of Montmartre. A right up rue Cortet (at Maison Rose restaurant) leads up an exclusive street with vine-covered homes to the Museum of Montmartre at #12. Utrillo once lived here with his mom. (Composer Erik Satie lived at #16.) The museum fills eight rooms in this creaky 17th-century manorhouse with paintings, posters, old photos, music, and memorabilia recreating the traditional cancan and caberet Montmartre scene (25F, no discount with museum pass, Tuesday–Sunday 11:00–18:00, closed Monday, reasonably well-described in English).
• *Walk past the Maison Rose restaurant one block down rue des Saules to Paris' last remaining vineyard.*

6. Clos Montmartre Vineyard: What drew artists to Montmartre originally was its country charm. With vineyards, wheat fields, windmills, animals, and a village tempo of life, it was the perfect escape from grimy Paris. Today's vineyard is off-limits to tourists except for the annual grape harvest fest (first Saturday in October) when a thousand costumed locals bring back the boisterous old days and the vineyard's annual production of 300 liters is auctioned off to support local charities.
• *Continue downhill to the foot of the vineyard.*

7. Lapin Agile Caberet: The faded poster above the door gives the place its name. A rabbit (*lapin*) makes an agile leap into a pot while balancing a bottle of wine. This was the village's hotspot. Picasso and other artists and writers would gather for performances and open-mikes that ranged from serious poetry, dirty limericks, sing-alongs, and parodies of famous people, to anarchist manifestos demanding that Montmartre secede from France. Once they tied a paintbrush to the tail of the owner's donkey and entered the "abstract painting" that resulted in the Salon—it won critical acclaim and sold for a nice price.
• *Return to the bakery at the top of the hill and go downhill hugging the*

buildings on your left—don't curve right on rue Lepic. Turn right on rue Ravignan and follow it to the "TIM Hotel." Next door, at 13 place Emile-Goudeau, is Bateau-Lavoir.

8. Bateau-Lavoir, Picasso's Studio: Modern art was born here in this humble artists' abode where as many as 10 artists lived and worked. The fading photos in the window show Picasso and the studio where he and his friends, Georges Braque and Juan Gris, revolutionized art. Sharing paints, ideas, and girlfriends, they created art like the *Demoiselles d'Auvignon* that shocked the world. Modigliani and the poet Apollinaire also lived here. The original wooden studio on this site burned in 1970. Picasso wrote, "I know one day we'll return to Bateau-Lavoir. It was there that we were really happy— where they thought of us as painters, not strange animals."

• *Walk back uphill one block, turn left on rue d'Orchampt, squirt out the end, and (at rue Lepic and rue d'Orchampt) come face-to-face with a wooden windmill.*

9. Moulin de la Galette: Only two windmills (*moulins*) remain on a hill that was once dotted with them. Originally, they pressed grapes and crushed stones. When the gypsum mines closed and vineyards became apartments, this one turned into a popular outdoor dance hall. Renoir's *Bal du Moulin de La Galette* (at the Orsay) shows it in its heyday—a sunny Sunday afternoon in the leafy gardens, with ordinary folk dancing, eating, and laughing. Some call it the quintessential Impressionist painting.

• *Rue Lepic winds down the hill. The green-latticed building to your right was all part of the Moulin de la Galette. Continue past the main entry of Moulin de la Galette down rue Lepic to #54 to find . . .*

10. Van Gogh's House: In the two short years he stayed here with his brother, Vincent van Gogh transformed from a gloomy Dutch painter of brown and grey peasant scenes into an inspired visionary with wild ideas and Impressionist colors.

• *Follow the rue Lepic downhill as it makes a 90-degree right to place Blanche; check out the horse butcher at 30 rue Lepic as you descend. Notice the happy horses on the price stickers. The local announcements taped to the walls (piano lessons, handy plumber, and so on) are an indication that this is a real neighborhood. Enjoy that notion as you enjoy the delightful last stretch of rue Lepic before it hits the big street and a big change. On busy place Blanche is the . . .*

11. Moulin Rouge: *Ooh la la!* People were awed by the new Eiffel Tower at the 1889 World's Fair, but it was nothing compared to the sight of pretty cancan girls spreading their legs at the

newly-opened "Red Wind-
mill." The nightclub seemed
to sum up the belle epoque,
the beautiful age of elegance,
opulence, sophistication, and
worldliness. On most nights,
you'd see a small man in a
sleek black coat, checked
pants, green scarf, and a
bowler hat peering through

his pince-nez glasses at the dancers and making sketches of them—
Henri Toulouse-Lautrec. Perhaps he'd order an *absinthe*, the dense,
green liqueur that was the toxic Muse for so many great and forgotten artists. Toulouse-Lautrec's sketches of the dancer Jane Avril
and comic La Goulue hang in the Orsay. Walk into the entryway,
mull over the photos, dinner-show options, and prices.

12. Pig Alley: The stretch of boulevard de Clichy from place
Blanche eastward (toward the Sacré-Coeur) to place Pigalle is the
den mother of all iniquities. Plaster of Paris from the gypsum found
on this mount was loaded sloppily at place Blanche . . . the white
place. Today, sex shops, peep shows, live sex shows, and hotdog
stands line the busy boulevard de Clichy. Dildos abound.

Although raunchy now, the area has always been the place
where bistros had tax-free status, the wine was cheap, and prostitutes roamed free. WWII GIs nicknamed Pigalle "Pig Alley."

End your tour at the place Blanche Métro stop (if you want to
skip the raunchiness) or hike through Pigalle, escaping home from
the fine Art Nouveau Métro stop, Pigalle.

LOUVRE
TOUR

Paris walks you through history in two world-class museums—
the Louvre (ancient world to 1850) and Orsay (1850 to 1914,
including Impressionism). Start your art-yssey at the Louvre. The
Louvre's collection—more than 300,000 works of art—is a full
inventory of Western civilization. To cover the entire collection in
one visit is in-Seine. We'll enjoy just three of the Louvre's specialties—Greek sculpture, Italian painting, and French painting.

Orientation

Cost: 45F, 26F after 15:00 and on Sunday; those under 18 enter
free. Tickets good all day. Re-entry allowed.

Hours: Wednesday–Monday 9:00–18:00, closed Tuesday, all wings
open Wednesdays until 21:45, Richelieu Wing (only) open until
22:00 on Mondays. Galleries start closing 30 minutes early. Closed
January 1, Easter, May 1, November 1, and Christmas Day. Crowds
are worst on Sundays, Mondays, Wednesdays, and mornings. Save
money and avoid crowds by visiting in the afternoon.

Getting There: The Métro stop "Palais Royale/Musée de
Louvre" is closer to the new entrance than the stop called
"Louvre Rivoli."

There is no grander entry than through the pyramid, but
metal detectors create a long line at times. There are two ways to
avoid the line. You can enter the Louvre underground, directly
from the Métro stop "Palais Royale/Musée de Louvre"; signs to
"Musée du Louvre" put you in a slick underground shopping mall
that connects with the pyramid. (Remember, don't get off at the
"Louvre Rivoli" Métro stop, which is farther away.) Or above
ground, you can enter at the little-known entrance at the southwest
corner of the intersection of rue de Rivoli and rue de Richelieu
(where the road enters the Louvre courtyard from the north).

——— THE LOUVRE–A BIRD'S EYE VIEW ———

Checkrooms: The coat check does not take bags. The bag check is separate from the coat check and may have a much shorter line.

Photography: Photography without a flash is allowed.

Length of Our Tour: Two hours.

Louvre Tours: The 90-minute English-language tours leave six times daily except Sunday (33F, tour tel. 01 40 20 52 09, Web site: www.louvre.fr.). Clever new 30F audio tours (after ticket booths, at top of stairs) give you a directory of about 130 masterpieces, allowing you to dial a rather dull commentary on included works as you stumble upon them; we recommend the free, self-guided tour described below.

Starring: *Vénus de Milo*, *Winged Victory*, Leonardo, the French painters, Raphael, Titian.

Surviving the Louvre

Pick up the free *Louvre Handbook* in English at the information desk under the pyramid as you enter. The Louvre, the world's largest museum, fills three wings in this immense U-shaped palace. The north wing (Richelieu) houses French, Dutch, and Northern art. The east wing (Sully) houses the extensive French painting collection. The underground shopping mall (under the inverted pyramid) has a post office, handy TI, SNCF train office, glittering boutiques, a dizzying assortment of good-value eateries (up the escalator), and the Palais-Royal Métro entrance. (Stairs at the far end take you right into the Tuileries Gardens, a perfect antidote to the stuffy, crowded rooms of the Louvre.)

For this tour, we'll concentrate on the Louvre's south wing (Denon), which houses the Louvre's superstars: ancient Greek sculpture, Italian Renaissance painting, and French neoclassical and Romantic painting.

Expect changes. The Louvre is in flux for several years as they shuffle the deck. If you can't find a particular painting, ask a guard. Point to the photo in your book and ask, *"Où est?"* (oo-ay).

• *From inside the big glass pyramid you'll see signs to the three wings. Head for the Denon wing.*

Escalate up several floors. At the top, go past four statues contemplating their. . . navels, and up the final few steps. Get oriented. The pyramid is outside the window. To the right is a staircase capped by the Winged Victory *(barely visible).*

Now turn left into "salle 4," with Italian sculpture. At the far end, you'll see a large, twisting male nude looking like he's just waking up after a thousand-year nap.

Michelangelo Buonarotti—*Slaves* (*L'Esclave Mourant* and *L'Esclave Rebelle*) (c. 1513)

These two statues by earth's greatest sculptor remind us that this museum spans both the ancient and modern worlds. Michelangelo, like his fellow Renaissance artists, learned from the Greeks. The perfect anatomy, twisting poses and idealized faces look like they could have been done 2,000 years earlier. But these definitely have the personal touch of Michelangelo.

The so-called *Dying Slave* (also called the *Sleeping Slave*, who looks like he should be stretched out on a sofa) twists listlessly against his T-shirt-like bonds, revealing his smooth skin. Compare the polished detail of the rippling, bulging left arm with the sketchy details of the face and neck. With Michelangelo, the body does the talking. Since Michelangelo rarely finished a work enough to get to the polishing stage, he must have loved this one, probably the most sensual nude ever done by the master of the male body.

The *Rebellious Slave* fights against his bondage. His shoulders turn one way while his head and leg turn the other, straining to get free. He even seems to be trying to free himself from the rock he's made of.

Michelangelo said that his purpose was to carve away the marble to reveal the figures God put inside. This *Slave* shows the agony of that process and the ecstasy of the result.

• *Now let's see the source of Michelangelo's inspiration—the classical world. Backtrack to the foot of the staircase with the* Winged Victory *on top. En route you'll see the* Borghese Gladiator.

GREEK STATUES (600 B.C.–A.D. 1)

Every generation defines beauty differently. For Golden Age Greeks, beauty was balance, combining opposites in just the right proportions. They thought that the human body—especially the female form—embodied the order they saw in the universe. In the Louvre, we'll see a series of "Venuses" throughout history. Their different poses and gestures tell us about the people that made them. We'll see how the idea of beauty (as balance) began in ancient Greece, how it evolved into Hellenism (tipping the balance from stability to movement), and then how it resurfaced in the Renaissance 2,000 years later.

Borghese Gladiator (*Guerrier Combattant, Dit Gladiateur Borghese*)

We see a fighting gladiator at the peak of action. He blocks a blow with the shield that used to be attached to his left arm while his right hand, weighted with an early version of brass knuckles, prepares to deliver the counterpunch. His striding motion makes a diagonal line from his left foot up his leg, along the body and out the extended arm. It's a dramatic, precariously balanced pose.

This is the motion and emotion of Greece's Hellenistic Age, the time after the culture of Athens was spread around the Mediterranean by Alexander the Great (c. 325 B.C.).

The earlier Golden Age Greeks might have considered this statue ugly. His rippling, knotted muscles are a far cry from the more restrained Parthenon sculptures and the soft-focus beauty of

Venus. And the statue's off-balance pose leaves you hanging, like an unfinished melody. But Hellenistic Greeks loved these cliff-hanging scenes of real-life humans struggling to make their mark. The artist himself made his mark, signing the work proudly on the tree trunk: "Agasias of Ephesus, son of Dositheos, did this."

• *At the foot of the staircase with the* Winged Victory, *go down the stairs (to the left) to see the earliest Greek statues, dating several centuries before the* Gladiator.

Pre-Classical Greece

These statues are noble but crude. A woman ("*Core*") is essentially a column with breasts. A young, naked man ("*Couros*") stands rigid like he's got a gun to his back—his hands at his sides, facing front, with sketchy muscles and a mask-like face.

"Don't move."

The early Greeks who admired such statues found stability more attractive than movement. Like their legendary hero, Odysseus, the Greek people had spent generations wandering, war-weary, and longing for the comforts of a secure home. The noble strength and sturdiness of these works looked beautiful.

• *Continue through the Greek section, where you'll find two relief sculptures from the Parthenon.*

Golden Age Greece

The great Greek cultural explosion that changed the course of history happened in a fifty-year stretch (around 450 B.C.) in Athens, a Greek town smaller than Muncie, Indiana. They dominated the ancient world through brain, not brawn, and the art shows their love of rationality and order.

In a sense, we're all Greek. Democracy, mathematics, theater, literature, and science were practically invented in ancient Greece. Most of the art that we'll see in the Louvre either came from Greece or was inspired by it.

Parthenon Frieze (Fragment de la Frise des Panathenees) (c. 440 B.C.)

These stone fragments once decorated the exterior of the greatest Athenian temple, the Parthenon. The right panel shows a half-man/half-horse creature sexually harassing a woman. It tells the story of how these rude Centaurs crashed a party of humans. But the Greeks fought back and threw the brutes out, just as Athens (metaphorically) conquered its barbarian neighbors and became civilized.

The other relief shows the sacred procession of young girls who marched up the hill every four years with an embroidered veil for the 40-foot statue of Athena—the goddess of wisdom. The maidens, carved in only a couple of inches of stone, are amazingly realistic and three-dimensional—more so than anything we saw in the Pre-Classical period. They glide along horizontally (their belts

GREEK STATUES

1 - MICHELANGELO: Slaves
2 - Downstairs to Pre-Classical Greek statues
3 - Parthenon Frieze
4 - Vénus de Milo
5 - Borghese Gladiator
6 - Melpomene, Muse of Tragedy
7 - Roman detour

WINGED VICTORY

ESCALATOR FROM
DENON WING ENTRANCE

DCH

and shoulders all in a line), while the folds of their dresses drape down vertically. The man in the center is relaxed and realistic—notice the veins in his arm.

Greeks of the Golden Age valued the Golden Mean, that is, balance. The ideal person was well-rounded—an athlete and a bookworm, a lover and a philosopher, a realtor who plays the piano, a warrior and a poet. In art, the balance between stability and movement made beauty. The maidens' pleated dresses make them look as stable as fluted columns, but their arms and legs step out naturally—the human form is emerging from the stone.

• *Now seek the Goddess of Love. You'll find her floating above a sea of worshipping tourists. It's been said that, among the war-like Greeks, this was the first statue to unilaterally disarm.*

Vénus de Milo (Aphrodite) (c. 100 B.C.)

The *Vénus de Milo* (or Goddess of Love from the Greek island of Milos) created a sensation when it was discovered in 1820. Europe was already in the grip of a classical fad, and this statue seemed to sum up all that ancient Greece stood for. The Greeks pictured their gods in human form, telling us they had an optimistic view of the human race.

Vénus de Milo is a harmonious balance of opposites. Venus is stable, resting her weight on one leg (called *contrapposto*, or "counter-pose"), yet her other leg is slightly raised, ready to take a step. This slight movement sets her whole body in motion, though she remains perfectly still.

Split *Vénus* down the middle (left and right) and see how the movement of the two halves balance each other. As she lifts her left leg, her right shoulder droops down. And as her knee points one way, her head turns the other. The twisting pose gives an S-curve to her body (especially noticeable from the back view) that the Greeks and succeeding generations found beautiful.

Other opposites balance as well, like the rough-cut texture of her (size 14) dress that sets off the smooth skin of her upper half. She's actually made from two different pieces of stone plugged together at the hips (the seam is visible). The face is realistic and anatomically accurate, but it's also idealized, a goddess, too generic and too perfect. This isn't any particular woman but Everywoman—all the idealized features that the Greeks found beautiful.

What were her missing arms doing? Several archeologists' theories are on a plaque nearby. Some say her right arm held her dress while her left arm was raised. Others say she was hugging a man statue or leaning on a column. I say she was picking her navel.

• *This statue is interesting and different from every angle. Remember the view from the back—we'll see it again later. Orbit* Vénus. *Make your re-entry to Earth as you wander among Greek statues. Try to find even one that's not contrapposto. Before heading back upstairs to the* Winged Victory, *take a . . .*

Roman Detour

The Romans were great conquerors, but bad artists. Fortunately for us, they had a huge appetite for Greek statues and made countless copies. They took the Greek style and wrote it in capital letters—like the huge statue of Melpomene, holding the frowning mask of tragic plays.

One area the Romans excelled in was realistic portrait busts, especially of their emperors, who were worshipped as gods on earth. Stroll among the Caesars and try to see the man behind the public persona—Augustus, the first emperor, and his wily wife, Livia; Nero ("Neron") who burned part of his own city; Hadrian (who popularized the beard), crazy Caligula, the stoic Marcus Aurelius, and Claudius of "I" fame.

The Roman rooms also contain sarcophagi and an impressive mosaic floor. Weary? Relax with the statues in the Etruscan Lounge.

• *Now ascend the staircase to the . . .*

Winged Victory of Samothrace (*Victoire de Samothrace*)

This woman with wings, poised on the prow of a ship, once stood on a hilltop to commemorate a great naval victory. Her clothes

are windblown and sea-sprayed, clinging to her body like the winner of a wet T-shirt contest. (Notice the detail in the folds of her dress around the navel, curving down to her hips.) Originally her right arm was stretched high celebrating the victory like a Super Bowl champion, waving a "we're-number-one" finger.

This is the *Vénus de Milo* gone Hellenistic—a balance of opposites that produces excitement, not grace. As *Victory* strides forward, the wind blows her and her wings back. Her feet are firmly on the ground, but her wings (and missing arms) stretch upward. She is a pillar of vertical strength while the clothes curve and whip around her. These opposing forces create a feeling of great energy making her the lightest two-ton piece of rock in captivity.

In the glass case nearby is *Victory*'s open right hand, discovered in 1950, a century after the statue itself was unearthed. Also in the case is *Victory*'s finger. When the French discovered this was in Turkey they negotiated with the Turkish government for rights to it. Considering all the other ancient treasures the French had looted from Turkey in the past, the Turks thought it only appropriate to give France the finger.

• *Enter the octagonal room to the left of the* Winged Victory *and bench yourself under a window. Look out towards the pyramid.*

FRENCH HISTORY

The Louvre as a Palace

The Louvre, a former palace, was built in stages over several centuries. On your right (the east wing) was the original medieval fortress. Next, another palace, the Tuileries, was built 500 yards to the west—in the open area past the pyramid and past the triumphal arch. Succeeding kings tried to connect these two palaces, each one adding another section onto the long, skinny north and south wings. Finally, in 1852 after three centuries of building, the two palaces were connected creating a rectangular Louvre. Soon after that, the Tuileries palace burned down during a riot, leaving the U-shaped Louvre we see today.

The glass pyramid was designed by the American architect I. M. Pei. Many Parisians hated the pyramid, like they used to hate another new and controversial structure 100 years ago—the Eiffel Tower.

The plaque above the doorway to the Apollo Gallery (Galerie d'Apollon) explains that France's Revolutionary National Assembly (the same people who brought you the guillotine) founded this museum in 1793. What could be more logical? You behead the king, inherit his palace and art collection, open the doors to the masses and, *Voilà!* you've got Europe's first public museum. Major supporters of the museum are listed on the walls—notice all the Rothschilds.

• *Enter the Apollo Gallery ("Galerie d'Apollon").*

Apollo Gallery

The Gallery gives us a feel for the Louvre as the glorious home of the French kings (before Versailles). Imagine a chandelier-lit party in this room: drenched in stucco and gold leaf, with tapestries of leading Frenchmen and paintings with mythological and symbolic themes.

In the glass case at the far end, you'll find the crown jewels. There's the jewel-studded crown of Louis XV; the 140-carat Regent Diamond, worn by Louis XV, Louis XVI, and Napoleon; and the dragon-shaped 107-carat Côte de Bretagne Ruby. You'll also see the pearl and diamond earrings worn by Napoleon's wife, Josephine, and the golden crown of the pin-headed Empress Eugenie.

In another glass case is the cameo crown of that great champion of democracy, Napoleon—we'll see this crown in a painting later.

The inlaid tables made from marble and semi-precious stones and many other art objects show the wealth of France, Europe's #1 power for two centuries.

• *The Italian collection is on the other side of the* Winged Victory. *Cross to the other side, past her damaged digit, and pause at the two fresco paintings on the wall to the left.*

Italian Renaissance

A thousand years after Rome fell, plunging Europe into the Dark Ages, the Greek ideal of beauty was "reborn" in 15th-century Italy. This was the Renaissance, the cultural revival of ancient art.

In these two frescoes by the Italian Renaissance artist Botticelli, we see echoes of ancient Greece. The maidens, with their poses, clear sculptural lines, and idealized beauty, are virtual *Vénus de Milo*s with clothes.

The key to Renaissance painting was realism, and for the Italians "realism" was spelled "3-D." Painters were inspired by the realism and balanced beauty of Greek sculpture.

• *The Italian collection—including* Mona Lisa—*is scattered throughout the next few rooms, in the long Grand Gallery, and in adjoining rooms. To see the paintings in chronological order may require a little extra shoe leather. When in doubt, show the photo to a guard and ask,* "Où est?"

Medieval and Early Renaissance Italian (1300–1500)

Painting a 3-D world on a 2-D surface is tough, and after a millennium of Dark Ages, artists were rusty. Living in a religious age, they mostly painted altarpieces full of saints, angels, Madonnas, and crucifixes floating in an ethereal gold-leaf heaven. Gradually, they brought these otherworldly scenes down to earth.

Painters like Giotto, Fra Angelico, and Uccello broke Renaissance ground by learning to paint realistic, 3-D humans. They placed them in a painted scene with a definite foreground, background, and middle ground to create the illusion of depth. Composition was simple but symmetrically balanced in the Greek style—two angels to the left, two to the right, and so on. Art was a visual sermon, appreciated for its moral message not its beauty.

Mantegna—*St. Sebastian*

No, this isn't the patron saint of porcupines. He's a Christian martyr, though he looks more like a classical Greek statue. Notice the *contrapposto* stance (weight on one leg) and the Greek ruins scattered around. His executioners look like ignorant medieval brutes bewildered by this enlightened Renaissance Man. Italian artists were learning how to create human realism and earthly beauty on the canvas. Let the Renaissance begin.

• *The long Grand Gallery displays Italian Renaissance painting, some masterpieces, some not.* Mona Lisa *is in a room about halfway down on the right.*

The Grand Gallery

The Grand Gallery was built in the late 1500s to connect the old palace with the Tuileries palace. From the doorway look to the far end and consider this challenge: I hold the world's record for the Grand Gallery Heel-Toe-Fun-Walk-Tourist-Slalom—end to end in one minute 58 seconds, two injured. Time yourself—it's a good break, if a bit of a detour.

Along the way, notice some of these features of Italian Renaissance painting: 1) *Religious*—lots of Madonnas, children, martyrs, and saints. 2) *Symmetrical*— the Madonnas are flanked by saints, two to the left, two to the right, and so on.

3) *Realistic*—Real-life human features are especially obvious in the occasional portrait.

4) *Three-Dimensional*—every scene gets a spacious setting with a distant horizon.

5) *Classical*—You'll see some Greek gods and classical nudes, but even Christian saints pose like Greek statues, and Mary is a "Vénus" whose face and gestures embody all that was good in the Christian world.

Italian High Renaissance (1500–1600)

The two masters of Renaissance grace and balance were Raphael and Leonardo da Vinci.

Leonardo was the consummate Renaissance Man. Musician, sculptor, engineer, scientist, and sometimes painter, he combined knowledge from all areas to create beauty. If he were alive today he'd create a Unified Field theory in physics—and set it to music.

• *Look for the following masterpieces by Leonardo and Raphael in the Grand Gallery.*

THE GRAND GALLERY

STAIRS DOWN TO SLAVES

WC

CAFÉ

SEINE RIVER

ITALIAN RENAISSANCE

GRAND GALLERY

COURT YARD

SALON DES ETATS

SALLE DENON

COURT YARD

SALLE DES SEPT MÈTRES

SALON CARRÉE

ROMAN MOSAIC BELOW

APOLLO GALLERY

ROTONDE

DARU STAIRCASE (DOWN EVENTUALLY TO PYRAMIDE)

FRENCH ROMANTICISM
(SALLE MOLLIEN)

1 – BOTTICELLI frescoes
2 – Early Italian
3 – High Renaissance: LEONARDO, RAPHAEL
4 – MONA LISA
5 – High Renaissance: TITIAN, RAPHAEL, etc.

6 – VERONESE: Marriage at Cana
7 – GERICAULT: Raft of the Medusa
8 – DELACROIX: Liberty Leading the People
9 – INGRES: La Grande Odalisque
10 – DAVID: Coronation of Napoleon

FRENCH NEOCLASSICISM
(SALLE DARU)

DCH

Leonardo da Vinci—*Virgin, Child, and St. Anne* (*La Vierge, l'Enfant Jésus, et Sainte Anne*)

Three generations—grandmother, mother, and child—are arranged in a pyramid form with Anne's face as the peak and the lamb as the lower right corner. Within this balanced structure, Leonardo sets the figures in motion. Anne's legs are pointed to our left. (Is Anne Mona? Hmm.) Her daughter Mary, sitting on her lap, reaches to the right. Jesus looks at her playfully while turning away. The lamb pulls away from him. But even with all the twisting and turning, this is still a placid scene. It's balanced.

There's a psychological kidney-punch in this happy painting. Jesus, the picture of childish joy, is innocently playing with a lamb—the symbol of his inevitable sacrificial death.

The Louvre has the greatest collection of Leonardos in the world—all five of them. Don't miss the neighboring *Madonna of the Rocks* and his androgynous *John the Baptist.*

Raphael—*La Belle Jardinière*

Raphael (roff-eye-ELL) perfected the style Leonardo pioneered. This Madonna, Child, and John the Baptist is also a balanced pyramid with hazy grace and beauty. Mary is a mountain of maternal tenderness (the title translates as "The Beautiful Kindergarten Teacher"), eyeing her son with a knowing look. Jesus looks up innocently, standing *contrapposto* like a chubby Greek statue.

With Raphael, the Greek ideal of beauty reborn in the Renaissance reached its peak. His work spawned so many imitators who cranked out sickly sweet generic Madonnas that we often take him for granted. Don't. This is the real thing.

While the *Jardinière* has an idealized beauty, Raphael could deliver photorealism, too. See his portrait of black-hatted, clear-eyed *Balthazar Castiglione.*

• *Have a seat and prepare for the* Mona Lisa *mob scene. Best to read ahead here. Then follow the crowds and signs to* Mona Lisa *in the Salle des Etats.*

Leonardo da Vinci—*Mona Lisa*

Leonardo was already an old man when François I invited him to France. He took a few paintings with him. One was a portrait of a Lisa del Giocondo, the wife of a wealthy Florentine merchant. When he arrived, François immediately fell in love with the painting, making it the centerpiece of the small collection of Italian masterpieces that would, in three centuries, become the Louvre museum. He called it *La Gioconda.* We know it as a contraction of the Italian for "my lady Lisa"—*Mona Lisa.*

Advance warning: *Mona* may disappoint you. She's smaller than you'd expect, darker, engulfed in a huge room, and hidden behind a glaring pane of glass. So, you ask, "Why all the hubbub?" Let's take a closer look. Like any lover, you've got to take her for what she is, not what you'd like her to be.

The famous smile attracts you first. Leonardo used a hazy

technique called *sfumato*, blurring the edges of Mona's mysterious smile. Try as you might, you can never quite see the corners of her mouth. Is she happy? Sad? Tender? Or is it a cynical supermodel's smirk? Every viewer reads it differently, projecting his own mood onto Lisa's enigmatic face. *Mona* is a Rorschach ink-blot . . . so how are you feeling?

Now look past the smile and the eyes that really do follow you (most portraits do) to some of the subtle Renaissance elements that make this work work. The body is surprisingly massive and statuelike, a perfectly balanced pyramid turned three-quarters angle so that we can see its mass. Her arm is resting lightly on the chair's armrest almost on the level of the frame itself, like she's sitting in a window looking out at us. The folds of her sleeves and her gently folded hands are remarkably realistic and relaxed. The typical Leonardo landscape shows distance by getting hazier and hazier.

The overall mood is one of balance and serenity, but there's also an element of mystery. Her smile and long-distance beauty are subtle and elusive, tempting but always just out of reach like strands of a street-singer's melody drifting through the Métro tunnel. *Mona* doesn't knock your socks off, but she winks at the patient viewer.

• *Near* Mona *look for* . . .

Titian—*Pastoral Symphony (Le Concert Champêtre)*

Venus enters the Renaissance in this colorful work by Titian the Venetian (they rhyme). The nymph turning toward the well at left

is like a Titian reconstruction of the *Vénus de Milo*, but what a difference! The Greek Venus was cold and virginal but these babes are hot, voluptuous, sensual.

The three seated figures form a pyramid, giving the scene a balanced, classical beauty, but this appeals more to the senses

than to the mind. The golden glow of the skin, the ample flesh, and hazy outlines became the standard for centuries of female nudes. French painters, especially, learned from Titian's rich colors and sensual beauty.

• *The huge canvas at the far end of the Salle des Etats is* . . .

Veronese—*Marriage at Cana*

Stand 10 steps away from this enormous canvas to where it just fills your field of vision, and suddenly . . . you're in a party! Pull up a glass of wine. This is the Renaissance love of beautiful things gone hog-wild. Venetian artists like Veronese painted the good life of rich, happy-go-lucky Venetian merchants.

In a spacious setting of Renaissance architecture we see colorful lords and ladies decked out in their fanciest duds, feasting on a great spread of food and drink while the musicians fuel the fires of good fun. Servants prepare and serve the food, jesters play, and animals roam. In the upper left, a dog and his master look on. A sturdy linebacker in yellow pours wine out of a jug, while nearby a ferocious cat battles a lion.

Believe it or not, this is a religious work showing the wedding celebration where Jesus turned water into wine. And there's Jesus in the dead center of 130 frolicking figures wondering if maybe wine coolers might not have been a better choice. With true Renaissance optimism, Venetians pictured Christ as a party animal, someone who loved the created world as much as they did.

Now, let's hear it for the band! On bass—the bad cat with the funny hat—Titian the Venetian! And joining him on viola—Crazy Veronese!

• *Exit behind the* Marriage at Cana *into the Salle Denon. The dramatic Romantic room is to your left and the grand neoclassical room is to your right. They feature the most exciting French canvases in the Louvre. In the neoclassical room, kneel before the largest canvas in the Louvre.*

FRENCH PAINTING—NEOCLASSICAL (1780–1850)

J. L. David—*The Coronation of Napoleon*

France's last kings lived in a fantasy world, far out of touch with the hard lives of their subjects. The people revolted, and this decadent world was decapitated—along with the head of state, Louis XVI. Then, after a decade of floundering under an inefficient revolutionary government, France was united by a charismatic, brilliant, temperamental upstart general who kept his feet on the ground, his eyes on the horizon, and his hand in his coat— Napoleon Bonaparte.

Napoleon quickly conquered most of Europe, and insisted on being made emperor (not merely king) of this "New Rome." He staged an elaborate coronation ceremony in Paris. The painter David (dah-VEED) recorded it for posterity.

We see Napoleon holding aloft the crown—the one we saw in the Apollo Gallery. He has just made his wife, Josephine, the empress, and she kneels at his feet.

Seated behind Napoleon is the Pope who journeyed from Rome to place the imperial crown on his head. But Napoleon felt that no one was worthy of the task. At the last moment, he shrugged the Pope aside, grabbed the crown, held it up for all to see . . . and crowned himself. The Pope looks p.o.'d.

The radiant woman in the gallery in the background center wasn't actually there. Napoleon's mother couldn't make it to see her boy become the most powerful man in Europe, so he had her painted in anyway. (There's a key on the frame telling who's who in the picture.)

The traditional place of French coronations was the ultra-Gothic Notre-Dame cathedral. But Napoleon wanted a setting that would reflect the glories of Greece and the grandeur of Rome. So interior decorators erected stage sets of Greek columns and Roman arches to give the cathedral the architectural political correctness you see in this painting. (The *Pietà* statue on the right edge of the painting is still in Notre-Dame today.)

David was the new republic's official painter and propagandist, in charge of costumes, flags, and so on for all public ceremonies and spectacles. His "neoclassical" style influenced French fashion. Take a look at his portrait of *Madame Récamier* nearby, showing a modern Parisian woman in ancient garb and Pompeii hairstyle reclining on a Roman couch. Nearby paintings such as *The Death of Socrates* and the *Oath of the Horatii (Le Serment des Horaces)* are fine examples of neoclassicism with Greek subjects, patriotic sentiment, and a clean, simple style.

Ingres—*La Grande Odalisque*

Take *Vénus de Milo*, turn her around, lay her down, and stick a hash pipe next to her and you have the *Grande Odalisque*. Okay, maybe you'd have to add a vertabra or two.

Using clean, polished, sculptural lines, Ingres (ANG-gruh, with a soft "gruh") exaggerates the S-curve of a standing Greek nude. As in the *Vénus de Milo*, rough folds of cloth set off her smooth skin. The face too has a touch of *Vénus'* idealized features (or like Raphael's kindergarten teacher), taking nature and improving on it. Also, contrast the cool colors of this statue-like nude with Titian's golden girls.

The link with *Vénus de Milo* is even more apparent in Ingres' *La Baioneuse*, where he preserves Venus' backside for posterior—I mean, posterity.

• *Cross back through the Salle Denon and into the opposite room gushing with . . .*

ROMANTICISM (1800–1850)

Géricault—*The Raft of the Medusa (Le Radeau de la Méduse)*

Not every artist was content to copy the simple, unemotional style of the Golden Age Greeks. Like the ancient Hellenists they wanted to express motion and emotion. In the artistic war between hearts and minds, the heart-style was known as Romanticism. It was the complete flip-side of neoclassicism, though they both flourished in the early 1800s.

What better setting for an emotional work than a shipwreck? This painting was based on the actual sinking of the ship *Medusa* off the coast of Africa. The survivors barely did, floating in open seas on a raft, suffering hardship and hunger, even resorting to cannibalism—all the exotic elements for a painter determined to shock the public and arouse their emotions.

That painter was young Géricault (zher-ee-KO). He'd honed his craft sketching dead bodies in the morgue and the twisted faces of lunatics in asylums. Here he paints a tangle of bodies and lunatics sprawled over each other. The scene writhes with agitated, ominous motion—the ripple of muscles, churning clouds, and choppy seas. On the right is a deathly-green corpse sprawled overboard. In the face of the man at left cradling a dead body, we see the despair of spending weeks stranded in the middle of nowhere.

But wait. There's a stir in the crowd. Someone has spotted something. The bodies rise up in a pyramid of hope culminating in a waving flag. They wave frantically trying to catch the attention of the tiny, tiny ship on the horizon, their last desperate hope . . . which did finally save them. Géricault uses rippling movement and powerful colors to catch us up in the excitement. If Art controls your heartbeat, this is a masterpiece.

Delacroix—*Liberty Leading the People (La Liberté Guidant le Peuple)*

France is the symbol of modern democracy. They weren't the first (America was), nor are they the best working example of it, but they've had to work harder to achieve it than any country. No sooner would they throw one king or dictator out than they'd get another. They're now working on their Fifth Republic.

In this painting, the year is 1830. The Parisians have taken to the streets once again to fight royalist oppressors. There's a hard-bitten proletarian with a sword (far left), an intellectual with a top hat and a sawed-off shotgun, and even a little boy brandishing pistols.

Leading them on through the smoke and over the dead and dying is the figure of Liberty, a strong woman waving the French flag. Does this symbol of victory look familiar? It's the *Winged Victory*, wing-less and topless. (You may also recognize it from the 100-franc note.)

Liberty stirs our emotions. Delacroix (dell-ah-KWAH) purposely uses only three major colors in the composition—the red, white, and blue of the French flag.

This symbol of freedom is a fitting end to a tour of the Louvre, the first museum ever opened to the common rabble of humanity. It's a reminder that the good things in life don't belong only to a small wealthy part of society, but to everyone—even us common rabble. And liberty is worth the fight. The motto of France is *"Liberté, Egalité, Fraternité"*—liberty, equality, and the brotherhood of all people.

• *Finished? I am.* Où est la sortie?

ORSAY
TOUR

The Musée d'Orsay (pron: mew-zay dor-say) houses French art of the 1800s (specifically, art from 1848 to 1914), picking up where the Louvre leaves off. For us, that means Impressionism, the art of sun-dappled fields, bright colors, and crowded Parisian cafés. The Orsay houses the best general collection of Manet, Monet, Renoir, Degas, van Gogh, Cézanne, and Gauguin anywhere. If you like Impressionism, visit this museum. If you don't like Impressionism, visit this museum. I personally find it a more enjoyable and rewarding place than the Louvre. Sure, ya gotta see Mona and Vénus de Milo, but after you get your gottas out of the way, enjoy the Orsay.

Orientation

Cost: 39F, 27F for ages 18–25 and over 60, under 18–free. Tickets are good all day.

Hours: Tuesday–Saturday 10:00–18:00, Thursday until 21:45, Sunday 9:00–18:00, closed Mondays. From June 20–September 20, the museum opens at 9:00. Last entrance 45 minutes before closing. Galleries start closing 30 minutes early. Note: The Orsay is very crowded Tuesdays, when the Louvre is closed.

Getting There: Directly at the RER-C stop called Musée d'Orsay; the nearest Métro stop is "Solferino," three blocks south of the Orsay. From the Louvre, it's a 10-minute walk downstream to the Orsay.

Information: The booth near the entrance gives free floor plans in English (tel. 01 40 49 48 48).

Photography: Photography without a flash is allowed.

Cuisine Art: The elegant second-floor restaurant has a buffet salad bar. A simple fourth-floor café is sandwiched between the Impressionists.

Length of Our Tour: Two hours.
Orsay Tours: English-language tours usually run daily except Sunday at 11:30. The 90-minute tours cost 38F and are available on audiotape; we recommend the free, self-guided tour described below. Starring: Manet, Monet, Renoir, Degas, van Gogh, Cézanne, and Gauguin.

Gare d'Orsay: The Old Train Station

• *Pick up the free English map at the info desk, buy your ticket, and check bags to the right. Belly up to the stone balustrade overlooking the main floor and orient yourself.*

Trains used to run right under our feet down the center of the gallery. This former train station, or *gare*, barely escaped the wrecking ball in the 1970s when the French realized it'd be a great place to house their enormous collections of 19th-century art scattered throughout the city in smaller museums.

The main floor has early 19th-century art (as usual, Conservative on the right, Realism on the left). Upstairs (not visible from here) is the core of the collection—the Impressionist rooms. Finally, we'll end the tour with "the other Orsay" on the mezzanine level you see to the left. Clear as Seine water? *Bon.*

THE ORSAY'S 19TH "CENTURY" (1848–1914)

Einstein and Geronimo. Abraham Lincoln and Karl Marx. The train, the bicycle, the horse and buggy, the automobile, and the balloon. Freud and Dickens. Darwin's Origin of Species and the Church's Immaculate Conception. Louis Pasteur and Billy the Kid. V. I. Lenin and Ty Cobb.

The 19th century was a mix of old and new side by side. Europe was entering the modern Industrial Age with cities, factories, rapid transit, instant communication, and global networks. At the same time it clung to the past with traditional, rural—almost medieval—attitudes and morals.

According to the Orsay, the "19th century" began in 1848 with the socialist and democratic revolutions (Marx's Communist Manifesto). It ended in 1914 with the pull of an assassin's trigger, igniting World War I and ushering in the modern world.

The museum shows art that is also both old and new, conservative and revolutionary. We'll start with the Conservatives and

— ORSAY GROUND FLOOR—OVERVIEW —

early rebels on the ground floor, then head upstairs to see how a few visionary young artists bucked the system and revolutionized the art world, paving the way for the 20th century.

• *Walk down the steps to the main floor, a gallery filled with statues.*

Conservative Art

No, this isn't ancient Greece. These statues are from the same century as the Theory of Relativity. It's the Conservative art of the French schools that was so popular throughout the 19th century. It was popular because it's beautiful. The balanced poses, perfect anatomy and sweet faces, the curving lines, the gleaming white stone—all this is very beautiful. (I'll be bad-mouthing it later, but for now appreciate the exquisite craftsmanship of this "perfect" art.)

——— CONSERVATIVE ART ———

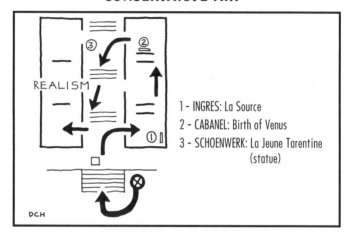

1 – INGRES: La Source
2 – CABANEL: Birth of Venus
3 – SCHOENWERK: La Jeune Tarentine
(statue)

• Take your first right into the small Room 1 marked "Ingres." Look for a nude woman with a pitcher of water.

Ingres—*The Source (La Source)*

Let's start where the Louvre left off. Ingres (pron: ANG-gruh, with a soft "gruh)", whose works help cap the Louvre collection, championed a Neoclassical style. The Source is virtually a Greek statue on canvas. Ingres worked on this over the course of 35 years and considered it his "image of perfection." Famous in its day, The Source influenced many artists whose classical statues and paintings are in the Orsay gallery.

In this and the next few rooms you'll see more of these visions of idealized beauty—nude women in languid poses, Greek myths, and so on. The "Romantics," like Delacroix, added bright colors, movement, and emotion to the classical coolness of Ingres.

• Walk uphill (quickly, this is background stuff) to the last room, with a pastel green painting.

Cabanel—*Birth of Venus (Naissance de Vénus)*

This goddess is a perfect fantasy, an orgasm of beauty. This is art of a pre-Freudian society, when sex was dirty and mysterious and had to be exalted into a more pure and divine form. The sex drive was channeled into an acute sense of beauty. French folk would literally swoon in ecstasy before these works of art.

Get a feel for the ideal beauty and refined emotion of these Greek-style works. You'll find a statue with a pose similar to Venus' back out in the gallery. Go ahead, swoon. If it feels good, enjoy it.

• *Now, take a mental cold shower, grab a bench in the main gallery of statues, and read on.*

Academy and Salon

Who liked this stuff? The art world was dominated by two conservative institutions: the Academy (the state art school) and the Salon, where works were exhibited to the buying public.

Now let's literally cross over to the "wrong side of the tracks" to the art of the early rebels.

• *Head back toward the entrance and turn right into Room 4 marked "Daumier" (opposite the Ingres room).*

Realism—Early Rebels

Daumier—Thirty-Six Caricature Busts (Ventre Legislatif)

This is a liberal's look at the stuffy bourgeois establishment that controlled the Academy and the Salon. In these 36 bust-lets, Daumier, trained as a political cartoonist, captures with vicious precision the pomposity and self-righteousness of these self-appointed arbiters of taste. The labels next to the busts give the name of the person being caricatured, his title or job (most were members of the French parliament), and an insulting nickname (like "gross, fat, and satisfied" and Monsieur "Platehead"). Give a few nicknames yourself. Can you find Reagan, Clinton, Yeltsin, Thatcher, and Gingrich?

These people hated what you're about to see. Their prudish faces tightened as their fantasy world was shattered by the Realists.

• *Go uphill four steps and through a few romantic and pastoral rooms to the final room, #6.*

REALISM—THE REBELS

ESCALATOR
UP TO IMPRESSIONISM

MANET

③

②

①

⑤

④

⑥

C
O
N
S
E
R
V
A
T
I
V
E

ART

DCH

1 – DAUMIER: 36 Caricature busts

2 – MILLET: The Gleaners

3 – COURBET: The Painter's Studio

4 – COUTURE: The Romans of the Fall

5 – MANET: Olympia

6 – Opera Exhibit

Millet—*The Gleaners* (*Les Glaneuses*)

Millet (pron: mee-YAY) grew up on a humble farm. He didn't attend the Academy and hated the uppity Paris art scene. Instead of idealized gods, goddesses, nymphs, and winged babies, he painted simple rural scenes. He was strongly affected by the Revolution of 1848 with its affirmation of the working class. Here he shows three gleaners, the poor women who pick up the meager leavings after a field has already been harvested by the wealthy. Millet captures the innate dignity of these stocky, tanned women who work quietly in a large field for their small reward.

This is "Realism" in two senses. It's painted "real"-istically, unlike the prettified pastels of Cabanel's Birth of Venus. And it's the "real" world—not the fantasy world of Greek myth, but the harsh life of the working poor.

• *Swoon briefly through the main gallery and hang a U-turn left, climbing the steps to a large alcove with two huge canvases. On the left . . .*

Courbet—*The Painter's Studio (L'Atelier du Peintre)*

Also rejected by the so-called experts, Courbet (pron: coor-BAY) held his own one-man exhibit. He built a shed in the middle of

Paris, defiantly hung his art out, and basically "mooned" the shocked public.

Here we see Courbet himself in his studio working diligently on a Realistic landscape, oblivious to the confusion around him. Looking on are a nude model— not a goddess but a real woman— and a little boy with an adoring look on his face. Perhaps it's Courbet himself as a child admiring the artist who sticks to his guns, whether it's popular or not.

• *Return to the main gallery. Back across the tracks, the huge canvas you see is . . .*

Couture—*The Romans of the Fall (Les Romains de la Décadence)*

We see a society that's stuffed with too much luxury, too much classical beauty, too much pleasure, wasted, burned-out, and in decay. The old, backward-looking order was about to be slapped in the face.

• *Continue up the gallery, then left into Room 14 ("Manet, avant 1870"). Find the reclining nude.*

Manet—*Olympia*

"This brunette is thoroughly ugly. Her face is stupid, her skin cadaverous. All this clash of colors is stupefying." So wrote a critic when Edouard Manet's nude hung in the Salon. The public hated it, attacking Manet (pron: man-NAY) in print and literally attacking the canvas.

Think back on Cabanel's painting, The Birth of Venus—an idealized, pastel, Vaseline-on-the-lens beauty. Cabenel's nude was soft-core pornography, the kind you see selling lingerie and

perfume. The public lapped it up
(and Napoleon III purchased it).
Manet's nude doesn't gloss over
anything. The pose is classic, used
by Titian, Goya, and countless
others. But the sharp outlines and
harsh contrasting colors are new
and shocking. Her hand is a clamp

and her stare is shockingly defiant, with not a hint of the seductive,
hey-sailor look of most nudes. This prostitute, ignoring the flowers
sent by her last customer, looks out to us as if to say "next." Manet
replaced soft-core porn with hard-core art.

Manet had an upper-class upbringing, some formal art training, and had been accepted by the Salon. He could have cranked
out pretty nudes and been a successful painter. Instead he surrounded himself with a group of young artists experimenting with
new techniques. With his reputation and strong personality, he was
their master, though he learned equally from them. Let the Impressionist revolution begin.

• *Continue to the end of the gallery. Before taking the covered escalator
up to the often-crowded Impressionist rooms, take a break and read ahead.
Or you could visit the nearby . . .*

Opera Exhibit

Float over to the Opera exhibit (near the escalator) where you can
hover over a scale model section of the city. There's the 19th-
century Garnier Opera House with its green roof in a diamond-
shaped block in the center.

You'll also see a cross-section model of the Opera House.
You'd enter from the right end, buy your ticket in the foyer, then
move into the entrance hall with its grand staircase. At curtain-
time, you'd find your seat in the auditorium, topped by a glorious
painted ceiling. (The current ceiling is even more wonderful than
the model, done by Marc Chagall.) Notice that the stage is as big as
the seating area, with elaborate riggings to raise and lower scenery.
Nearby, there are models of set designs from some famous produc-
tions. These days, Parisians enjoy their Verdi and Gounod mostly
at a new opera house at place Bastille.

IMPRESSIONISM

The camera threatened to make artists obsolete. A painter's original function was to record reality faithfully like a journalist. Now a
machine could capture a better likeness faster than you could say
Etch-a-Sketch.

EARLY IMPRESSIONISM

But true art is more than just painting reality. It gives us reality from the artist's point of view, putting a personal stamp on the work. It records not only the scene—a camera can do that—but the artist's impressions of the scene. Impressions are often fleeting, so you have to work quickly.

The Impressionist painters rejected camera-like detail for a quick style more suited to capturing the passing moment. Feeling stifled by the rigid rules and stuffy atmosphere of the Academy, the Impressionists' motto was "out of the studio, into the open air." They grabbed their scarves and took excursions to the country, setting up their easels on riverbanks and hillsides or sketching in cafés and dance halls. Gods, goddesses, nymphs, and fantasy scenes were out, common people and rural landscapes were in.

The quick style and simple subjects were ridiculed and called childish by the "experts." Rejected by the Salon, the Impressionists staged their own exhibition in 1874. They brashly took their name from an insult thrown at them by a critic who laughed at one of Monet's "Impressions" of a sunrise. For the next decade they exhibited their own work independently. The public, opposed at first, was slowly drawn in by the simplicity, the color, and the vibrancy of Impressionist art.

• *Ride the escalator to the top floor. Take your first left for a commanding view of the Orsay. Second left takes you between a bookshop and a giant "backwards" clock to the art.*

The Impressionist collection is scattered somewhat randomly through the next 10 or so rooms. Shadows dance and the displays mingle. You'll find nearly all of these paintings, but exactly where they're hung is a lot like their brushwork . . . delightfully sloppy. (If you don't see a described painting, move on. It's either hung farther down or on holiday.) Now, let there be . . .

Impressionism—Manet, Degas, Monet, Renoir

Light! Color! Vibrations! You don't hang an Impressionist canvas—you tether it. Impressionism features: light colors, easygoing open-air scenes, spontaneity, broad brush strokes, and the play of light.

The Impressionists made their canvases shimmer by a simple but revolutionary technique. If you mix, say, red, yellow, and blue together you'll get brown, right? But Impressionists didn't bother to mix them. They'd slap a thick brushstroke of yellow down, then a stroke of green next to it, then red next to that. Up close all you see are the three messy strokes, but as you back up . . . *voilà!* Brown! The colors blend in the eye at a distance. But while your eye is saying "bland brown" your subconscious is shouting, "Red! Yellow! Blue! Yes!"

There are no lines in nature. Yet someone in the classical tradition (Ingres, for example) would draw an outline of his subject, then fill it in with color. But the Impressionists built a figure with dabs of paint . . . a snowman of color.

Manet—*Luncheon on the Grass*
(Le Déjeuner sur l'Herbe)
Manet really got a rise out of people with this one. Once again the public judged a painting on moral terms rather than artistic ones.

What are these scantily clad women doing with these fully clothed men, they wondered? Or rather, what will they be doing after the last baguette is eaten?

A new revolutionary movement is budding: Impressionism. Notice the messy brushwork of the trees and leaves in the background, and the play of light on the pond in back and filtering through the trees onto the hazy woman stooping behind. And the strong contrasting colors (white skin, black clothes, green grass). And the fact that this is a true out-of-doors painting, not a studio production. The first shot had been fired.

Whistler—*Whistler's Mother (Portrait de la mére de l'Auteur)*

Why so famous? I don't know either. It shouldn't be, of course, but it is. Perhaps because it's by an American, and we see in his mother some of the monumental solidity of our own ancestral moms made tough by pioneering the American wilderness.

Or perhaps because it was so starkly different in its day. In a roomful of golden goddesses, it'd stand out like a fish in a tree. The experts hated it and didn't understand it. (If music is the fear of silence, is art the fear of reality?) The subtitle is "Arrangement in Grey and Black," and the whole point is the subtle variations on dark shades, but the critics kept waiting for it to come out in Colorization.

Degas—*The Dance Class (La Classe de Danse)*

Edgar Degas (pron: day-GAH) was a rich kid from a family of bankers who got the best classical-style art training. Adoring Ingres' pure lines and cool colors, he painted in the Conservative style. His work was exhibited in the Salon. He gained success and a good reputation and then . . . he met the Impressionists.

Degas blends classical lines with Impressionist color and spontaneity. His dancers have outlines, and he's got them in a classic 3-D setting—with the floor lines slanting to the upper right.

So why is Degas an Impressionist? First off, he's captured a candid, fleeting moment, a momentary "impression"—look at the girl on the left scratching her back restlessly and the cuddly little

bundle of dog in the foreground.
Degas loved the unposed "snapshot" effect, catching his models
off guard.

Clearly, Degas loved dance
and the theater. (Catch his statue,
Tiny Dancer, 14 Years Old, in
the glass case.) The play of stage
lights off his dancers, especially
the halos of ballet skirts, is made to order for an Impressionist.

Finally, he's got that Impressionistic "fury" of the brush. In The
Dance Class, look at the bright green bow on the girl with her back
to us. Not only are the outlines sketchy, but see how he slopped
green paint onto her dress and didn't even say, "*Excusez-moi.*"

Degas—*The Glass of Absinthe (Au Café, dit L'Absinthe)*

Degas hung out with low-life Impressionists
discussing art, love, and life in the cheap
cafés and bars in Montmartre (the original
Bohemia-ville). He painted Impressionistic
snapshots of everyday people. Here a weary
lady of the evening meets morning with a last
lonely coffin-nail drink in the glaring light of
a four-in-the-morning café.

Look across the room at some later
works by Manet. The old dog was learning
new tricks from his former disciples.

• *The next rooms feature works by two Impressionist masters at their
peak, Monet and Renoir. You're looking at the quintessence of Impressionism.*

Monet—*La Gare St. Lazare*

Claude Monet (pron: mo-NAY)
is the father of Impressionism.
He learned from Manet (a before
o) but quickly went beyond even
Manet's shocking slabs of colors.
Monet fully explored the possi-
bilities of open-air painting and
lighter, brighter colors. He could
even make this drab train station glow with reflected light. The sun
diffuses through the skylight and mingles with the steam from the
engine.

Stand a good six feet from the canvas and look at the tall

building with the slanted Mansard roof behind the station. Looks fine? Now get close up. At six inches it's a confusing pile of color blobs. Light on!

Monet—*The Cathedral of Rouen* (*La Cathédrale de Rouen*) (series of five paintings)

Monet went to Rouen, rented a room across from the cathedral, set up his easel . . . and waited. He wanted to catch "a series of differing impressions" of the cathedral facade at different times of day and

year. He often had several canvases going at once. In all he did 30 canvases, and each is unique. These five are labeled: In the morning, in grey weather, morning sun, full view, full sunlight.

As Monet zeroes in on the play of the colors and the light, the physical subject—the cathedral—is dissolving. It has become only a rack upon which to hang the light and color. Later artists would boldly throw away the rack, leaving purely abstract modern art in its place.

Monet—Paintings from Monet's Garden at Giverny

One of Monet's favorite places to paint was the garden of his home in Giverny, west of Paris (and worth a visit if you like Monet more than you hate crowds). You'll find several different views of it along with the painter's self-portrait. The Blue Water Lilies is similar to the large and famous water lily paintings you'll find in the nearby L'Orangerie Museum (open only May–August in 1999) across the river in the Tuileries Gardens.

Renoir—*Dance at the Moulin de la Galette* (*Bal du Moulin de la Galette*)

On Sunday afternoons, working-class folk would dress up and head for the fields on Butte Montmartre (near the Sacré-Coeur church) to dance, drink, and eat little cakes (*galettes*) till dark. Renoir (pron: ren-WAH) liked to go there to paint the common Parisians living and loving in the afternoon sun. The sunlight filtering through the trees creates a kaleidoscope of colors, like a 19th-century mirrored ball throwing darts of light on the dancers.

This dappled light is the "impression" that Renoir came away with. He captures it with quick blobs of yellow. Look at the sun-dappled straw hat (right of center) and the glasses (lower right). Smell the powder on the ladies' faces. The painting glows with bright

colors. Even the shadows on the ground, which should be grey or black, are colored a warm blue. As if having a good time was required, even the shadows are caught up in the mood, dancing. Like a photographer uses a slow shutter speed to show motion, Renoir paints a waltzing blur.

Renoir—*The City Dance/The Country Dance* (*La Danse à la Ville/La Danse à la Campagne*)

In contrast to Monet's haze of colors, Renoir clung to the more traditional technique of drawing a clear outline, then filling it in.

This two-panel "series" by Renoir shows us his exquisite draftsmanship, sense of beauty, and smoother brushwork. Like Degas, Renoir had classical training and exhibited at the Salon.

Renoir's work is light-hearted with light colors, almost pastels. He seems to be searching for an ideal, the pure beauty we saw on the ground floor. In later years he used more and more red tones as if trying for even more warmth.

• *On the divider in the center of the room, you'll find . . .*

Pissarro and Others

We've neglected many of the founders of the Impressionist style. Browse around and discover your own favorites. Pissarro is one of mine. He's more subtle and subdued than the flashy Monet and Renoir, but as someone said, "He did for the earth what Monet did for the water."

You may find the painting Young Girl in the Garden (*Jeune Fille en Jardin*) with a pastel style as pretty as Renoir's. It's by Mary Cassatt, an American who was attracted to the strong art magnet that was and still is Paris.

• *Take a break. Look at the Impressionist effect of the weather on the Paris skyline. Notice the skylight above you—these Impressionist rooms are appropriately lit by ever-changing natural light. Then carry on . . .*

POST-IMPRESSIONISM

Take a word, put "-ism" on the end, and you've become an intellectual. Commune-ism, sex-ism, Cube-ism, computer-ism . . . Post-Impressionism.

"Post-Impressionism" is an artificial and clumsy concept to describe those painters who used Impressionist techniques after Monet and Renoir. It might just as well be called something like "Pre-Modernism," because it bridged Impressionism with the 20th century . . . or you could call it bridge-ism.

• *The Orsay's Post-Impressionist collection (we'll see van Gogh, Cézanne, Gauguin, Rousseau, Seurat, and Toulouse-Lautrec) flip-flops back and forth between here and the end of this gallery. Be prepared to skip around.*

Van Gogh

Impressionists have been accused of being lightweights. The colorful style lends itself to bright country scenes, gardens, sunlight on the water, and happy crowds of simple people. It took a remarkable genius to add profound emotion to the Impressionist style.

Vincent van Gogh (pron: van-GO, or van-GOCK by the Dutch and the snooty) was the son of a Dutch minister. He too felt a religious calling, and he spread the gospel among the poorest of the poor—peasants and miners. When he turned to painting, he channeled this same spiritual intensity into his work. Like Michelangelo, Beethoven, Rembrandt, Wayne Newton, and a select handful of others, he put so much of himself into his work that art and life became one. In this room you'll see both van Gogh's painting style and his life unfold.

Van Gogh—*Peasant (Paysanne près de l'Atre)*

As a young man, van Gogh left his steady clerking job to work with poor working people in overcast Belgium and Holland. He painted these hardworking, dignified folks in a crude, dark style reflecting the oppressiveness of their live . . . and the loneliness of his own as he roamed northern Europe in search of a calling.

Van Gogh—*Self-portrait, Paris (Portraite de l'Artiste)* (1887)

Encouraged by his art-dealer brother, van Gogh moves to Paris, and *voilà!* The color! He meets Monet and hobnobs with Gauguin and Toulouse-Lautrec. He rents a room in Montmartre, learning the Impressionist style. (See how he builds a bristling brown beard using thick strokes of reds and greens side by side.)

POST-IMPRESSIONISM

At first he paints like the others but soon develops his own style. By using thick swirling brushstrokes he infuses life into even inanimate objects. Van Gogh's brushstrokes curve and thrash around like a garden hose pumped with wine.

Van Gogh—*Mid-day (La Méridienne)*, based on a painting by Millet (1890)

The social life of Paris becomes too much for the solitary van Gogh. He moves to the south of France. At first in the glow of the bright spring sunshine, he has a period of incredible creativity and happiness, overwhelmed by the bright colors—an Impressionist's dream. Here again we see his love of the common people taking a glowing siesta in the noon sun.

Van Gogh—*Van Gogh's Room at Arles (La Chambre de Van Gogh à Arles)* (1889)

But being alone in a strange country begins to wear on him. The distorted perspective of this painting makes his tiny rented room look even more cramped. He invites his friend Gauguin to join him, but after two months together arguing passionately about art, nerves get raw. Van Gogh threatens Gauguin with a knife, driving him back to Paris. In crazed despair, van Gogh mutilates his own ear.

The people of Arles realize they have a madman on their hands, and convince van Gogh to seek help. He enters a mental hospital.

Van Gogh—*The Church at Auvers-sur-Oise* (*L'Église d'Auvers-sur-Oise*) (1890)

Van Gogh's paintings done in the peace of the mental hospital are more meditative— fewer bright landscapes, more closed-in scenes with deeper and almost surreal colors.

There's also a strong sense of mystery. What's behind this church? The sky is cobalt blue and the church's windows are also blue, like we're looking right through the church to an infinite sky. There's something myste-rious lurking on the other side. You can't see it, but you feel its presence like the cold air from an approaching Métro train still hidden in the tunnel. There's a road that leads from us to the church, then splits to go behind. A choice must be made. Which way?

Van Gogh—*Self-portrait, St. Remy* (*Portrait de l'Artiste*) (1889)

Van Gogh wavered between happiness and madness. He despaired of ever being sane enough to continue painting.

This self-portrait shows a man engulfed in a confused but beautiful world. The back-ground brushstrokes swirl and rave, setting in motion the waves of the jacket. He's caught in the current, out of control. But in the midst of this rippling sea of mystery floats a still, detached island of a face with probing, questioning, wise eyes.

Do his troubled eyes know that only a few months later he would take a pistol and put a bullet through his chest?

Cézanne

Cézanne's art brought Impressionism into the 20th century. There's less color here, less swirling brushwork, less passion. It's cleaner, chunkier, more intellectual. Cézanne (pron: say-ZAHN) can be difficult to appreciate after the warmth of Renoir and he won't give you the fireworks of van Gogh. But he's worth the effort.

Cézanne—*Self-portrait (Portrait de l'Artiste)*

Cézanne was virtually unknown and unappreciated in his lifetime. He worked alone, lived alone, and died alone, ignored by all but a few revolutionary young artists who understood his efforts.

And Cézanne couldn't draw. His brush was a blunt instrument. With it, he'd bludgeon reality into submission, drag it across a canvas and leave it there to dry. But Cézanne, the mediocre painter, was a great innovator. His works are not perfected, finished products but revolutionary works-in-progress—gutter balls with wonderful spin. His work spoke for itself—which is good because, as you can see here, he had no mouth.

Cézanne—*Landscape (Rochers près des Grottes au dessus de Château-Noir)*

Cézanne used chunks of color as blocks to build three-dimensional forms. The rocky brown cliffs here consist of cubes of green, tan, and blue that blend at a distance to create a solid 3-D structure. It only makes sense from a distance. Try this: start at six inches and fade back. At some point the messy slabs become reality on the rocks.

Why is this revolutionary? Past artists created the illusion of 3-D with lines (like when we draw receding lines to turn a square into a cube). The Impressionists pioneered the technique of using blobs of color, not lines, to capture a subject. But most Impressionist art is flat and two-dimensional, a wall of color like Monet's Rouen Cathedral series. Cézanne went 3-D with chunks.

These chunks are like little "cubes." No coincidence that his experiments in reducing forms to their geometric basics influenced the . . . Cubists.

Cézanne—*The Card Players (Les Joueurs de Cartes)*

These aren't people. They're studies in color and pattern. The subject matter—two guys playing cards—is less important than the pleasingly balanced pattern they make on the canvas, two sloping forms framing a cylinder (a bottle) in the center. Later abstract artists would focus solely on the shapes and colors.

Again, notice how the figures are built with chunks of color. The jacket of the player at right consists of tans, greens, and browns. As one art scholar put it: "Cézanne confused intermingled forms and colors, achieving an extraordinarily luminous density in which lyricism is controlled by a rigorously constructed rhythm." Just what I said—chunks of color.

Cézanne—*A Modern Olympia (Une Moderne Olympia)*

Is this Cézanne himself paying homage to Manet? And dreaming up a new, more radical style of painting? We've come a long way since Manet's Olympia, which seems tame to us now.
• *From the café, continue ahead, walking under the large green beam.*
A hallway leads to . . .

Redon

Now flip out the lights and step into his mysterious world. If the Orsay's a zoo, this is the nocturnal house. Prowl around. This is wild, wild stuff, intense—imagine Richard Nixon on mushrooms playing sax.
• *At cockcrow pass into the gallery lined with metal columns containing the Primitive art of Rousseau and Gauguin. Start in the first alcove to the left.*

PRIMITIVISM

Henri Rousseau—*War (Le Guerre ou La Chevauchée de la Discorde)*

Some artists, rejecting the harried, scientific, and rational world, remembered a time before "-isms" when works of art weren't scholarly "studies in form and color" but voodoo dolls full of mystery and magic power. They learned from the art of primitive tribes in Africa and the South Seas, trying to recreate a primal Garden of Eden of peace and wholeness. In doing so they created another ism: "Primitivism."

One such artist was Rousseau, a man who painted like a child. He was an amateur artist who palled around with all the great painters, but they never took his naive style of art seriously.

This looks like a child's drawing of a nightmare. The images are primitive—flat and simple, with unreal colors—but the effect is both beautiful and terrifying. War in the form of a woman with a sword flies on horseback across the battlefield, leaving destruction in her wake—broken bare trees, burning clouds in the background, and heaps of corpses picked at by the birds.

Gauguin—*The Beautiful Angel (La Belle Angele)*

A woman in peasant dress, sits in a bubble like the halos in a medieval religious painting. Next to it is a pagan idol. This isn't a scene, but an ordered collage of images with symbolic overtones. It's left to us to make the connection.

Paul Gauguin (pron: go-GAN) learned the bright clashing colors from the Impressionists, but diverged from this path about the time van Gogh waved a knife in his face.

Gauguin simplifies. His figures are two-dimensional with thick dark outlines filled in with basic blocks of color. He turned his back on the entire Western tradition of realism begun in the Renaissance, which tried to recreate the 3-D world on a 2-D canvas. Instead he returns to an age where figures become symbols.

Gauguin—*Arearea (Pleasantries) (Joyeusetes)*

Gauguin got the travel bug early in childhood and grew up wanting to be a sailor. He became a stockbroker instead. In his spare time he painted and was introduced to the Impressionist circle. At the age of 35, he got fed up with it all, quit his job, abandoned his wife and family, and took refuge in his art. He traveled to the South Seas in search of the exotic, finally settling on Tahiti.

In Tahiti, Gauguin found his Garden of Eden. He simplified his life to the routine of eating, sleeping, and painting. He simplified his painting still more to flat images with heavy black outlines filled in with bright, pure colors. He painted the native girls in their naked innocence (so different from Cabanel's seductive Venus!). But this simple style had a deep undercurrent of symbolic meaning.

Arearea shows native women and a dog. In the "distance" (there's no attempt at traditional 3-D here) a procession goes by with a large pagan idol. What's the connection between the idol and the foreground figures who are apparently unaware of it? Gauguin makes us dig deep down into our medulla oblongata to make a mystical connection between the beautiful women, the dog, and religion. In primitive societies, religion permeates life. Idols, dogs, and women are holy.

Seurat—*The Circus (Le Cirque)*

With "pointillism," Impressionism is brought to its logical conclusion— little dabs of different colors placed side by side to blend in the viewer's eye. Using only red, yellow, blue, and green points of paint, Seurat (pron: sur-RAH) creates a mosaic of colors that shimmers at a distance.

Toulouse-Lautrec—*The Clownesse Cha-U-Kao*

Henri de Toulouse-Lautrec was the black sheep of a noble family. At age 15 he broke both legs, which left him a cripple. Shunned by his family, a freak to society, he felt more at home in the underworld of other outcasts—prostitutes, drunks, thieves, dancers, and actors. He painted the nightlife low-life in the bars, cafés, dance halls, and brothels he frequented. Toulose-Lautrec died young of alcoholism.

This is one of his fellow freaks, a fat lady clown who made her living being laughed at. She slumps wearily after a performance, indifferent to the applause, and adjusts her dress to prepare for the curtain call.

Toulouse-Lautrec was a true "impression"-ist, catching his models in candid poses. He worked spontaneously, never correcting his mistakes, as you can see from the blotches on her dark skirt and the unintentional yellow sash hanging down. Can you see a bit of Degas here? In the subject matter, the snapshot pose and the colors?

Toulouse-Lautrec—*Jane Avril Dancing*

Toulouse-Lautrec hung out at the Moulin Rouge dance hall in Montmartre. One of the most popular dancers was this slim, graceful, elegant, and melancholy woman who stood out above the rabble of the Moulin Rouge. Toulouse-Lautrec the artistocrat might have identified with her noble face—sad and weary of the nightlife, but stuck in it.

• *You've seen the essential Orsay and are permitted to cut out (the exit is straight below you). But there's an "Other Orsay" I think you'll find entertaining.*

To reach the mezzanine ("niveau median"), cross to the other side of the gallery and go down three flights. At the foot of the escalator, the mezzanine (which overlooks the main floor) is to your right. But first, go left to the palatial room of mirrors and chandeliers, marked "Salle des Fetes", or "Arts et Decors de la IIIème République" (Room 52).

THE "OTHER" ORSAY—MEZZANINE

The beauty of the Orsay is that it combines all the art of the 1800s (1848–1914), both modern and classical, in one building. The classical art, so popular in its own day, has been maligned and forgotten in the 20th century. It's time for a reassessment. Is it as gaudy and gawdawful as we've been led to believe? From our end-of-century perspective, let's take a look at the opulent, *fin de siècle* ("end of the century") French high society and its luxurious art.

The Grand Ballroom (Arts et Decors de la IIIème République)

This was one of France's most luxurious night spots when the Orsay hotel was here. You can easily imagine gowned debutantes and white-gloved dandies waltzing the night away to the music of a chamber orchestra. Notice:

1) The interior decorating: Raspberry marble-ripple ice-cream columns, the pastel ceiling painting, gold work, mirrors, and leafy strands of chandeliers.

2) The statue Bacchante Couchée sprawled in the middle of the room. Familiar pose? If not, you flunk this tour.

3) The statue Aurore, with her canopy of hair, hide-and-seek face, and silver-dollar nipples.

4) The large painting, The Birth of Venus (*La Naissance de Vénus*) by William Bouguereau. Van Gogh once said: "If I painted like Bouguereau, I could hope to make money. The public will never change—they love only sweet things."

5) Le Souvenir, with the only see-through veil of marble I've ever seen through.

So here's the question—is this stuff beautiful or merely gaudy? Divine or decadent?

• *Return to the mezzanine overlooking the main gallery, turn left "vers Naturalisme et le Symbolisme." Head toward the far end. Enter the first room on the left (#55).*

Art Worth a Second Look

We've seen some great art, now let's see some not-so-great art—at least, that's what modern critics tell us. This is realistic art with a subconscious kick, art from a neurotic society before Freud articulated its demons.

• *Working clockwise, you'll see . . .*

Cain

The world's first murderer is exiled with his family. Archeologists had recently discovered a Neanderthal skull, so the artist shows them as a prehistoric hunter/gatherer tribe.

The Dream (Le Rêve)

Soldiers sleep, while visions of gattling-guns dance in their heads.

Payday (La Paye des Moissonneurs)

Peasants getting paid, painted by the man called "the grandson of Courbet and Millet." The subtitle of the work should be, "Is this all there is to life?"

The Excommunication of Robert Le Pieux

The bishops exit after performing the rite. The king and queen are stunned, the sceptre dropped. The ritual candle has been snuffed out, it falls, fuming, echoing through the huge hall . . . Again, is this art or only cheap theatrics?

• *Return to the mezzanine. Skip the next room, then left into Room 55 labeled "Symbolisme."*

Art Not Worth a Second Look

The Orsay's director said: "Certainly we have bad paintings. But we have only the greatest bad paintings." And here they are.

Serenity

An idyll in the woods. Three nymphs with harps waft off to the right. These people are stoned on something.

The School of Plato (L'École de Platon)

Subtitled, "The Athens YMCA." A Christ-like Plato surrounded by adoring, half-naked nubile youths gives new meaning to the term "Platonic relationship."

Will the pendulum shift so that one day art like *The School of Plato* becomes the new, radical avant-garde style?

• *Return to the mezzanine and continue to the far end. Enter the last room on the left (#65) and head for the far corner.*

ART NOUVEAU

The Industrial Age brought factories, row houses, machines, train stations, geometrical precision—and ugliness. At the turn of the century some artists reacted against the unrelieved geometry of harsh, pragmatic iron-and-steel, Eiffel-Tower art with a "new art"—Art Nouveau (pron: art new-VO). Hmm. I think I had a driver's ed teacher by that name.

Charpentier—*Dining Room of Adrien Benard* (Boiserie de la Salle à Mangé de la Propriété Benard)

Like Nature, which also abhors a straight line, Art Nouveau artists used the curves of flowers and vines as their pattern. They were convinced that "practical" didn't have to mean "ugly" as well. They turned everyday household objects into art.

This wood-paneled dining room with its organic shapes is one of the finest examples of the Art Nouveau style (called Jugendstil in Germanic countries). Another is the curvy wrought iron work of some of Paris' early Metro entrances (some survive) built by the same man who commissioned this dining room for his home.

• *Browse through the Art Nouveau rooms to the left. You'll spill out back onto the mezzanine. Grab a seat in front of the Rodin statue of a man missing everything but his legs.*

Auguste Rodin

Rodin completes the tour—from classical sculpture to Impressionist painting to an artist who brought them both together. Rodin

THE OTHER ORSAY

1 - Grand Ballroom
2 - Art worth a second look
3 - Art NOT worth a second look
4 - Art Nouveau
5 - RODIN - The Walking Man
6 - CLAUDEL - L'Age Mur
7 - RODIN - The Gates of Hell
8 - RODIN - Balzac

DCH

FANCY REST.

combined classical solidity with Impressionist surfaces to become the greatest sculptor since Michelangelo.

Rodin—*The Walking Man (L'Homme qui Marche)*

This muscular, forcefully striding man could be a symbol of the Renaissance Man with his classical power. But Rodin also learned a thing or two from the comparatively lightweight Impressionist painters. Get close and look at the statue's surface. This rough "unfinished" look reflects light like the rough Impressionist brushwork, making the statue come alive, never quite at rest in the viewer's eye.

• *Near the far end of the mezzanine you'll see a small bronze couple (L'Age Mur) by Camille Claudel, a student of Rodin's.*

Claudel - *L'Age Mur*

Camille Claudel, Rodin's student and mistress, may have portrayed their doomed love affair here. A young girl desperately reaches out to an older man, who is led away reluctantly by an older woman. The center of the composition is the empty space left when their hands separate. In real life, Rodin refused to leave his wife, and Camille (see her head sticking up from a block of marble) ended up in an insane asylum.

Rodin—*The Gates of Hell (Porte de l'Enfer)*

Rodin worked for decades on these doors, and it contains some of his greatest hits, small statues that he later executed in full size. Find "The Thinker" squatting above the doorway, contemplating Man's fate. And in the lower left is the same kneeling man eating his children ("Ugolin") you'll see in full size nearby. Rodin paid models to run, squat, leap, and spin around his studio however they wanted. When he saw an interesting pose he'd yell "freeze" (or "statue maker") and get out his sketch pad. Many of these snap-shots found their way into these doors based on Dante's Inferno.

Rodin—*Balzac*

The great French novelist is given a heroic, monumental ugliness. Wrapped in a long cloak, he thrusts his head out at a defiant angle, showing the strong individualism and egoism of the 19th-century Romantic move-ment. Balzac is proud and snooty—but his body forms a question mark, and underneath the twisted features we can see a touch of per-sonal pain and self-doubt. This is hardly cam-era-eye realism—Balzac wasn't that grotesque—but it captures a personality that strikes us even if we don't know the man.

From this perch, look over the main floor at all the classical statues between you and the big clock and realize how far we've come—not in years, but in style changes. Many of the statues below—beautiful, smooth, balanced, and idealized—were done at the same time as Rodin's powerful, haunting works. Rodin is a good place to end the tour. With a stable base of 19th-century stone, he launched art into the 20th century.

MORE MUSEUM TOURS

L'Orangerie • Rodin Museum • Napoleon's Tomb and Les Invalides • Cluny Museum

L'ORANGERIE

Step out of the tree-lined, sun-dappled Impressionist painting that is the Tuileries Gardens and into L'Orangerie Museum, a little bijou of select works. Upstairs you'll find a line of eight rooms dedicated to Utrillo, Cézanne, Renoir, Matisse, and Picasso. Downstairs is the finale: Monet's *Water Lilies.* The museum's collection is small and enjoyable but complete, showing enough to see the bridge from Impressionism to the Moderns. And it's all beautiful.

Orientation

Cost and Hours: 30F, Wednesday–Monday 9:45–17:15, closed Tuesday, tel. 01 42 97 48 16. *L'Orangerie is open only May–August in 1999; it closes in September for a two-year renovation.*
Getting There: Head to the Tuileries Gardens near place de la Concorde, Mo: Concorde.
Tour Length: One hour.

Maurice Utrillo (1883–1955)

Postcard views of Montmartre by the hard-drinking, streetwise bohemian. Whitewashed buildings under perennially cloudy skies.

Cézanne (1839–1906)

These small canvases of simple subjects reinvented the way modern artists painted. In his landscapes, Cézanne the Impressionist creates "brown" rocks out of red, orange, and purple, and "green" trees out of green, lime, and purple.

L'ORANGERIE

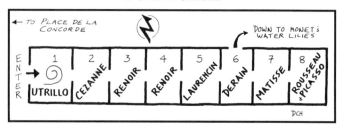

TO PLACE DE LA CONCORDE →

DOWN TO MONET'S WATER LILIES

ENTER → | 1 UTRILLO | 2 CÉZANNE | 3 RENOIR | 4 RENOIR | 5 LAURENCIN | 6 DERAIN | 7 MATISSE | 8 ROUSSEAU & PICASSO

DCH

Cézanne the proto-Cubist builds the rocks and trees out of blocks of thick brushstrokes.

The fruits of his still-lifes are also "built" out of patches of color. There's no traditional shading to create the illusion of 3-D, but these fruits bulge out like cameos from the canvas. The fruits are clearly at eye level, yet they're also clearly placed on a table seen from above. Picasso was fascinated with Cézanne's strange new world that showed multiple perspectives at once.

Renoir (1841–1919)

Renoir loved to paint *les femmes*—women and girls, nude and innocent, all with rosy-red cheeks and a relaxed grace. We get a feel for the happy family life of middle-class Parisians during the belle epoque—the beautiful age. Renoir's warm, sunny colors (mostly red) are Impressionist, but he adds a classical touch with his clearer lines and, in the later nudes, the voluptuousness of classical statues and paintings.

Marie Laurencin (1883–1956)

Pink, blue, and grey pastels of women and animals.

Andre Derain (1880–1954)

Still-lifes, nudes, harlequins, portraits, landscapes—all of them in odd, angular poses. Contrast his sharp lines with the fuzziness of the earlier, Impressionist style.

Matisse (1869–1954)

Languid women in angular rooms with arabesque wallpaper. Matisse, the original Fauve ("wild beast"), has tamed his colors a bit here. These paler tones evoke the sunny luxury of the Riviera.

Traditional 3-D perspective is thrown out the occasional hotel window as the women and furnishings in the "foreground" blend with the wallpaper "background" to become part of the decor.

Picasso (1881–1973)

Pablo Picasso is a shopping-mall of 20th-century artistic styles. In this room alone he passes through his "Blue" Period (sad and tragic), "Rose" Period (red-toned nudes with timeless, mask-like faces), and Cubism (flat planes of interwoven perspectives). He even seems a lover of women in the tradition of Renoir with his massive, sculptural nudes—warm blow-up dolls with substance. If all roads lead to Paris, all art styles flowed through Picasso.

Rousseau (1812–1867)

Henri Rousseau, a simple government official, never traveled outside France, but he created an exotic, dreamlike, completely unique world. A Parisian wedding is set amid tropical trees. Figures are placed in a 3-D world, but the lines of perspective recede so steeply into the distance that everyone is in danger of sliding down the canvas. The way he put familiar images in bizarre settings influenced the Surrealists. Enjoy France's biggest collection of Rousseaus.

• *Downstairs in two large rooms is L'Orangerie's highlight.*

Claude Monet's Water Lilies

Hall I

These mammoth, curved, panels immerse you in Monet's garden. We're looking at the pond in his garden at Giverny—dotted with water lilies, surrounded by foliage—and at the reflections of the sky, clouds, and trees on the surface. The water lilies (*nympheas*) range from plain green lilypads to flowers of red, white, yellow, lavender, and various combos.

The true subject is the play of light on the water. Monet (1840–1926) would work on several canvases at once, each one dedicated to the pond at a different time of day. He'd move with the sun from one to the next. Pan slowly around this hall. Watch the pond turn from pre-dawn to bright sunlight to twilight.

Get close to the yellow panel and see how Monet worked. Starting from the grey of blank canvas (lower right), he'd lay down big, thick brushstrokes of a single color, weaving them in a (mostly) horizontal and vertical pattern to create a dense mesh of foliage. Then, over this, he'd add more color for the dramatic highlights, until (in the center) he got a dense paste of piled-up paint. Up close it's a mess, but back up and the colors begin to resolve into a luminous scene of sunlight and trees on the water. The panel (to the right) on one of the long walls shows green lilies floating among lavender clouds reflected in blue water. Staring into Monet's pond, we see the intermingling of the four classical elements—earth (foliage), air (the sky), fire (sunlight) and water—the primordial soup from which all life springs.

• *Between the two halls—use the passageway on the right—is a bust of Monet with his Impressionist beard. Opposite the bust is a glass case filled with old photos of the artist in his Giverny garden and studio.*

Hall II

Here the pond is framed by pillar-esque tree trunks and overhanging foliage. The compositions are a little more symmetrical and the color schemes more muted, with blue-and-lavender and green-brown.

But as you get close, you'll see that even a "brown" tree is a tangled Impressionist beard of purple, green, blue, and red. Each leaf is a long brushstroke and each lilypad a dozen smudges.

The darkest panel (at the end) is a mess of paint made symmetrical by the one rosy lily in the center. Get close to the lily, and you'll see that, yes, it's made of many brushstrokes, but also that each brushstroke is itself a mix of red, white, and pink paints. In order to make Monet's colors fully resolve, you'd have to back up all the way to Giverny (50 miles west of Paris). Monet, who personally planned for these paintings to hang in this location, wanted the vibrant colors to keep firing your synapses. As the subjects become fuzzier, the more important are the colors and patterns alone. Monet builds a bridge between Impressionism and modern, abstract art.

RODIN MUSEUM

Auguste Rodin (1840–1917) is a modern Michelangelo, sculpting human figures on an epic scale, revealing through the body their deepest thoughts and feelings. Like many of Michelangelo's unfinished works, Rodin's statues rise from the raw stone around them,

─── RODIN MUSEUM AND GARDENS ───

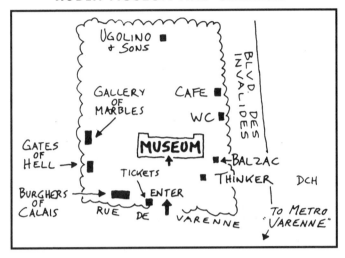

driven by the life force. With missing limbs and scarred skin, these are pre-fab classics, making ugliness noble. Rodin's people are always moving restlessly. Even the famous *Thinker* is moving. While plopped down solid . . . his mind is a million miles away. The museum presents a full range of Rodin's work, housed in a historic mansion where he once lived and worked. The gardens are picnic-perfect.

Orientation

Cost: 28F, 18F on Sundays and for seniors, students, and those under 18; 5F for garden only. Tel. 01 44 18 61 10.

Hours: April–September Tuesday–Sunday 9:30–17:45, garden closes at 18:45. October–March Tuesday–Sunday 9:30–16:45, garden closes at 17:00. Closed Mondays.

Getting There: It's near Napoleon's Tomb (77 rue de Varennes, Mo: Varenne).

Tour Length: One hour.

The Museum

Entrance Hall: Two bronze men stride forward, as bold as the often-controversial Rodin. Just ahead, a white-marble couple locks lips in *The Kiss*, one of many statues of lovers entwined. We don't need to see their faces to tell us what they feel.

• *Pick up a museum plan with room numbers, and walk through the shop and to the far corner to start a circular tour of the ground floor.*

Room 1: These are his early works. Born of working-class roots, Rodin taught himself art by sketching statues at the Louvre and then sculpting copies. *The Man with the Broken Nose* (*L'homme au nez casse*) was one of the live models the struggling sculptor could afford. Also see a painting of Rodin's future wife (*Portrait de Madame Rodin*).

Room 2: To feed his new family, Rodin cranked out small works—portraits, ornamental vases, nymphs, and knickknacks.

Room 3: He moved to Brussels, where his first major work, *The Bronze Age* (*L'age d'arain*), brought attention and controversy. This nude youth, awakening to a new world, was so life-like that Rodin was accused of not sculpting it himself but simply casting it directly from a live body.

Room 4: Like the hand of a sculptor, *The Hand of God* (*La main de Dieu*) shapes Adam and Eve from the mud of the earth to which they will return. Rodin left many works "unfinished," reminding us that all creating is a hard process of dragging a form out of chaos. Other works in this room show embracing couples who seem to emerge from the stone just long enough to love.

Room 5: The two hands that form the arch of *The Cathedral* (*La Cathedrale*) are actually two right hands (a man's and a woman's?).

Rodin worked with many materials—he chiseled marble *(The Kiss)*, used clay (the smaller, red-brown "Kiss"—opposite the big kiss), cast bronze, worked plaster, painted, and sketched. He often did different versions of the same subject in a different medium.

Room 6: This is the Camille Claudel Room. The 44-year-old Rodin took 17-year-old Camille as his pupil, muse, colleague, and lover. This room displays her work, obviously in the style of her master. *The Mature Age* (*L'Age Mur*)—perhaps the story of their own relationship—shows a young girl on her knees, begging the man not to leave her, as he's led away reluctantly by an older woman. The center of the composition is the hole left when their hands drift apart. Rodin did leave Camille (see Camille's portrait bust of a steely-eyed Rodin, the cad by the door). She went crazy and was institutionalized until she died.

Rooms 7–8: What did Rodin think of women? Here are many different images from which you can draw conclusions.

Room 9: This dimly lit room is filled with Rodin's sketches. The first flash of inspiration for a huge statue might be a single line sketched on notepaper. Rodin wanted nude models in his studio at all times—walking, dancing and squatting—in case they struck some new and interesting pose.

• *Upstairs you'll find a glass display case that explains how . . .*

Rodin made his bronze statues by pouring molten bronze into the narrow space between an original clay model and the mold around it. Once you had a mold, you could produce other copies, which is why there are famous Rodin bronzes all over the world.

Rooms 10–11: For decades, Rodin wrestled with a massive project—a doorway encrusted with characters from Dante's *Inferno*. These *Gates of Hell* were never completed, but these studies created some of Rodin's masterpieces—including *The Thinker*, who was to be the centerpiece. (You'll see the unfinished *Gates of Hell* outside in the garden.)

Room 12: A virtual unknown until his mid-30s, Rodin slowly began receiving major commissions for public monuments. *The Burghers of Calais* depicts the actual event in 1347 when, in order to save their people, the city fathers surrender the keys of the city—and their own lives—to the enemy. Rodin portrays them, not in some glorious pose drenched in pomp and allegory but as a simple example of men sacrificing their lives together. As they head to the gallows, with ropes already around their necks, each shows a distinct emotion: from courage to despair. Compare the small plaster model in the glass case with the final, life-size bronze group out the window in the garden (near the street behind the ticket booth).

Room 15: Rodin's feverish attempts to capture a portrait of the novelist Balzac range from a pot-bellied Bacchus to a headless nude cradling an erection. In a moment of inspiration, Rodin threw a plaster-soaked robe over the nude and watched it dry into

what would become the final, definitive version (*Balzac: Avant-dernier étude pour le monument, 1897*).

Room 17: Legendary lovers kiss, embrace, and intertwine in yin-yang bliss.

Room 14: Rodin's portrait busts of celebrities and some paintings by (yawn, are we through yet?) van Gogh, Monet, and Renoir.

Room 13: Film clips of Rodin in the studio making the marble chips fly.

The Gardens

Leaving the house, there are four more stops: two on the left and two on the right. Beyond these stops is a big breezy garden ornamented with statues, a cafeteria, and WC.

Balzac: This final version also stands in the Musée d'Orsay and on a street median in Montparnasse.

The Thinker: Leaning slightly forward, tense and compact, every muscle working toward producing that one great thought, Man

contemplates his fate. No constipation jokes, please.
• *Follow the Thinker's gaze to the opposite side of the house. Standing before a tall white backdrop is a big dark door—the Gates of Hell. To the right is a glass outbuilding and on the left are the Burghers of Calais.*

Various Works in White Marble: Unfinished, they show human features emerging from the rough stone. We can imagine Rodin in his studio working, like Michelangelo, to free them and give them life.

The Gates of Hell: These doors (never meant to actually open) were never finished for a museum that was never built. But the vision of Dante's trip into hell is peopled by some familiar faces we've seen earlier. Pondering the whole scene from the middle of it all is the Thinker.

It's been said that all of Rodin's work shows the struggle of mind over matter, of brute creatures emerging from the mud and evolving into a species of thinkers.

NAPOLEON'S TOMB AND LES INVALIDES ARMY MUSEUM

If you've ever considered being absolute dictator of a united Europe, come here first. Hitler did, before going out and making the same mistakes as his mentor. (Hint: Don't invade Russia.)

Napoleon's tomb rests beneath the golden dome of Les Invalides church. In addition, you can visit various military museums housed in this former veterans' hospital built by Louis XIV.

Orientation

Cost and Hours: 37F, daily 10:00–18:00, closes off-season at 17:00, tel. 01 44 42 37 67.

Getting There: The tomb is at Hôtel Les Invalides (near Rodin Museum, Mo: La Tour Maubourg or Varennes).

Tour Length: Women–one hour, men–two hours, Republican men–all day.

NAPOLEON'S TOMB

Enter the church, lean over the railing and bow to the emperor lying inside the red porphyry, scrolled tomb. If the lid were opened, you'd find an oak coffin inside, which holds another ebony coffin, housing two lead ones, then mahogany, then tinplate . . . until finally you'd find Napoleon himself staring at you, with his feet towards the door and head to the altar. When his body was exhumed from the original gravesite and transported here, even after 19 years in the ground, it was found to be perfectly preserved.

Born of humble Italian heritage on the French-owned isle of Corsica, Napoleon Bonaparte (1769-1821) went to school at Paris' École Militaire (Military School), then rose quickly through the ranks amid the chaos of the Revolution. The charismatic "Little Corporal" won fans by fighting for democracy at home and abroad. In 1799, he assumed power and, within five short years, conquered most of Europe. The great cham-

pion of the Revolution had become a dictator, declaring himself emperor of a new Rome. He installed his big brother Joseph as king of Spain (turn around to see Joseph's tomb in the alcove to the left of the door), his little brother Jerome became

LES INVALIDES

king of Westphalia (facing out, to right of door), and his baby boy, Napoleon Junior, sat in diapers on the throne of Rome.

The Crypt

• *The stairs behind the altar take you down to crypt level for a closer look at the tomb.*

The red tomb on its green base stands 15 feet high in the center of a marble floor. Wandering clockwise, read the names of Napoleon's battles inlaid on the floor. His victories in Italy (*Rivoli*) and Egypt (*Pyramides*) mark his rise to power. *Austerlitz* made him Europe's top dog.

Gaze at the grand statue of Napoleon the emperor in the alcove at the foot of the tomb—royal sceptre and orb of the earth in his hands. And continue around to Moscow (*Moscova*). . . .

Napoleon invaded Russia with 600,000 men and returned to Paris with 100,000 frostbitten survivors. Two years later, the Russians marched into Paris, and Napoleon's days were numbered. After a brief exile on the isle of Elba, he skipped parole, sailed to

France, bared his breast and said, "Strike me down or follow me!" For a hundred days they followed him, finally into Belgium where the British finished him off at the Battle of Waterloo (conspicuously absent on the floor decor). Exiled again by a war tribunal, he spent his last days on the small South Atlantic island of St. Helena.

Around the crypt are relief panels showing Napoleon's constructive side. Dressed in toga and laurel leaves, he dispenses justice, charity, and pork-barrel projects to an awed populace. In the alcove opposite the stairway, Napoleon II (*Roi de Rome*) is buried at his father's feet.

Back upstairs, you'll find more dead war heroes (including WWI's Marshall Foch) and many painted saints, making this the French Valhalla in the Versailles of churches.

LES INVALIDES AND THE ARMY MUSEUM (MUSÉE DE L'ARMÉE)

Your tomb ticket also admits you to several military museums scattered around the complex (listed in the free English map/guide in the ticket hall). If you like dummies in uniforms and endless glass cases full of swords and muskets, without a lot of historical context, you'll love the Army Museum. Hike behind the church, past the ticket hall, and down a long hallway.

Halfway down the hall, on the right, you'll see the three bare stone slabs under weeping willows that originally marked Napoleon's grave on St. Helena island. There was no epitaph, since the French and British wrangled over what to call the hero/tyrant. The stones read simply, "Here Lies . . . ."

Army Museum: East Wing

This traces uniforms, swords, and muskets through French history, from Louis XIV up to WWI. This is interesting for Napoleo-philes.

• *Cross the Courtyard of Honor, enter the East Wing under golden letters, and go upstairs to the second floor. As you circle this floor, you'll follow the history and art of French warfare from about 1700 to 1850: Pre-Revolution, Revolution, Napoleon, Restoration.*

The "First Republic: 1793–1804" (*Première République*) section is interesting for its early Napoleonic exhibits. Don't miss the tent of the emperor (room: *Salle Boulogne*) showing his bivouac equipment—bed with mosquito netting, a collapsible director's chair, and a table that you can imagine his generals hunched over, making battle plans.

In the rooms covering "Napoleon and The Empire 1804-1814," you'll find the famous portrait by Ingres of Napoleon at his peak of power, stretching his right arm to supernatural lengths (first room: *Salle Austerlitz*). Then comes Napoleon's beloved horse, Le Vizir, who weathered many a campaign and grew old with him in exile (stuffed in a glass case, third room: *Salle Eylau*). Later (room: *Salle Montmirail*) there's a portrait of a dejected Napoleon after his first abdication in 1814.

Napoleon's big white dog suffered the same fate as his horse (in a glass case after you turn the corner into the long, blue *Corridor de Tarascon*). Directly behind the dog, in the Waterloo section, a shining breastplate shows the effectiveness of British artillery in 1815. In about the middle of the long blue room, you'll find Napoleon's death mask and a reconstruction of his final home on St. Helena.

After the *Salle Restauration* (covering the mid-1800s when France brought back the royalty), you've come full circle. Next to the stairs leading to the exit is an American flag in a big glass case, marking the General La Fayette exhibit—with the only English-language description in the entire place.

The Musée des Plans Reliefs (on top floor of West Wing) has original 18th-century models of fortified cities. Their strategic importance is explained in a flier at the door.

Army Museum: West Wing

Across the courtyard a twin museum in the West Wing features armor, more weapons, and the 20th century. The ground floor covers military implements from stone axes to Axis powers. Near the entry, two huge, interesting rooms of armor and medieval weaponry have some good English descriptions.

Hitler-phobes will want to climb to the second floor where General de Gaulle greets you as if to say, "WWI on your left, WWII on your right." Photos and film footage spice up the uniforms and guns.

The Musee de l'Ordre de la Liberation tells the story of de Gaulle and the Resistance in WWII. The French refer to WWII as the War of '39–'40. But this proud memorial collection makes it clear that the French were busy during the Nazi occupation (free, without a word of English, off the hallway back near the ticket hall).

CLUNY MUSEUM (MUSÉE NATIONAL DU MOYEN AGE)

The new name of this museum means the National Museum of the Middle Ages. The Middle Ages don't seem quite so boring as I myself approach middle age. Aside from the solemn religious art, there is some lively stuff here.

Paris emerged on the world stage in the Middle Ages. Europe was awakening from a thousand-year slumber. Trade was booming, people actually owned chairs, and the Renaissance was moving in like a warm front from Italy.

Orientation

Cost and Hours: 30F, 20F on Sunday, Wednesday–Monday 9:15–17:45, closed Tuesday, tel. 01 53 73 78 00.

Getting There: It's at 6 place Paul-Painlevé, near the corner of boulevards St. Michel and St. Germain (Mo: Cluny, St. Michel, or Odéon).

Tour Length: One hour.

The Museum

Room 2: The first art you see is not some grim grey crucifixion, but a colorful tapestry of grape-stomping peasants during the *Vendange* (the autumn harvest/party).

Room 6: Stained glass from the cathedral of light, Sainte-Chapelle, but here you can get close (on the wall immediately to the left as you enter). The round panel right next to the door shows the angel Gabriel blasting his horn on Resurrection morning, rousting the grateful dead from their coffins.

Room 8: These 21 stone heads (sculpted 1210–1230) of the kings of Judah from the Bible once decorated the facade of Notre-Dame. Then in 1793, an angry and misinformed mob of revolutionaries mistook the kings of Judah for the kings of France and decapitated the statues. (Today's heads on the Notre-Dame statues are reconstructions.) Someone gathered up the heads and buried them in his backyard near the present-day Opéra. There they slept, unknown and nose-less, for two centuries, until 1977 when some diggers accidentally unearthed them and brought them to an astounded world.

Room 9: This was a Roman frigidarium. The museum is located on the site of a Roman bath house, a reminder of the Romans' centuries of occupation. After hot baths and exercise in adjoining rooms, ordinary Romans would cool off here, cheek to cheek with notables like the Emperor Julian the Apostate (see statue), who lived right next door. The ceiling is the largest Roman vault in France, and it took the French another thousand years to improve on that technology. Near Julian is a slice of a column (*Pilier des Nautes*) that may once have stood in the Temple of Jupiter, where Notre-Dame now stands.

• *Go upstairs to . . .*

"The Lady and the Unicorn" Tapestries

As Europeans emerged from the Dark Ages, they rediscovered the beauty of the world around them.

Designed by an unknown (but probably French) artist before 1500 and woven in Belgium out of wool and silk, these six mysterious tapestries—loaded with symbols, some serious, some playful—have been interpreted many ways, but the series deals with each of the five senses.

• *Moving clockwise around the room . . .*

Taste: A blonde lady takes candy from a servant's dish to feed it to her parakeet. A unicorn and a lion look on. At her feet, a monkey also tastes something, while her little white dog wishes he had something.

Hearing: Wearing a stunning dress, the lady plays sweet music on an organ, soothing the savage beasts around her. These creatures live in a blue, enchanted garden filled with flowers.

Sight: The unicorn cuddles up and looks at himself in the lady's mirror, pleased with what he sees. The lion turns away and snickers. Despite the great artistic skill of some of the detail work (such as the necklace and the patterns in her dress), the tapestry is crude by Renaissance standards. The fox and rabbits, supposedly in the distance, simply float overhead as big as the animals at the lady's feet.

Smell: The lady picks flowers and weaves them into a sweet-smelling wreath. On a bench behind, the monkey apes her.

Touch: This is the most basic and dangerous of the senses. The lady "strokes the unicorn's horn," if you know what I mean, and the lion gets the double-entendre. Middle-Age Europeans were exploring the wonders of love and the pleasures of sex.

Tapestry #6: The most talked-about tapestry gets its name from the words on our lady's tent: *A Mon Seul Desir* ("To My Sole Desire"). What *is* her only desire?

Is it jewelry, as she grabs a necklace from the jewel box? Or is she putting the necklace away, renouncing material things in order to follow her only desire? Is her desire love? Her friends the unicorn and lion open the tent doors; perhaps she's going in to meet the object of her desire. An old, dark age is ending and a new Renaissance world is coming.

VERSAILLES TOUR

12

paris

If you've ever wondered why your American passport has French writing in it, you'll find the answer at Versailles (vehr-sigh). The powerful court of Louis XIV at Versailles set the standard of culture for all of Europe right up to modern times. Versailles was every king's dream palace, and today, if you're planning to visit just one palace in all of Europe, make it Versailles.

Orientation

Cost: 45F (35F after 15:30, on Sunday, or for those over 60 or ages 18–25; under 18 free). To supplement this with a guided tour through the other sections, you'll need to pay the 45F base price, then add 25F for a one-hour guided tour, 37F for a 90-minute guided tour, or 30F for a self-guided Walkman-cassette tour. Individuals join the longest line (door A1). Those with the Paris Museum Pass (or who took the private guided tour) are allowed in through A2 without a wait.

The grounds are free, except for fountain-filled Sundays (25F, every Sunday from May through October, 11:15-11:35 and 15:30–17:00). The Grand Trianon costs 25F and the Petit Trianon is 15F.

Hours: Tuesday–Sunday 9:00–18:30, closed Monday, October–April 9:00–17:30, last entry 30 minutes before closing. In summer, Versailles is especially crowded around 10:00 and 13:00, Tuesday, and Sunday. Remember, the crowds gave Marie-Antoinette a pain in the neck too, so relax and let them eat cake. It's less crowded early and late. To minimize crowds and get a reduced entry ticket, arrive after 15:30. Tour the gardens after the palace closes. The palace is great late. On my last visit, at 18:00, I was the only tourist in the Hall of Mirrors . . . even on a Tuesday.

Getting There: Take the RER-C train (26F round-trip, 30 min) to "Versailles R.G." (not "Versailles C.H."). Trains, usually named "Vick," leave about five times an hour for the palace. Get off at Versailles Rive Gauche (the end of the line). RER-C trains leave from these RER/Metro stops: "Invalides" (Napoleon's Tomb, Rodin museum), "Champ de Mars" (Eiffel Tower), "Musée d'Orsay," "St. Michel" (Notre-Dame, Latin Quarter), and "Gare d'Austerlitz." Then walk 10 minutes to the palace. Your Eurailpass is not good on the RER trains (instead get a ticket for the turnstiles; keep this ticket to get out upon arrival). When returning, look through the windows past the turnstiles for the departure board. Any train leaving Versailles goes as far as downtown Paris (they're marked "all stations until d'Austerlitz").

Information: There's a helpful tourist information office across the street from Versailles' R.G. station (tel. 01 39 50 36 22), two information desks on the approach to the palace, and a very helpful TI at entrance C. The useful brochure, "Versailles Orientation Guide," explains your sightseeing options. Versailles info: tel. 01 30 84 76 18 or 01 30 84 74 00. WC and phones are near the main entrance.

Cuisine Art: The cafeteria is near the general entrance. Restaurants line the street to right of equestrian statue. There's a handy McDonald's immediately across from the train station (WC without crowds).

Tour Length: Allow two hours for the palace and two for the gardens. Including two hours to cover your round-trip transit time, it's a six-hour day trip from Paris.

Starring: Louis XIV and the Old Regime.

KINGS AND QUEENS AND GUILLOTINES

• *Read this on the train ride out there. Relax, the palace is the last stop.*
Come the Revolution, when they line us up and make us stick out our hands, will you have enough calluses to keep them from shooting you? A grim thought, but Versailles raises questions like that. It's the symbol of the Old Regime, a time when society was divided into rulers and rulees, when you were born to be rich or to be poor. To some it's the pinnacle of civilization, to others the sign of a civilization in decay. Either way it remains one of Europe's most impressive sights.

Versailles was the residence of the king and seat of France's government for a hundred years. Louis XIV (reigned 1643–1715) moved out of the Louvre in Paris, the previous royal residence, and built an elaborate palace in the forests and swamps of Versailles, 12 miles west. The reasons for the move were partly personal—Louis loved the out-of-doors and disliked the sniping environs of stuffy Paris—and partly politics.

VERSAILLES

Louis was creating the first modern, centralized state. At Versailles he consolidated Paris' scattered ministries so he could personally control policy. More important, he invited to Versailles all of France's nobles so he could control them. Living a life of almost enforced idleness, the "domesticated" aristocracy couldn't interfere with the way Louis ran things. With 18 million people united under one king (England had only 5.5 million), a booming economy and a powerful military, France was Europe's #1 power.

Versailles was also the cultural heartbeat of Europe. Every king wanted a palace like Versailles. Everyone learned French. French taste in clothes, hairstyles, table manners, theater, music, art, and kissing spread across the Continent. That cultural dominance has continued to some extent right up to our century.

Louis XIV

At the center of all this was Europe's greatest king. He was a true Renaissance Man a century after the Renaissance—athletic, good-looking, a musician, dancer, horseman, statesman, art lover, lover. For all his grandeur he was one of history's most polite and approachable kings, a good listener who could put even common-ers at ease in his presence.

Louis called himself the Sun King, because he gave life and warmth to all that he touched. He was also thought of as Apollo, the Greek god of the sun. Versailles became the personal temple

of this god on earth, decorated with statues and symbols of Apollo, the sun, and
Louis himself.

Louis was a hands-on king who personally ran affairs of state. All decisions
were made by him. Nobles, who in other
countries were the center of power,
became virtual slaves dependent on Louis'
generosity. For 70 years he was the perfect embodiment of the absolute
monarch. He summed it up best himself
with his famous rhyme—*"L'etat, c'est moi!"*
("The state, that's me!").

Only Two More Louis To Remember

Three kings lived in Versailles during its century of glory. Louis
XIV built it and established French dominance. Louis XV, his
great-grandson (Louis XIV reigned for 72 years), carried on the
tradition and policies but without the Sun King's flair. During
Louis XV's reign, France's power abroad was weakening and there
were rumblings of rebellion from within.

France's monarchy was crumbling, and the time was ripe for a
strong leader to re-establish the old feudal order. They didn't get
one. Instead, they got Louis XVI, a shy, meek bookworm, the kind
of guy who lost sleep over Revolutionary graffiti . . . because it was
misspelled. Louis XVI married a sweet girl from the Austrian royal
family, Marie-Antoinette, and together they retreated into the
idyllic gardens of Versailles while revolutionary fires smoldered.

They finally got their rude awakening in October 1789, when a
mob of angry Parisians stormed the palace, trashed it, and kidnapped the Royal Family, taking them back to Paris. Four years
later they lost their heads under the guillotine. The Old Regime was
dead. No longer the center of Europe, Versailles became a museum.

Arriving at Versailles

• *Leave the Versailles R.G. train station and turn right, following signs
to "château." Walk about a hundred yards, turn left and make the
grand approach over Europe's biggest cobblestones up to the palace. Enter
the iron-work gates and stop at the equestrian statue in the middle of the
large court.*

This tour covers the ceremonial center of the palace (The State
Apartments) and the extensive grounds.

The only way to see the "King's Apartments"—the actual
bedroom and private rooms—is to pay for a guided tour (Tour C).
The advantages of Tour C are 1) these rooms are more lavishly

furnished than the ones we'll
see; 2) you visit the Opera
House, the single most stunning place in the whole complex; and 3) it gets you into
the palace (where you can
then take this self-guided
tour) without standing in line
quite so long.

The disadvantages: 1) it costs more; 2) it takes 90 minutes,
sometimes with a boring guide; and 3) you see pretty much the
same kinds of things covered in this tour. If you do it, do it first to
get into the palace quicker. For true Versailles-o-philes, two more
guided tours feature the queen's apartments and the royal opera
and chapel.

• *Locate the entrances. The self-guided tour we'll take starts at door*
"A," located on the right side of the courtyard—where the line is. The
guided tour (door C) is ahead on the left, in an alleyway. Remember,
those with a museum pass can crowd ahead and enter door A2. (If the
lines are long, get in line now, but orient yourself from the statue.)

The central palace, the part we'll tour, forms a U around the
courtyard in front of you. The right half (King's Wing) is separat-
ed from the left half (Queen's Wing) by the Hall of Mirrors ahead
of you. Then two long wings shoot out to the right and left (north
and south) of this U. In this tour, we'll walk counterclockwise
through the U-shaped part on the middle floor.

The Original Château

The part of the palace directly behind the horse in the statue, at
the far end of the courtyard, is the original château. Louis XIV's
dad used to come out to the forests of Versailles to escape the
worries of kingship. Here he built this small hunting lodge. His
son spent the happiest times of his boyhood at the lodge, hunting
and riding. Louis XIV's three arched bedroom windows (beneath
the clock) overlooked the courtyard. Naturally, it faced the rising
sun. The palace and grounds are laid out on an east-west axis.

When he became king, Louis XIV spent more and more time
here, away from the hubbub of Paris. He expanded the lodge,
planted gardens, and entertained guests. The reputation spread
about this "Enchanted Island," a kind of Disneyworld for dukes
and duchesses. As visitors flocked here, Louis expanded around the
original hunting château, attaching wings to create the present U-
shape. Then, the long north and south wings were built. The total
cost of the project has been guesstimated to be half of France's
entire GNP for one year.

Think how busy this courtyard must have been 300 years ago. There were as many as 5,000 nobles here at any one time, each with an entourage. They'd buzz from games to parties to amorous rendezvous in sedan-chair taxis. Servants ran about delivering secret messages and roast legs of lamb. Horse-drawn carriages arrived at the fancy gate with their finely-dressed passengers, having driven up the broad boulevard that ran direct from Paris. (You can still see the horse stables lining the boulevard.) Incredible as it seems, both the grounds and most of the palace were public territory where even the lowliest peasant could come to gawk. Of course this meant that there were, then as now, hordes of tourists, pickpockets, and dark-skinned men selling wind-up children's toys.

• *Enter at Entrance A (or at A2 if you have a museum pass) and buy your ticket. After showing your ticket, you first pass through the 21 rooms of the history museum, with paintings on the background of Versailles and its kings.*

Our tour starts upstairs, in the room that overlooks the lavish Royal Chapel. If you took the guided tour, you may spill out here, looking at the upper level of the Royal Chapel.

The State Apartments

Royal Chapel

In the vast pagan "temple" that is Versailles, built to glorify one man, Louis XIV—the Sun King and Apollo on earth—this Royal Chapel is a paltry tip of the hat to that "other" god, the Christian one. It's virtually the first, last, and only hint of Christianity you'll see in the entire complex. Versailles celebrates Man, not God, by raising Louis to almost godlike status, the personification of all good human qualities. In a way, Versailles is the last great flowering of Renaissance humanism and revival of the classical world.

Louis attended Mass here every morning. While he sat on the upper level, the lowly nobles below would turn their backs to the altar and look up—worshiping Louis worshiping God. Important religious ceremonies took place here, including the marriage of young Louis XVI to Marie-Antoinette.

• *Take a seat in the next room, a large room with a fireplace and a colorful painting on the ceiling.*

Hercules Drawing Room

Pleasure ruled at Versailles. The main suppers, balls, and official receptions were held in this room. Picture elegant party-goers in fine silks, wigs, rouge, and lipstick (and that's just the men) dancing to the strains of Mozart played by a string quartet.

On the wall opposite the fireplace is an appropriate painting, showing Christ in the middle of a Venetian party. The work by Veronese, a gift from the Republic of Venice, was one of Louis' favorites, so they decorated the room around it.

The ceiling painting of Hercules being crowned a god gives the room its name. Hercules (with his club) rides up to heaven on a chariot, where the king of the gods is ready to give him his daughter in marriage. Louis XIV built the room for his own daughter's wedding reception.

• *The following rooms are listed in order. The names of the rooms generally come from the paintings on the ceiling. From here on it's a one-way tour—getting lost is not allowed. Follow the crowds into the small green room with a goddess in pink on the ceiling.*

The King's Wing

Cornucopia Room

If the party in the Hercules Room got too intense, you could always step in here for some refreshments. Silver trays were loaded up with liqueurs, coffee, juice, chocolates, and on really special occasions, three-bean salad.

The ceiling painting shows the cornucopia of riches poured down on invited guests. Around the edges of the ceiling are painted versions of the king's actual dinnerware and treasures.

Louis himself might be here. He was a gracious host who enjoyed letting his hair down at night. If he took a liking to you, he might sneak you through those doors there (in the middle of the wall), into his own private study where he'd show off his collection of dishes, medals, jewels or . . . the *Mona Lisa*, which hung on his wall.

Venus Room

Love ruled at Versailles. In this room, couples would cavort beneath a canopy of golden garlands (on the ceiling) sent down to earth by the goddess of love to ensnare mortals in love. Notice how a painted garland goes "out" the bottom of the central painting, becomes a gilded wood garland held by a satyr, then back to a painting again—Baroque artists loved to mix their media to fool the eye. Another illusion is in the paintings at both ends of the room that extend this grand room into mythical courtyards.

Don't let the statue of a confident Louis as a Roman emperor fool you. He started out as a poor little rich kid with a chip on his shoulder. His father had died before he was old enough to rule, and during the regency period the French Parliament treated little Louis and his mother like trash. They were virtual prisoners, humiliated in their home (the Louvre), surviving on bland meals, hand-me-down leotards, and pointed shoes. Once he attained power and wealth, there was one topic you never discussed in Louis' presence—poverty. Maybe Versailles was his way of saying, "Living well is the best revenge."

Diana Room

This was the billiards room. Men played on a table that stood in the center of the room, while ladies sat surrounding them on Persian-carpet cushions.

The famous bust of Louis by Bernini (now in the center) shows a handsome, dashing, 27-year-old play-boy-king. His gaze is steady amid his wind-blown cloak and hair. Young Louis loved life. He hunted by day (notice Diana the Huntress on the ceiling) and partied by night.

Games were actually an important part of Louis' political strategy known as "the domestication of the nobility." By distracting the nobles with the pleasures of courtly life, he was free to run the government his way. Billiards, dancing, and concerts were popular, but the biggest was gambling, usually a card game similar to "21." Louis lent money to the losers, making them even more indebted to him. The good life was an addiction, and Louis kept the medicine cabinet well-stocked.

Mars Room

Decorated with a military flair, this was the room for Louis' Swiss bodyguards. On the ceiling, there's Mars, the Greek god of war, in a chariot pulled by wolves. The bronze cupids in the corners are escalating from love-arrows to heavier artillery. Notice the fat walls that hid thin servants who were to be at their master's constant call—but out of sight when not needed. Don't miss the view of the sculpted gardens out the window.

Mercury Room

Louis' life was a work of art, and Versailles was the display case. Everything he did was a public event designed to show his subjects how it should be done. This room served as Louis' official bedroom, where the Sun King would ritually rise each morning to warm his subjects.

The tapestry on the wall shows how this ceremony might have looked. From a canopied bed, Louis would rise, dress, and take a seat for morning prayer. Meanwhile, the nobles (on the left), stand behind a balustrade, in awe of his piety, nobility, and clean socks. When Louis went to bed at night, the nobles would fight over who got to hold the candle while he slipped into his royal jammies. Bedtime, wake-up, and meals were all public rituals.

The two chests that furnish the room, with their curved legs, gilding, and heavy animal feet, are done in the "Louis the XIVth" style. Later furniture found in other rooms is lighter, straighter, and less ornamented. The clock dates from Louis' time. When the cocks crowed at the top of the hour and the temple doors opened, guess who popped out?

Apollo Room

This was the grand throne room. Louis held court from a 10-foot silver-canopied throne on a raised platform placed in the center of the room. (Notice the four metal bolts in the ceiling that once supported the canopy.)

Everything in here reminds us that Louis was not just any ruler, but the Sun King who lights the whole world with his presence. The ceiling shows Apollo in his chariot, dragging the sun across the heavens every day. Notice the ceiling with its beautifully gilded frame and Goldfinger maidens.

In the corners are the four corners of the world, all, of course, warmed by the sun. Counterclockwise from above the exit door are 1) Europe, with a sword; 2) Asia, with a lion; 3) Africa, with an elephant; and 4) good old America, an Indian maiden with a crocodile.

The famous portrait by Rigaud over the fireplace gives a more human look at Louis. He's shown in a dancer's pose, displaying the legs that made him one of the all-time dancing fools of kingery. At night, they often held parties in this room, actually dancing around the throne.

Louis (who was 63 when this was painted) had more than 300 wigs like this one, changing them many times a day. This fashion "first" started when his hairline began to recede, then sprouted all over Europe, spreading even to the American colonies in the time of George Washington.

Louis may have been treated like a god, but he was not an overly arrogant man. His subjects adored him because he was a symbol of everything a man could be, the fullest expression of the Renaissance Man.

The War Room

Versailles was good propaganda. It showed the rest of the world how rich and powerful Louis was. One look at this eye-saturating view of the gardens sent visitors reeling.

But France's success also made other countries jealous and

nervous. The semi-circles on the ceiling show
Germany (with the double eagle), Holland
(with its ships), and Spain (with a red flag and
roaring lion) ganging up on Louis. Two guess-
es who won. Of course, these mere mortals
were no match for the Sun King. The stucco
relief on the wall shows Louis on horseback triumphing over his fallen enemies.

But Louis' greatest triumph may be the
next room, the one that everybody wrote home
about.

The Hall of Mirrors

No one had ever seen anything like this hall when it was opened.
Mirrors were still a great luxury at the time, and the number and
size of these monsters were astounding. The hall is almost 250
feet long. There are 17 arched
mirrors matched by 17 windows with that breathtaking
view of the gardens. Lining
the hall are 24 gilded cande-
labras, eight busts of Roman
emperors, and eight classical-
style statues (seven of them
ancient). The ceiling decora-

tion chronicles Louis' military accomplishments, topped off by
Louis himself in the central panel (with cupids playing cards at his
divine feet) doing what he did best—triumphing.

This was where the grandest festivities were held for the most
important ambassadors and guests. The throne could be moved
from the Apollo room and set up at the far end of the hall. Imagine
this place filled with guests dressed in silks and powdered wigs, lit
by the flames of thousands of candles. The mirrors are a . . . reflec-
tion of an age when beautiful people loved to look at themselves. It
was no longer a sin to be proud of good looks or fine clothes or to
enjoy the good things in life: laughing, dancing, eating, drinking,
flirting, and enjoying the view.

From the center of the Hall, you can fully appreciate the epic
scale of Versailles. The huge palace (by architect Le Brun), the
fantasy interior (Le Vau), and the endless gardens (Le Notre)
made Versailles *le* best.

In more recent times, the Hall of Mirrors is where the Treaty
of Versailles was signed ending World War I (and, some say,
starting WWII).

• *Enter the small Peace Room and grab a bench.*

The Peace Room

"Louis Quatorze was addicted to wars . . . ." but by the end of his life, he was tired of fighting. In this sequel to the War Room, peace is granted to Germany, Holland, and Spain as cupids play with the discarded cannons, armor, and swords.

The oval painting above the fireplace shows 19-year-old Louis bestowing an olive branch on Europe. Beside him is his wife, Marie Therese, cradling their two-year-old twin daughters. If being a father at 17 seems a bit young, remember that Louis was married when he was . . . four.

The Peace Room marks the beginning of the queen's half of the palace. On Sundays the queen held chamber music concerts here for family and friends.

• *Enter the first room of the Queen's Wing, with its canopied bed.*

The Queen's Wing

The Queen's Bedchamber

This was the queen's official bedroom. Sometimes the queen actually slept here, and it was here that she rendezvoused with her husband. Two queens died here. This is where 19 princes were born. The chandelier is where two of them were conceived. Just kidding.

True, Louis was not the most faithful husband. There was no attempt to hide the fact that the Sun King warmed more than one bed, for he was above the rules of mere mortals. Adultery became acceptable—even fashionable—in court circles. The secret-looking doors on either side of the bed were for Louis' late-night liaisons—they lead straight to his rooms.

Some of Louis' mistresses became more famous and powerful than his rather quiet queen, but he was faithful to the show of marriage and had genuine affection for his wife. Their private apartments were connected, and Louis made a point of sleeping with the queen as often as possible, regardless of whose tiara he tickled earlier in the evening.

This room looks like it did in the days of the last queen, Marie-Antoinette. That's her bust over the fireplace, and the double-eagle of her native Austria in the corners. The big chest to the left of the bed held her jewels.

The queen's canopied bed is a reconstruction. The bed, chair, and wall coverings switched with the seasons. This was the cheery summer pattern.

Drawing Room of the Nobles

The queen's circle of friends met here, seated on the stools. Discussions ranged from politics to gossip, food to literature, fashion to philosophy. The Versailles kings considered themselves enlightened monarchs who promoted the arts and new ideas. Folks like Voltaire—a political radical—and the playwright Moliére participated in the Versailles court. Ironically, these discussions planted the seeds of liberal thought that would grow into the Revolution.

Queen's Antechamber

This is where the Royal Family dined publicly while servants and nobles fluttered around them, admiring their table manners and laughing at the king's jokes like courtly Paul Shaeffers. A typical dinner consisted of four different soups, two whole birds stuffed with truffles, mutton, ham slices, fruit, pastry, compotes, and preserves.

The portrait in the center is of luxury-loving, "Let-them-eat-cake" Marie-Antoinette, who became a symbol of decadence to the French peasants. The portrait at the far end is a P.R. attempt to soften her image, showing her with three of her nine children.

On the ceiling is a scene showing pilgrims bowing before Darius, with the world's shortest legs. (If you think that's a stretch, try looking for levity in the palace guidebook.)

Queen's Guard Room

On October 6, 1789, a mob of revolutionaries—appalled by their queen's taste in wallpaper—stormed the palace. They were fed up with the life of luxury led by the ruling class in the countryside while they were starving in the grimy streets of Paris.

The king and queen locked themselves in. Some of the revolutionaries got access to this upper floor. They burst into this room, where Marie-Antoinette had taken refuge, then killed three of her bodyguards and dragged her and her husband off. (Some claim that, as they carried her away, she sang "Louis, Louis, oh-oh . . . we gotta go now.")

The enraged peasants then proceeded to ransack the place, taking revenge for the years of poverty and oppression they'd suffered. Marie-Antoinette and Louis XVI were later taken to the Place de la Concorde in Paris, where they knelt under the guillotine and were made a foot shorter at the top.

Did the king and queen deserve it? Were the revolutionaries destroying civilization or clearing the decks for a new and better one? Was Versailles progress or decadence?

Coronation Room

No sooner did they throw out a king than they got an emperor.

The Revolution established democracy, but it was shaky in a country that wasn't used to it. In the midst of the confusion, the upstart general Napoleon Bonaparte took control and soon held dictatorial powers. This room captures the glory of the Napoleon years when he conquered most of Europe. In the huge canvas on the left-hand wall, we see him crowning himself emperor of a new, revived "Roman" Empire. (This is a lesser quality copy of a version hanging in the Louvre.)

Catch the portrait of a dashing, young, charismatic Napoleon by the window on the right. This shows him in 1796 when he was just a general in command of the Revolution's army in Italy. Compare this with the portrait next to it from 10 years later—looking less like a revolutionary and more like a Louis. Above the young Napoleon is a portrait of Josephine, his wife and France's empress. In David's Distribution of Eagles (opposite the Coronation) the victorious general (in imperial garb) passes out emblems of victory to his loyal troops. In The Battle of Aboukir (opposite the window), Napoleon looks rather bored as he slashes through a tangle of dark-skinned warriors. His horse, though, has a look of "What are we doing in this mob?! Let's get out of here!" Let's.

• *Pass through a couple of rooms to the exit staircase on your left. The long Battle Gallery ahead of you shows 130 yards of scenes from famous French battles arranged chronologically clockwise around the gallery. The exit staircase puts you outside on the left (south) side of the palace.*

The Gardens—Controlling Nature

Louis was a divine-right ruler. One way he proved it was by controlling nature like a god. These lavish grounds, so elaborately planned out, pruned and decorated, showed everyone that Louis was in total command.

• *Exiting the palace into the gardens, veer to the left toward the* concrete railing about 75 yards away. You'll pass through flowers, cookie-cutter patterns of shrubs and green cones. Stand at the railing overlooking the courtyard below and the Louis-made lake in the distance.

The Orangerie

The warmth from the Sun King was so great that he could even grow orange trees in chilly France. Louis had a thousand of these and other exotic plants to amaze his visitors. In wintertime they were kept warm in the long greenhouses (beneath your feet) that surround the courtyard. On sunny days they were wheeled out in their silver planters and scattered around the grounds.

• *From the stone railing, turn about-face and walk back toward the palace, veering left toward the two large pools of water. Sit on the top stair and look away from the palace.*

View Down the Royal Drive

This, to me, is the most impressive spot in all of Versailles. In one direction, the palace. Stretching out in the other, the endless grounds. Versailles was laid out along an eight-mile axis that included the grounds, the palace, and the town of Versailles itself, one of the first instances of urban planning since Roman times and a model for future capitals like Washington, D.C., and Brasilia.

Looking down the Royal Drive (also known as "The Green Carpet") you see the round Apollo fountain way in the distance. Just beyond that is the Grand Canal. The groves on either side of the Royal Drive were planted with trees from all over, laid out in an elaborate grid and dotted with statues and fountains. Of the original 1,500 fountains, 300 remain.

Looking back at the palace you can see the Hall of Mirrors—it's the middle story, with the arched windows.

• *Stroll down the steps to get a good look at the frogs and lizards that fill the round Latona Basin.*

The Latona Basin

The theme of Versailles is Apollo, the god of the sun, associated with Louis. This round fountain tells the story of the birth of Apollo and his sister Diana. On top of the fountain are Apollo and Diana as little kids with their mother Latona (they're facing toward the Apollo fountain). Latona, an unwed mother, was insulted by the local peasants. She called on the king of the gods, Zeus (the children's father), to avenge the insult. Zeus swooped down and turned all the peasants into the frogs and lizards that ring the fountain.

• *As you walk down past the basin toward the Royal Drive, you'll pass by "ancient" statues done by 17th-century French sculptors. The Colonnade is hidden in the woods on the left-hand side of the Royal Drive about three-fourths of the way to the Apollo Basin.*

The Colonnade

Versailles had no prestigious ancient ruins so they built their own. This pre-fab Roman ruin is a 100-foot circle of 64 marble columns supporting arches. Beneath the arches are small birdbath fountains. Nobles would picnic in the shade to the tunes of a string quartet, pretending they were the enlightened citizens of the ancient world.

The Apollo Basin

The fountains of Versailles were its most famous attraction, a marvel of both art and engineering. This one was the centerpiece, showing the Sun God—Louis—in his sunny chariot starting his journey across the sky. The horses are half-submerged, giving the impression, when the fountains play, of the sun rising out of the mists of dawn. Most of the fountains were only turned on when the king walked by, but this one played constantly for the benefit of those watching from the palace.

All the fountains are gravity-powered. They work on the same principle as when you block a hose with your finger to make it squirt. Underground streams, flowing from basins up at the palace, feed into smaller pipes at the fountains that shoot the water high into the air.

Looking back at the palace from here, realize that the distance you just walked is only a fraction of this vast complex of buildings, gardens, and waterways. Be glad you don't have to mow the lawn.

The Grand Canal

Why visit Venice when you can just build your own? In an era before virtual reality, this was the next-best thing to an actual trip. Couples in gondolas would pole along the waters accompanied by barges with orchestras playing "O Sole Mio." The Canal is actually cross-shaped, this being the long arm, a mile from end to end. Of course, this too is a man-made body of water with no function other than pleasing.

The Trianon Area—Retreat from Reality

Versailles began as an escape from the pressures of kingship. In a short time, the palace was as busy as Paris ever was. Louis needed an escape from his escape and built a smaller palace out in the tulies. Later, his successors retreated still farther into the garden, building a fantasy world of simple pleasures from which to ignore the real world, which was crumbling all around them.

• *You can rent a bike or catch the tourist tram (5/hrly, 4 stops), but the walk is half the fun. It's about a 30-minute walk from here to the end of the tour, plus another 30 minutes to walk back to the palace. The Grand Trianon (TREE-ah-non) is 10 minutes northwest of the Apollo Basin (the palace is due east).*

The Grand Trianon

This was the king's private residence away from the main palace. Louis usually spent a couple nights a week here, but the two later Louis spent more and more time retreating.

The facade of this one-story building is a charming combination of pink, yellow, and white, a cheery contrast to the imposing Baroque facade of the main palace. Ahead you can see the gardens through the columns. The king's apartments were to the left of the columns.

The flower gardens were changed daily for the king's pleasure—so he'd have new color combinations to look at, but also to create interesting new "nasal cocktails."

Walk around the palace (to the right) if you'd like, for a view of the gardens and rear facade.

• *Facing the front do an about-face. The Summer House is not down the driveway, but about 200 yards away along the smaller pathway at about 10 o'clock.*

The Summer House of the French Garden

This small white building with four rooms fanning out from the center was one more step away from the modern world. Here the queen spent summer evenings with family and a few friends listening to music or playing parlor games. All avenues of *la douceur de vivre*—"the sweetness of living"—were explored. To the left are the buildings of the Menagerie where cows, goats, chickens, and ducks were bred.

• *Continue frolicking along the path until you run into . . .*

The Petit Trianon

Louis XV developed an interest in botany. He wanted to spend more time near the French Gardens, but the Summer House just wasn't big enough. He built the Petit Trianon (the "small" Trianon), a masterpiece of neoclassical architecture. This grey, cubical building has four distinct facades, each a perfect and harmonious combination of Greek-style columns, windows, and railings. Walk around it and find your favorite.

Louis XVI and his wife Marie-Antoinette made this their home base. Marie-Antoinette was a sweet girl from Vienna who never quite fit in with the fast, sophisticated crowd at Versailles. Here at the Petit Trianon she could get away and recreate the simple home life she remembered from her childhood. On the lawn outside she installed a merry-go-round.

• *Five minutes more will bring you to . . .*

The Temple of Love

A circle of 12 marble Corinthian columns supporting a dome, decorating a path where lovers would stroll. Underneath, there's a statue of Cupid making a bow (to shoot arrows of love) out of the club of Hercules. It's a delightful monument to a society whose rich could afford that ultimate luxury, romantic love. When the Revolution came, I bet they wished they'd kept the club.

• *And finally you'll reach . . .*

Le Hameau—The Hamlet

Marie-Antoinette longed for the simple life of a peasant. Not the hard labor of real peasants—who sweated and starved around her—but the fairy-tale world of simple country pleasures. She built this complex of 12 buildings as her own private village.

This was an actual working farm with a dairy, a waterwheel mill, and domestic animals. The harvest was served at Marie's table. Marie didn't do much work herself, but she "supervised," dressed in a plain white muslin dress and a straw hat.

The Queen's House is the main building, actually two buildings connected by a wooden gallery. Like any typical peasant farmhouse it had a billiard room, library, elegant dining hall, and two living rooms.

Nearby was the small theater. Here Marie and her friends acted out plays far from the rude intrusions of the real world. . . .

• *The real world and the main palace are a 30-minute walk to the southeast. Along the way, stop at the Neptune Basin near the palace, an impressive mini-lake with fountains, and indulge your own favorite fantasy.*

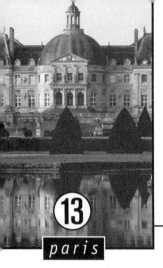

DAY TRIPS
FROM PARIS

*Grand Châteaus • Chartres •
Giverny • Disneyland Paris*

GRAND CHÂTEAUS NEAR PARIS

The region around Paris (the Île de France) is dotted with sumptuous palaces. Paris's booming upper class made this the heartland of European château-building in the 16th and 17th centuries. Most of these châteaus were lavish hunting lodges—getaways from the big city. The only thing they defended were noble and royal egos.

Consider four very different châteaus:

▲▲▲Versailles - for grandeur
▲▲▲Vaux-le-Vicomte - for intimacy
▲▲Fontainebleau - for its intimate interior
▲Chantilly - for its serene setting

If you only have time for one château, choose between Versailles and Vaux-le-Vicomte. Except for Versailles, these châteaus are quiet on weekdays.

Palace of Versailles

✪ See Versailles Tour on page 137. Versailles was the residence of French kings for about 100 years—until the Revolution of 1789 ended the notion that God deputized some people to rule for Him on Earth. Louis XIV spent half a year's income of Europe's richest country turning his dad's hunting lodge into a palace fit for a divine monarch. Louis XV and Louis XVI spent much of the 18th century gilding Louis XIV's lily. In 1837, about 50 years after the royal family was evicted, King Louis Philippe opened the palace as a museum. Europe's next-best palaces are Versailles wannabes.
Cost: Admission to the palace costs 45F (35F after 15:30, on Sunday, or for those over 60 or aged 18–25; under 18 free). Guided tours cost extra (60 minutes–25F, 90 minutes–37F, walkman–30F). The Grand Trianon is 25F, Petit Trianon is 15F. On Sunday only, the gardens cost 25F and the fountains perform.

DAY TRIPS FROM PARIS

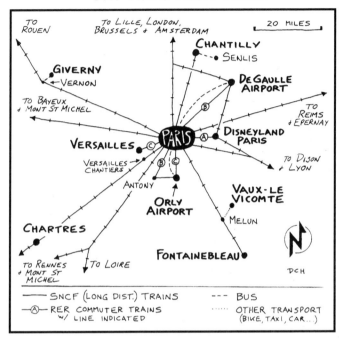

TO ROUEN

TO LILLE, LONDON, BRUSSELS & AMSTERDAM

20 MILES

CHANTILLY
SENLIS

GIVERNY
VERNON

DE GAULLE AIRPORT

TO BAYEUX & MONT ST MICHEL

TO REIMS & EPERNAY

VERSAILLES

PARIS

DISNEYLAND PARIS

VERSAILLES CHANTIERS

TO DIJON & LYON

ANTONY

ORLY AIRPORT

VAUX-LE VICOMTE

MELUN

CHARTRES

FONTAINEBLEAU

TO RENNES & MONT ST MICHEL

TO LOIRE

DCH

—— SNCF (LONG DIST.) TRAINS   - - - BUS
—Ⓐ— RER COMMUTER TRAINS   .... OTHER TRANSPORT
       w/ LINE INDICATED   (BIKE, TAXI, CAR...)

Hours: Tuesday–Sunday 9:00–18:30, closed Monday, October–April 9:00–17:30, last entry 30 minutes before closing.
Time to Allow: Six hours round-trip from Paris (an hour each way in transit, two hours for the palace, two for the gardens).
Getting to Versailles: From Paris, take the RER-C train (26F round-trip, 30 min) to "Versailles R.G.," not "Versailles C.H.," which is farther from the palace. Versailles makes a fine home base (see accommodations under Sleeping).

Vaux-le-Vicomte

While Versailles is most travelers' first choice for its sheer historic weight, Vaux-le-Vicomte (voh-luh-vee-komt) offers a more lavish interior and a far better sense of 17th-century château life. Sitting in a huge forest with magnificent gardens and no urban sprawl in sight, Vaux-le-Vicomte gave me just a twinge of palace envy.

Vaux-le-Vicomte was the architectural inspiration of Versailles and set the standard for European châteaus to come. The proud owner, Nicolas Fouquet (Louis XIV's finance minister) threw a château-warming party. Louis was so jealous that he

arrested his host; took his
architect (Le Vau), artist (Le
Brun), and landscaper (Le
Notre); and proceeded with the
construction of the bigger and
costlier (but not necessarily
more splendid) palace of Versailles. Monsieur Fouquet is
thought to be Alexandre
Dumas' man in *The Man in the
Iron Mask*, which was recently filmed here.

Vaux-le-Vicomte is expensive to get to (because of cab fare)
but a joy to tour. While the gift shop's 25F souvenir booklet has
helpful information, the château's rooms have English explanations. Start with the fine horse carriages exhibit (*equipages*) in the
old stables. Wax figures and an evocative soundtrack get you in
the proper mood. Next, stroll like a wide-eyed peasant across the
drawbridge and up the front steps into the château. You'll notice
candles. Over 1,300 flicker for candle-lit night visits.

As you wander through Fouquet's dream-home, you'll understand Louis' jealousy. Versailles was a rather simple hunting lodge
when this was built. Since Louis confiscated everything; the furniture is not original. It's from other palaces in the area. You'll see
cozy bedrooms upstairs, and grand living rooms downstairs,
including a billiards room, library, card room, and a dining room.
The kitchen and wine cellar are in the basement.

Survey the garden from the back steps of the palace. This was
the landscaper Le Notre's first claim to fame. This garden was the
cutting edge of sculpted French gardens. He integrated ponds,
shrubbery, flowers, and trees in a style that would be copied in
palaces all over Europe. Take the 30-minute walk (one way) to the
Hercules viewpoint, atop the grassy hill way in the distance. Rent
golf carts (Club Cars, 80F for 45 minutes) to make the trip easier.
Picnics are not allowed.

Cost and Hours: Steep 56F admission; 30F for gardens only. The
château is open daily March–October 10:00–13:00, 14:00–18:00
(gardens don't close midday), less in winter, tel. 01 64 14 41 90.

The candle-lit visits (*visites aux chandelles*) are worth the 75F
entry. (Open 20:30–24:00 on Saturdays May–October and holidays
except July 14—call to ask about any upcoming holidays; there are
many in May. The last train to Paris leaves Melun at about 22:00.)

The fountains run April–October on the second and last Saturday of each month 15:00–18:00. A good indoor/outdoor café-
restaurant, offering reasonable prices and good salads, is inside the
first courtyard.

Getting to Vaux-le-Vicomte: To reach Vaux-le-Vicomte by car or by a train and taxi combination, head for the city of Melun. RER trains run to Melun from Paris' Gare du Nord and Chatelet stations. Faster Banlieue trains leave from Paris' Gare de Lyon (43F one-way, 35 min). Taxis make the 10-minute drive from Melun's station to Vaux-le-Vicomte (85F weekdays, 100F evenings and Sundays, taxi phone number posted above taxi stand). Ask a staff person at the château to call a cab for your return or schedule a pick-up time with your driver. In either direction, split the cab fare with other travelers. Melun's TI is a block from the train station, past the ugly concrete building (Tuesday–Saturday 10:00–12:00, 14:00–18:00, closed Sunday and Monday, 2 avenue Gallieni, tel. 01 64 37 11 31).

Adding Fontainebleau: Vaux-le-Vicomte and Fontainebleau can be combined into a full, though manageable, daytrip by car or train from Paris. Fountainebleau is 12 minutes by train from Melun.

Sleeping near Vaux-le-Vicomte: The modern but handy IBIS Hotel is between Melun and the château (Db-300F, less on weekends, tel. 01 60 68 42 45, fax 01 64 09 62 00).

Château of Fontainebleau

Fontainebleau's history rivals Versailles'. Another glamorous hunting lodge, many French kings have called this home. Napoleon welcomed the pope here during his coronation celebration and it was here that he abdicated his rule when exiled to Elba in 1814. General Patton set up headquarters here on his way to Berlin.

While Vaux-le-Vicomte and Versailles are French-designed, Fountainebleau (fohn-ten-bloh) was built—a century earlier—by an Italian. The palace you see today is largely the work of Renaissance King Francois I. Inspired by his travels through Renaissance Italy, he hired Italian artists to build his palace.

Orient with a quick visit to the château information room with its huge model of the château (first door on your right in the grand courtyard). The palace entry is next door. Your ticket provides access to the Chinese rooms and the main rooms of the château. Napoleon buffs will enjoy the little museum of Napoleonic history, which requires an additional ticket and a guided tour (16F; ask about tour times at the ticket window). While 20F guidebooklets give excellent room-by-room descriptions, you'll find adequate English explanations posted throughout.

Start downstairs with the small but impressive Chinese collection of the Empress of Napoleon III, then climb to the main rooms of the palace. Highlights include the stunning Renaissance hall of Francois I, the opulent dance hall with piped-in music (*Salle de bal*), Napoleon's throne room, and the Trinity chapel. The idyllic gardens, designed a century later by the landscaper Le Notre, are worth a stroll. Rent a rowboat in the *etang des carpes* (carp pond) or walk its path for a good view of the château complex.

Cost and Hours: 35F, Wednesday–Monday 9:30–18:00, closed Tuesday, November–May 9:30–12:30, 14:00–17:00, last entry 45 minutes before closing.

Getting to Fontainebleau: Catch a train from Paris' Gare de Lyon in the direction of Montereau (47F one-way, 40 min) to the Fontainebleau-Avon station where a bus goes to the château (Cars Verts, 4/hrly, 10F, pay on board; schedules posted in English). Or from the station, you could take a taxi to the château (40F) and to Vaux-le-Vicomte (200F).

Town of Fontainebleau: The helpful TI has hiking maps, bike rental information, and hotel listings (daily 9:30–17:30, at the bus stop a block from château, tel. 01 64 74 99 99). You can rent a bike at the station, the TI, or best at La Petite Reine (85F/day, 50F/half-day, 32 rue des Sablons, tel. 01 64 74 57 57).

Sleeping in Fontainebleau: Hotels offer good values in this pleasant town. Hotel de Londres***, in business since 1850, has Old World character on a busy square next to the TI (Db-350F, deluxe Db-450–550F, CC:VM, place General de Gaulle, tel. 01 64 22 20 21, fax 01 60 72 39 12). One block from the château gardens, Hotel Legris et Parc*** is a quiet, dreamy getaway with a courtyard and elegant restaurant (Db-460–570F, CC:VMA, 36 rue Paul Seramy, tel. 01 64 22 24 24, fax 01 64 22 22 05). Hotel a la Carpe d'Or** is a simpler option (Db-200–225F, 21 bis rue Paul Seramy, tel. 01 64 22 28 64).

Château of Chantilly

Chantilly (shan-tee-yee), 35 minutes north of Paris, floats serenely on a reflecting pond amid grand gardens. Unfortunately, the château interior is disappointing. Its best rooms are visitable only on a boring French-only guided tour and the fine works of art in the picture galleries are poorly displayed. Still, Chantilly can be a pleasant experience if approached in the right way. Allow most of a day for Chantilly.

This extravagant hunting palace was destroyed during the

Revolution. Today's château was largely rebuilt during the 19th century. It's divided into two parts: the painting gallery (with paintings by Raphael, Titian, Poussin, Delacroix, and others) and the private apartments (requiring a French-language tour). The highlight of the apartments is the first stop, the Prince's library, lined with more than 13,000 books and beautiful copies of pages from *Les Tres Riches Heures du Duc du Berry*, a much-admired illuminated 15th-century manuscript. Unfortunately the tour continues through room after room of look-alike furniture and endless portraits of *le* Prince.

The gardens immediately behind the château are formal and austere. With your back to the château, follow the signs to the right to *le Hameau*. This little hamlet was the prototype for the more famous *hameau* at Versailles (and has a delightful garden café). Just beyond is a small kiosk, offering a tethered hot air balloon ride (45F, great view) and electric boat trips along the canals (35F, tel. 03 44 57 35 35).

Cost and Hours: 39F, 17F for gardens only, Wednesday–Monday 10:00–18:00, closed Tuesday, off-season 10:30–12:45, 14:00–17:00, tel. 01 44 57 08 00.

Live Horse Stables (*Les Ecuries Vivant*): The Prince de Conde built this horse château for himself, as he believed he'd be reincarnated as a horse. You'd have to have similar beliefs to pay the 50F entry for this albeit impressive and thorough horse museum, featuring 40 live horses in their stables and a daily demonstration generally at 15:30, more often in summmer (April–October Wednesday–Monday 10:30–17:30, also open Tuesdays in summer; November–March 14:00–17:30, closed Tuesday, weekends 10:30–17:30, tel. 03 44 57 13 13).

Getting to Chantilly: Leave from Paris' Gare du Nord for Chantilly-Gouvieux. The RER, Banlieue, and main train lines all leave from different tracks (41F one-way, 35 min). Upon arrival in Chantilly, confirm your return times. The TI is a block in front of the station. To get to the château, it's a 40F taxi ride, a free bus ride on a rare city bus (ask at the station), or a 30-minute walk (follow signs, stay on path, turn right before BP gas station, cross grass field, "château" in distance is stables, château is beyond that). The well-preserved medieval town of Senlis is a 30-minute bus ride (110F taxi) from the Chantilly station.

MORE DAY TRIPS FROM PARIS

▲▲▲**Chartres**—In 1194 a terrible fire destroyed the church at Chartres with the much-venerated veil of Mary. With almost unbelievably good fortune, the monks found the veil miraculously preserved in the ashes. Money poured in for the building of a bigger and better cathedral—decorated with 2,000 carved figures and some of France's best stained glass. The cathedral feels too large for the city because it was designed to accommodate huge crowds of pilgrims. One of those pilgrims, an impressed Napoleon, declared after a visit in 1811: "Chartres is no place for an atheist." Rodin called it "the Acropolis of France." British Francophile Malcolm Miller or his impressive assistant give great "Appreciation of Gothic" tours Monday–Saturday, usually at noon and 14:45 (verify times in advance, no tours off-season, call TI at tel. 02 37 21 50 00). Each 40F tour is different; many stay for both tours. Just show up at the church (open daily 7:00–19:00).

Explore Chartres' pleasant city center and discover the picnic-friendly park behind the cathedral. The helpful TI, next to the cathedral, has a map with a self-guided tour of Chartres (daily 9:30–18:45). Chartres is a one-hour train trip from the Gare Montparnasse (71F one-way, 10/day, last train on Saturday departs at about 19:00). Upon arrival, confirm your return schedule to avoid an unplanned night in Chartres.

▲**Giverny**—From 1883–1926, Monet spent 43 of his most creative years at Giverny (zhee-vayr-nee), the Camp David of Impressionism. Monet's gardens and home are split by a busy road. Buy your ticket, walk through the gardens, and take the underpass into the artist's famous lilypad land. The path leads you over the Japanese Bridge, under weeping willows, and past countless scenes that leave artists aching for an easel. For Monet fans, it's strangely nostalgic. Back on the other side, continue your visit with a wander through his more robust and structured garden and his mildly interesting home. The jammed gift shop at the exit is the actual skylit studio where Monet painted his waterlily masterpieces.

While lines may be long and tour groups may trample the flowers, true fans still find magic in those lilypads. Avoid crowds by arriving after 16:00 (35F, 25F for gardens only, April–October Tuesday–Sunday 10:00–18:00, closed Monday and off-season, tel. 02 32 51 28 21).

Take the Rouen-bound train from Paris' Gare St. Lazare station to Vernon (about 140F round-trip, long gaps in service, know schedule before you go). To get from the Vernon train station to Monet's garden (four km away), take the Vernon–Giverny bus (5/day, scheduled to meet most trains), hitch, taxi (60F), or rent a bike at the station (55F, busy road). Get return bus times from the ticket office in Giverny or ask them to call a taxi. Big tour companies do a Giverny day trip from Paris for around $60.

The new American Impressionist Art Museum (100 yards from Monet's place) is devoted to American artists who followed Claude to Giverny. Giverny had a great influence on American artists of Monet's day. This bright, modern gallery is well-explained in English, has a good little Mary Cassatt section, and gives Americans a rare chance to see French people appreciating our artists (same price and hours as Monet's home, pleasant café).

▲▲**Disneyland Paris**—Europe's Disneyland is basically a modern remake of California's, with most of the same rides and smiles. The main difference is that Mickey Mouse speaks French (and you can buy wine with your lunch). My kids went ducky. Locals love it. It's worth a day if Paris is handier than Florida or California. Crowds are a problem. If possible, avoid Saturday, Sunday, Wednesday, school holidays, and July and August. The park can get very crowded. When 60,000 have entered, they close the gates (tel. 01 64 74 30 00 for the latest). After dinner, crowds are gone, and you'll walk right on to rides that had a 45-minute wait three hours earlier. Food is fun but expensive. To eat cheaply, smuggle in a picnic.

Disney brochures are in every Paris hotel. The RER (40F each way, direct from downtown Paris to Marne-la-Vallee in 30 minutes) drops you right into the park. The last train back into Paris leaves shortly after midnight. (200F for adults, 155F for kids 3–11, 25F less in spring and fall. Daily 9:00–23:00 in late June–early September and Saturday and Sunday off-season, shoulder-season weekdays 9:00–19:00, off-season 10:00–18:00, tel. 01 60 30 60 30, fax 01 60 30 60 65 for park and hotel reservations.)

To sleep reasonably at the huge Disney complex, try Hotel Sante Fe (780F family rooms for two to four people includes breakfast, less off-season; ask for their hotel and park package deal). If all this ain't enough, a new Planet Hollywood restaurant opened just outside the park a five-minute walk from the RER stop.

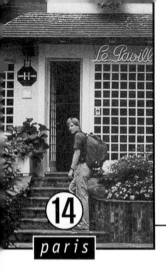

SLEEPING
IN PARIS

I've focused on three safe, handy, and colorful neighborhoods: rue Cler, Marais, and Contrescarpe. For each, I list good hotels, helpful hints, and restaurants (see Eating). At the end of the chapter, you'll find accommodations listed for Versailles, as well as apartments in Paris for longer stays.

Reserve ahead for Paris, the sooner the better. Conventions clog Paris in September (worst), October, May, and June. Most hotels accept telephone reservations, require prepayment with a credit-card number, and prefer a faxed follow-up to be sure everything is in order. For more information, see Making Reservations in this book's introduction.

French hotels are rated by stars (indicated in this book by an *). One star is simple, two has most of the comforts, and three is, for this book, plush. If you need maximum comfort, go for the three-star places.

Old, characteristic, budget Parisian hotels have always been cramped. Retrofitted with elevators, toilets, and private showers (as most are today), they are even more cramped. Even three-star hotel rooms are small, and generally not worth the extra expense in Paris. Some hotels include the hotel tax (*taxe de sejour*, about 5F per person per day), though most will add this to your bill. Two-star hotels are required to have an English-speaking staff. Nearly all hotels listed will have someone who speaks English.

Quad rooms usually have two double beds. Recommended hotels have an elevator unless otherwise noted. Because rooms with double beds and showers are cheaper than rooms with twin beds and baths, room prices vary within each hotel.

You can save about 100F by finding the increasingly rare room without a private shower, though some hotels charge for down-the-hall showers. Breakfasts cost 20F to 50F extra. Café or picnic breakfasts are cheaper. Singles (except for the rare closet-type rooms that fit only one twin bed) are simply doubles used by one person. They rent for only a little less than a double.

Get advice for safe parking from your hotel. Meters are free in August. Garages are plentiful (90–140F per day, with special rates through some hotels). Self-serve Laundromats are common; ask your hotelier for the nearest one (*Où est un laverie automatique?*; ooh ay uh lah-vay-ree auto-mah-teek).

Sleep Code
S = Single, **D** = Double/Twin, **T** = Triple, **Q** = Quad, **b** = bathroom, **t** = toilet only, **s** = shower only, **CC** = Credit Card (**V** = Visa, **M** = MasterCard, **A** = Amex), ***** = French hotel rating system (0–4 stars). **Exchange rate:** 5.5F = about $1

Sleeping in the Rue Cler Neighborhood
(7th *arrondissement*, Mo: École Militaire, zip code: 75007)
Rue Cler, a village-like pedestrian street, is safe, tidy, and makes me feel like I must have been a poodle in a previous life. How such coziness lodged itself between the high-powered government/business district and the expensive Eiffel Tower and Invalides areas, I'll never know. Living here ranks with the top museums as one of the city's great experiences. (But if you're into nightlife, consider one of the other two neighborhoods I list.)

The street called rue Cler is the glue that holds this pleasant neighborhood together. From rue Cler you can walk to the Eiffel Tower, Napoleon's Tomb, the Seine, and the Orsay and Rodin museums. The first six hotels listed below are within Camembert-smelling distance of the rue Cler; the others are within a five-minute stroll. Warning: The first two hotels are popular with my readers.

Hôtel Leveque** has been entirely renovated. But, with a helpful staff and a singing maid, it's still cozy. It's a fine value with the best location on the block, comfortable rooms, cable TV, hair dryers, safes, an ice machine, and tasteful decor throughout (Sb-270F, Db-380–450F, Tb-550F, breakfast-30F but free for readers of this book, CC:VMA, 29 rue Cler, tel. 01 47 05 49 15, fax 01 45 50 49 36, Web site: http://interresa.ca/hotel/leveque/fr, e-mail: leveque@hotellerie.net). Laurence at the front desk speaks English.

Hôtel du Champs de Mars**, with charming, pastel rooms and helpful English-speaking owners, Françoise and Stephane, is an even cosier rue Cler option. The hotel has a Provence-style

RUE CLER HOTELS

1. HOTEL LEVEQUE
2. HOTEL DU CHAMPS DU MARS
3. HOTEL LA SERRE
4. HOTEL RELAIS BOSQUET
5. HOTEL LE VALADON
6. HOTEL PRINCE
7. HOTEL DE L'ALMA
8. HOTEL LONDRES EIFFEL
9. MARS HOTEL
10. HOTEL LA TOUR MAUBOURG
11. HOTEL EIFFEL RIVE GAUCHE
12. HOTEL KENSINGTON
13. HOTEL DE LA TULIPE
14. HOTEL LE PAVILLION
15. HOTEL ROYAL PHARE
16. HOTEL DE LA MOTTE PIQUET
17. HOTEL DE LA PAIX
18. HOTEL BEAUGENCY
19. HOTEL DE LA TOUR EIFFEL

small-town feel from top to bottom. Rooms are comfortable and a very good value. Single rooms can work as tiny doubles (Db-390–420F, Tb-505F, CC:VMA, cable TV, hair dryers, etc., 30 yards off rue Cler at 7 rue du Champs de Mars, tel. 01 45 51 52 30, fax 01 45 51 64 36, Web site: www: adx.fr/hotel-du-champ-de-mars, e-mail: stg@club-internet.fr).

Hôtel la Serre*, across the street from the Hotel Leveque, is a simple hotel with basic rooms, well-worn hallways, no elevator, and a charming location. Regrettably, you may be expected to pay in advance before seeing the room (D-270F, Db-390–400F, Tb-520F, cable TV, CC:VM, 24 rue Cler, tel. 01 47 05 52 33, fax 01 40 62 95 66, e-mail: laserre@easynet.fr).

Hôtel Relais Bosquet*** is bright, spacious, and a bit upscale with sharp, comfortable rooms (Db-550–900F, most at 750F, CC:VMA, 19 rue de Champs de Mars, tel. 01 47 05 25 45, fax 01 45 55 08 24, e-mail: Webmaster@relais-bosquet.com). The similar **Hotel Beaugency***** offers similar comfort for less (Db-720F, includes a buffet breakfast, 21 rue Duvivier, tel. 01 47 05 01 63, fax 01 45 51 04 96).

Hôtel Le Valadon**, on a quiet street with a plain lobby and spacious, comfy rooms, has a shy, modern Parisian cuteness and a friendly staff (Db-410–530F, Tb-560F, CC:VM, 16 rue Valadon, tel. 01 47 53 89 85, fax 01 44 18 90 56).

These listings are a five-minute walk west of the rue Cler and are listed in order of proximity.

Hotel Prince** just across avenue Bosquet from École Militaire Métro, has a "we try harder" spirit and good value rooms, many overlooking a busy street (Db-430–510F, CC:VM, 66 avenue Bosquet, tel. 01 47 05 40 90, fax 01 47 53 06 62, friendly owner Christof speaks English).

Hotel le Tourville**** is the most classy and expensive of my Paris listings. This four-star gem is surprisingly intimate and friendly from its welcoming lobby to ultra-polished rooms (standard Db-600–900F, superior Db-800–1,150F, Db with private terrace-1,450F, 16 avenue de Tourville, Mo: École Militaire, tel. 01 47 05 62 62, fax 01 47 05 43 90, e-mail: hotel@tourville.com).

Hôtel de l'Alma*** is a tight and tidy place with 32 delightful look-alike rooms all with TV and minibar (Sb-400F, Db-450F, breakfast included, no triples but a kid's bed can be moved in for free, popular with Mexican and Russian groups, CC:VMA, 32 rue de l'Exposition, tel. 01 47 05 45 70, fax 01 45 51 84 47).

Hôtel Eiffel Rive Gauche** is quiet, unassuming, and is being renovated into a fair value (Ds-260F, Db-420–460F, CC:VM, 6 rue du Gros-Caillou, tel. 01 45 51 24 56, fax 01 45 51 11 77).

Hotel Londres Eiffel*** is just renovated with cheerful attention to detail. Its small, cozy rooms are comfortable, and its friendly owners seem eager to please (Sb-495F, Db-595F, Tb-725F, extra bed-70F, CC:VMA, 1 rue Augerau, tel. 01 45 51 63 02, fax 01 47 05 28 96).

Mars Hôtel** has a richly decorated lobby, spacious—if well-worn—rooms, and a beam-me-up-Maurice coffin-sized elevator. The front rooms look out on the Eiffel Tower (large Sb-320F, Db-380F, Twin/b-480F, CC:VM, 117 avenue de la Bourdonnais, tel. 01 47 05 42 30, fax 01 47 05 45 91).

Hôtel La Tour Maubourg*** is particularly romantic. It lies alone five minutes east of the rue Cler, just off the Esplanade des Invalides and feels like a slightly faded, elegant manor house with spacious Old World rooms. It overlooks a cheery green lawn within sight of Napoleon's tomb (Sb-550–650F, Db-690–850F, suites for up to four 900F–1,400F, prices include breakfast with fresh-squeezed juice, prices reduced from mid-July–mid-August, CC:VM, immediately at the La Tour Maubourg Métro stop, 150 rue de Grenelle, tel. 01 47 05 16 16, fax 01 47 05 16 14, e-mail: victor@worldnet.fr).

These places are lesser values but, in this fine area, acceptable last choices: **Hôtel de la Tour Eiffel**** (Sb-330F, Db-380F, Tb-480F, CC:VMA, 17 rue de l'Exposition, tel. 01 47 05 14 75, fax 01 47 53 99 46, Muriel speaks English); **Hôtel Kensington****, near the Mars Hotel (Sb-315F, Db-400–500F, extra bed-80F, CC:VMA, 79 avenue de La Bourdonnais, tel. 01 47 05 74 00, fax 01 47 05 25 81); **Hôtel de la Tulipe**** (Db-580F, overpriced and wood-beamed with a leafy courtyard, no elevator, 33 rue Malar, tel. 01 45 51 67 21, fax 01 47 53 96 37); quiet **Hotel le Pavillon** with a small courtyard (Db-460F, family suites-575F, 54 rue St. Dominique, tel. 01 45 51 42 87, fax 01 45 51 32 79); **Hôtel Royal Phare**** (Db-310–410F, facing École Militaire Métro stop, 40 avenue de la Motte Piquet, tel. 01 47 05 57 30, fax 01 45 51 64 41); **Hôtel la Motte Piquet**** (Db-350–440F, duplex suites-730F, CC:VM, 30 avenue de la Motte Piquet, tel. 01 47 05 09 57, fax 01 47 05 74 36); and simple, quiet **Hôtel de la Paix**, run agreeably by English-speaking Noël (S-175F, Ds-310F, Db-345F, Tb-475F, no elevator, 19 rue du Gros-Caillou, tel. 01 45 51 86 17).

Rue Cler Orientation

✪ See the Rue Cler Walk, page 68, for more information on this area. Become a local at a rue Cler café for breakfast or join the afternoon crowd for *une bière pression* (a draft beer). On rue Cler you can eat and browse your way through a street full of tart shops, delis, cheeseries, and colorful outdoor produce stalls. (For cafés and restaurants, see Eating.) For an after-dinner cruise on the Seine, it's just a short walk to the river to the Bâteaux Mouches.

Your neighborhood TI is at the Eiffel Tower (daily May–September 11:00–18:00, tel. 01 45 51 22 15). The Métro station (École Militaire) and a post office with phone booths are at the end of rue Cler, on avenue de la Motte Piquet. Taxi stands are on avenue de Tourville at avenue la Motte Piquet (near Métro stop), and on avenue Bosquet at rue St. Dominique. The Banque

Populaire (across from Hôtel Leveque) changes money and has an ATM. Rue St. Dominique is the area's boutique street.

The American Church and College is the community center for Americans living in Paris (65 quai d'Orsay, tel. 01 47 05 07 99). The interdenominational service at 11:00 on Sunday, the coffee hour after church, and the free Sunday concerts (18:00) are a great way to make some friends and get a taste of émigré life in Paris. Stop by and pick up copies of the *Free Voice* for a monthly review of Paris entertainment and *France–U.S.A. Contacts* for information on housing and employment through the community of 30,000 Americans living in Paris.

Afternoon *boules* (lawn bowling) on the esplanade des Invalides is a relaxing spectator sport. Look for the dirt area to the upper right as you face the Invalides.

Helpful bus routes: Line 69 runs along rue St. Dominique and serves Les Invalides, Orsay, Louvre, Marais, and Père-Lachaise cemetery. Line 92 runs along avenue Bosquet and serves the Arc de Triomphe and Champs-Élysées in one direction and the Montparnasse tower in the other. Line 49 runs on boulevard La Tour Maubourg and serves St. Lazare and Gare du Nord stations.

Sleeping in the Marais Neighborhood
(4th *arrondissement*, Mo: St. Paul or Bastille, zip code: 75004)
Those interested in a more Soho/Greenwich, gentrified, urban-jungle locale would enjoy making the Marais their Parisian home. The Marais is a more happening locale than rue Cler. It's narrow medieval Paris at its finest. Only 15 years ago it was a forgotten Parisian backwater, but now the Marais is one of Paris' most popular residential areas. It's a 15-minute walk to Notre-Dame, Île St. Louis, and the Latin Quarter. The St. Paul Métro stop puts you right in the heart of the Marais.

Hôtel Castex** is pleasant, clean, cheery, and run by the friendly Perdigao family (Miguel and Vasco). This place is a great value, with comfortable rooms, many stairs, and a great location on a relatively quiet street (Ss-240F, Sb-260–290F, Ds-320–340F, Db-340–360F, Tb-460F, CC:VM, no elevator, 5 rue Castex, just off place de la Bastille and rue Saint Antoine, Mo: Bastille, tel. 01 42 72 31 52, fax 01 42 72 57 91). Reserve by phone and leave your credit-card number. The security code marked on your key opens the front door after hours.

Grand Hôtel Jeanne d'Arc**, a cozy, welcoming place with thoughtfully appointed rooms on a quiet street, is a fine value and a haven for connoisseurs of the Marais (small Db-310F, Db-400–490F, Tb-530F, Qb-590F, extra bed 75F, CC:VM, 3 rue Jarente, Mo: St. Paul, tel. 01 48 87 62 11, fax 01 48 87 37 31).

MARAIS HOTELS

Sixth-floor rooms have a view. Corner rooms are wonderfully bright in the city of light.

Hotel Bastille Speria*** feels family-run while offering a serious business-type service. Its spacious lobby and 45 rooms are modern, cheery, and pastel and it's English language–friendly, from the Herald Tribunes in the lobby to the history of the Bastille in the elevator (Sb-525–550F, Db-570–635F, Tb-770F, extra bed-120F, CC:VMA, 1 rue de la Bastille, Mo: Bastille, tel. 01 42 72 04 01, fax 01 42 72 56 38, e-mail: speria@micronet.fr).

Hôtel de la Place des Vosges** , quasi-classy with a linoleum/antique feel, is ideally located on a quiet street (Sb-350F, Db-450–510F, CC:VMA, 12 rue de Biraque, just off the elegant place des Vosges and just as snooty, Mo: St. Paul, tel. 01 42 72 60 46, fax 01 42 72 02 64).

Hotel des Chevaliers*** , one block northwest of the place des Vosges, offers pleasant and comfortable rooms with all the comforts from hair dryers to cable TV (Db-630–820F, CC:VMA, skip the over-priced breakfast, 30 rue de Turenne, Mo: St. Paul, tel. 01 42 72 73 47, fax 01 42 72 54 10).

Hotel de la Herse D'Or is industrial-strength, three-coats-of-paint simple, with a good location, tortured floor plan, and hard-to-beat prices (S-160F, D-200F, Db-280F, showers 10F, no elevator, 20 rue Saint Antoine, Mo: Bastille, tel. 01 48 87 84 09, fax 01 48 87 94 01).

Hotel Sévigné** provides basic two-star comfort at fair prices with the cheapest breakfast in Paris: 16F (Sb-355F, Db-375F, CC:VM, 2 rue Malher, Mo: St. Paul, tel. 01 42 72 76 17, fax 01 42 78 68 26).

Hôtel Pratic* has a slightly Arabic feel in its cramped lobby. The tidy rooms are simple but not confined, stairs are many, and it's right on a great people-friendly square. Single rooms are bare, tiny, and depressing (S-180F, D-245F, Ds-290F, Db-340F, no elevator, 9 rue d'Ormesson, Mo: St. Paul, tel. 01 48 87 80 47, fax 01 48 87 40 04).

The bare-bones and dumpy **Hôtel Moderne**, next to the Hôtel Pratic, might be better than a youth hostel if you need privacy. The only thing "moderne" about it is the name—which is illegible on the broken sign (D-170F, Ds-190F, Db-220F, 3 rue Caron, Mo: St. Paul, tel. 01 48 87 97 05).

Grand Hotel du Loiret** is a fair value with easy-going management, and while popular with American students, is renovating many of its rooms out of a student price range (S-190F, Sb-250–350F, D-220F, Db-300–400F, Tb-400F, Qb-500F, CC:VMA, 8 rue des Garcons Mauvais, Mo: Hotel de Ville, tel. 01 48 87 77 00, fax 01 48 04 96 56).

Hôtel de 7ème Art**, a Hollywood-nostalgia place, is run by young, hip Marais types, with average rooms, a full service café/bar, and Charlie Chaplin murals (Sb-300F, Db-420–490F, a few large double rooms at 670F, CC:VMA, 20 rue St. Paul, Mo: St. Paul, tel. 01 44 54 85 00, fax 01 42 77 69 10).

Hôtel de Nice** is a cozy "Marie Antoinette does tie-dye" place with lots of thoughtful touches on the Marais' busy main drag (Sb-380F, Db-480F, Tb-600F, CC:VM, 42 bis rue de Rivoli, Mo: Hotel de Ville, tel. 01 42 78 55 29, fax 01 42 78 36 07). Twin rooms, which cost the same as doubles, are roomier but on the street side (effective double-pane windows).

Hotel de la Bretonniere*** is my favorite splurge in the Marais with elegant decor, tastefully decorated rooms with an antique, open beam coziness and an efficient, helpful staff (standard Db-640F, Db with character-790F and elegant suites at 980F, the standard Db has enough character for me, CC:VMA, between the rue du Vielle du Temple and the rue des Archives at 22 rue Sainte Croix de la Bretonnerie, Mo: Hotel de Ville, tel. 01 48 87 77 63, fax 01 42 77 26 78, Web site: www. HoteldelaBretonnerie.com).

Hotel Caron de Beaumarchais***, renovated into an 18th-century Marais manor house, is charming from the Louis XVI fireplace in the lobby to the period furniture in each room (Db-690–770F, CC:VMA, air-con, 12 rue Vielle du Temple, Mo: Hotel de Ville, tel. 01 42 72 34 12, fax 01 42 72 34 63).

Hotel Rivoli Notre Dame***, another nicely remodeled three-star place with all the comforts, is centrally located in the Marais (Db-660–715F, CC:VMA, 19 rue du Bourg Tibourg, Mo: Hotel de Ville, tel. 01 42 78 47 39, fax 01 40 29 07 00, Web site: www.hotelrivolinotredame.com).

Hotel de Vieux Marais**, tucked away on a quiet street near the Pompidou Center, will offer renovated rooms with air-conditioning in 1999 (Sb-500F, Db-660–690F, extra bed-100F, CC:VM, just off rue des Archives at 8 rue du Platre, Mo: Hotel de Ville, tel. 01 42 78 47 22, fax 01 42 78 34 32).

MIJE "Youth Hostels": The Maison Internationale de la Jeunesse des Étudiants (MIJE) runs three classy old residences in the Marais for travelers under age 30. Each offers simple, clean, single-sex, mostly four-bed rooms for 126F per bed, including shower and breakfast. Singles cost 200F. Rooms are locked from 12:00–15:00 and at 01:00. MIJE Fourcy (cheap dinners, 6 rue de Fourcy, just south of the rue Rivoli), MIJE Fauconnier (11 rue Fauconnier), and the best, MIJE Maubisson (12 rue des Barres), share one telephone number (01 42 74 23 45) and Métro stop (St. Paul). Reservations are accepted.

Marais Orientation

✪ See the Marais Walk, page 64, for more information on this area. The nearest TIs are in the Louvre and Gare de Lyon (arrival level, open 8:00–20:00, tel. 01 43 43 33 24). The Banque de France changes money, offering good rates and sometimes long lines (where rue Saint Antoine hits place de la Bastille, Monday–Friday 9:00–11:45, 13:30–15:30). Most banks, shops, and other services are on rue Saint Antoine between Métro stops St. Paul and Bastille. You'll find one taxi stand on the north side of Saint Antoine where it meets rue Castex, and another on the south side of Saint Antoine in front of the St. Paul church.

The new Bastille opera house, Promenade Plantée Park, place des Vosges (Paris' oldest square), and the Jewish Quarter (rue des Rosiers) are all nearby. The Marais' main drag, rue Saint Antoine, starts at the Bastille and leads west towards the hopping Beaubourg/Les Halles area. A fine budget department store is

BHV, next to the Hôtel de Ville. Marais post offices are on rue Castex and on the corner of rues Pavée and Francs Bourgeois.

Helpful bus routes: Line 69 on rue Saint Antoine takes you to the Louvre, Orsay, Rodin, and Napoleon's Tomb and ends at the Eiffel Tower. Line 86 runs down boulevard Henri IV crossing the Île St. Louis and serving the Latin Quarter along boulevard St. Germain. Line 65 serves the train stations Austerlitz, Est, and Nord from place de la Bastille.

Sleeping in the Contrescarpe Neighborhood
(5th *arrondissement*, Mo: place Monge, zip code: 75005)
This lively, colorful neighborhood—just over the hill from the Latin Quarter and behind the Panthéon—is walking distance from Notre-Dame, Île de la Cité, Île St. Louis, Luxembourg Gardens, and the grand boulevards St. Germain and St. Michel. The rue Mouffetard and delightfully Parisian place Contrescarpe are the heart and soul of this area. Rue Mouffetard is a market street by day and touristy restaurant row by night. Fewer tourists sleep here and I find the hotel values consistently better than most other neighborhoods. These hotels are listed in order by proximity to the Seine river.

The low-energy, bare-bones **Hôtel du Commerce** is run by Monsieur Mattuzzi, who must be a pirate gone good (S-130F, D-140F, Ds-150F, Ts-210F, Qs-260F, showers-15F, no elevator, takes no reservations, call at 10:00 and he'll say "*oui*" or "*non*," 14 rue de La Montagne Ste. Geneviève, Mo: Maubert-Mutualité, tel. 01 43 54 89 69). This 300-year-old place (with vinyl that looks it) is a great rock-bottom deal and as safe as any dive next to a police station can be. In the morning, the landlady will knock and chirp, "*Restez-vous?*" (Are you staying tonight?)

Hôtel des Grandes Écoles** is as good as a two-star Parisian hotel gets (and better than most three-star hotels). It's idyllic and peaceful, with three buildings protecting a flowering garden courtyard. This romantic place is deservedly popular, so call well in advance (Db-520–670F, Tb-620–770F, Qb-670–870F, 75 rue de Cardinal Lemoine, Mo: Cardinal Lemoine, tel. 01 43 26 79 23, fax 01 43 25 28 15, mellow Marie).

Hôtel Central* is unprententious with a charming location, a steep and slippery castle-like stairway, simple rooms (all with shower, though toilets are down the hall), so-so beds, and plenty of smiles. It's a fine budget value (Ss-165–190F, Ds-240–270F, no elevator, 6 rue Descartes, Mo: Cardinal Lemoine, tel. 01 46 33 57 93).

The hotels listed below lie on or at the bottom of the rue Mouffetard and often have rooms when others don't.

Hotel Comfort Inn**, with its modern hotel chain rooms,

CONTRESCARPE HOTELS

CLUNY MUSEUM

BLVD.

SAINT

GERMAIN

SEINE

QUAI

TOURNELLE

BERNARDINS

TO NOTRE DAME

Maubert Mutualite

RUE DE LA MONT ST GENEVIEVE

SAINT JACQUES

PANTHEON

RUE DES ECOLES

DESCARTES

Cardinal Lemoine

SOUFFLOT

TO LUXEMBOURG GARDENS

RUE

RUE CARD.

RUE MONGE

ARENES DE LUTECE

N

PLACE CONTRESCARPE

ROLLIN

LACEPEDE

MOUFFETARD

ORTOLAN

POT DE FER

Monge

PLACE MONGE

RUE

R. CENSIER

CENSIER - DAUBENTON

❶ HOTEL DU COMMERCE
❷ HOTEL DES GRANDES ECOLES
❸ HOTEL CENTRAL
❹ HOTEL COMFORT INN
❺ Y & H HOSTEL
❻ HOTEL DE L'ESPERANCE
❼ HOTEL PASCAL
❽ HOTEL DE FRANCE
❾ HOTEL PORT ROYAL

100 YDS.

DCH

R. BERNARD

R. PASCAL

MONGE

seems out of place in this non-conformist area, but it's brilliantly located right on the rue Mouffetard, a stone's throw from the place Contrescarpe and late night action (Sb-535F, Db-620F, CC:VM, 56 rue Mouffetard, Mo: Cardinal Lemoine, tel. 01 43 36 17 00, fax 01 43 36 25 78).

Y&H Hostel offers a great location, easygoing English-speaking management, and basic but acceptable hostel-like conditions (100F-beds in four-bed rooms, 120F-beds in double rooms, 15F for sheets, rooms closed 11:00–17:00 though reception stays open, reservations must be paid in advance, 80 rue Mouffetard, Mo: Cardinal Lemoine, tel. 01 45 35 09 53, fax 01 47 07 22 24).

Hotel de l'Esperance** gives you nearly three stars for the price of two. It's quiet, fluffy, and comfortable, with thoughtfully appointed rooms complete with canopy beds, hair dryers, cable TV, and a flamboyant owner (Sb-380–410F, Db-410–480F, Tb-550F, CC:VM, 15 rue Pascal, Mo: Censier-Daubenton, tel. 01 47 07 10 99, fax 01 43 37 56 19).

Hotel Pascal* is a good value with simple, clean rooms, small double beds, and miniscule bathrooms (S-200F, Db-300F, Tb-450F, Qb-600F, funky studio lofts with kitchenettes-450F, 20 rue Pascal, Mo: Censier-Daubenton, tel. 01 47 07 41 92, fax 01 47 07 43 80, e-mail: hotpascal@mail.opsion.fr).

Hotel de France**, on a busy street, has fine, modern rooms and hardworking, helpful owners (Sb-360F, Db-410–430F, CC:VM, 108 rue Monge, Mo: Censier-Daubenton, tel. 01 47 07 19 04, fax 01 43 36 62 34). The best and quietest rooms are *sur le cour* (on the courtyard).

Hotel Port Royal* is a budget traveler's dream with helpful owners and spotless, comfortable rooms at great prices (S-180–225F, D-225F, Db-335–350F, CC:VM, 8 boulevard de Port Royal, Mo: Gobelins, tel. 01 43 31 70 06, fax 01 43 31 33 67).

Contrescarpe Orientation

The nearest TI is at the Louvre Museum. The post office (PTT) is between rue Mouffetard and rue Monge at 10 rue de l'Épée du Bois. Place Monge hosts a colorful outdoor market on Wednesday, Friday, and Sunday until 13:00. The street market at the bottom of rue Mouffetard bustles daily 8:00–12:00 and 15:30–19:00 (five blocks south of the place Contrescarpe), and the lively place Contrescarpe hops in the afternoon and well after dark.

The flowery Jardin des Plantes park is close by and great for afternoon walks, as are Luxembourg Gardens, which justify the 15-minute walk. The doorway at 49 rue Monge leads to a hidden Roman arena (Arènes de Lutèce). Today, *boules* players occupy the stage while couples cuddle on the seats. Walk to the Panthéon, admire it from the outside (it's not worth paying to go in), and go into the wildly beautiful St. Étienne-du-Mont church.

Sleeping near Paris, in Versailles
(zip code: 78000)

For a laid-back alternative to Paris within easy reach of the big city by RER train (5/hrly, 30 min), with free and safe parking, Versailles can be a good overnight stop.

Hôtel Le Cheval Rouge**, built in 1676 as Louis XIV's stables, now houses tourists comfortably. It's a block behind place du Marche in a quaint corner of town on a large quiet courtyard (Ds-275F, Db-340–390F, extra bed-90F, CC:VMA, 18 rue Andre Chenier, tel. 01 39 50 03 03, fax 01 39 50 61 27).

Ibis Versailles**, a slick business-class place, offers all the comfort with none of the character (Db-390–490F, CC:VMA, across from RER station, 4 avenue du Gen. de Gaulle, tel. 01 39 53 03 30, fax 01 39 50 06 31).

Hotel du Palais, facing the RER station, has cheap and handy beds; get one off the street. It's a pink and funky place, dumpy enough to lack stars but proud enough to put candy on the beds (D-170F, Ds-220F, Db-250F, 30F per additional person, miles of stairs, 6 place Lyautey, tel. 01 39 50 39 29, fax 01 39 50 80 41).

Hotel d'Angleterre** is a peaceful, well-worn old place near the palace (Db-300–350F, extra bed-60F, CC:VM, first-floor rooms are best, 2 rue de Fontenay, tel. 01 39 51 43 50, fax 01 39 51 45 63).

For Longer Stays

Staying a week or longer? Consider the advantage of renting a furnished apartment. Complete with a small equipped kitchen and living room, this option is family friendly. Among the many English-speaking organizations ready to help, the following have proven most reliable.

Paris Appartements Services rents studios and one-bedroom apartments in the Opéra, Louvre, and Marais neighborhoods (2 rue d'Argout, 75002 Paris, tel. 01 40 28 01 28, fax 01 40 28 92 01, Web site: www.paris-appartements-services.fr).

Apalachee Bay is British-owned and offers "an extensive range of carefully selected furnished apartments" (21 rue de Madrid, 75008 Paris, tel. 01 42 94 13 13, fax 01 42 94 83 01, Web site: www.apalachee.com).

Locaflat offers accommodations ranging from studios to five-room apartments (tel. 01 43 06 78 79, fax 01 40 56 99 69, Web site: http://locaflat.com).

EATING
IN PARIS

Paris is France's wine and cuisine melting pot. While it lacks a style of its own, it draws from the best of France. Paris could hold a gourmet's Olympics—and import nothing.

Picnic or go to bakeries for quick take-out lunches, or stop at a café for a lunch salad or *plat du jour*, but linger longer over dinner. You can eat well, restaurant-style, for 100–140F. Your hotel can also recommend small nearby restaurants in the 60–100F range. Remember, cafés and simple small restaurants are happy to serve a *plat du jour* (garnished plate of the day, about 60F) or a chef-like salad (35–50F) day or night. Famous places are often overpriced, overcrowded, and overrated. Find a quiet neighborhood and wander, or follow a local recommendation. Restaurants open for dinner around 19:00, and small local favorites get crowded after 21:00. To save piles of francs, review the budget eating tips in this book's introduction.

Carve time out of your busy day to relax at a Parisian café. Sound good? See Les Grand Cafés de Paris, at the end of this chapter.

Restaurants

The Parisian eating scene is kept at a rolling boil. Entire books (and lives) are dedicated to the subject. If you are traveling outside of Paris, save your splurges for the countryside, where you'll enjoy better cooking for less money. I've listed places that conveniently fit a busy sightseeing schedule and places near recommended hotels. If you'd like to visit a district specifically to eat, consider the many romantic restaurants that line the cozy Île St. Louis' main street and the colorful, touristic but fun string of eateries along rue Mouffetard behind the Panthéon (in Contrescarpe neighborhood).

Cafeterias and Picnics

Many Parisian department stores have huge supermarkets hiding in the basement and top-floor cafeterias offering not really cheap but low-risk, low-stress, what-you-see-is-what-you-get meals.

For picnics, you'll find handy little groceries (*épiceries*) and delis (*charcuteries*) all over town but rarely near famous sights. Good picnic fixings include roasted chicken, drinkable yogurt, fresh bakery goods, melons, and exotic pâtés and cheeses. Great take-out deli-type foods like gourmet salads and quiches abound. *Boulangeries* make good cheap mini-quiches and sandwiches. While wine is taboo in public places in the United States, it's *pas de problème* in France.

Good Picnic Spots: The pedestrian bridge, Pont des Arts, with unmatched views and plentiful benches, and the park under the Eiffel Tower are my favorite dinner-picnic places. Bring your own dinner feast and watch the riverboats or the Eiffel Tower light up the city for you. The Palais Royal (across the street from the Louvre) is a good spot for a peaceful, royal picnic. Also try the little triangular Henry IV Park on the west tip of the Île de la Cité, people-watching at the Pompidou Center, the elegant place des Vosges (closes at dusk) in the Marais neighborhood, the gardens at the Rodin Museum, and Luxembourg Gardens.

Eating in the Rue Cler Neighborhood

Restaurants: The rue Cler neighborhood isn't famous for its restaurants. That's why I eat here. Several small family-run places serve great dinner menus for 100F and *plats du jour* for 60–80F.

Café du Marché, with the best seats, coffee, and prices on rue Cler, serves hearty salads and great 60F *plats du jour* for lunch or dinner. Arrive before 19:30 or wait at the bar. A chalkboard listing the plates of the day—each a meal—will momentarily be hung in front of you (at the corner of rue Cler and rue Champs de Mars).

Leo le Lion has been run by Mimi for 20 years and must be the friendliest place in the neighborhood. A warm, charming souvenir of old Paris, it's popular with locals. The 105F menu comes with a first course that could feed two for an entire meal (but no splitting) and a fully garnished main course (closed Sunday, 23 rue Duvivier, tel. 01 45 51 41 77).

Vegetarians will appreciate the Mediterranean cuisine at **7ème Sud**, though it can be smoky (at the corner of rue de Grenelle and rue Duvivier).

Thoumieux, the neighborhood's classy, traditional Parisian brasserie, is deservedly popular (82F and 160F menu, complete *á la carte*, 79 rue St. Dominique, tel. 01 47 05 49 75).

For a special dinner, survey the handful of fine places that line the rue de l'Exposition (between rue St. Dominique and rue de Grenelle): **Restaurant La Serre**, at #29, has fun ambience (*plats* 50–70F, daily from 19:00, often a wait after 21:00, good onion soup and duck specialties, tel. 01 45 55 20 96, Marie-Alice and Philippe speak English). Across the street at #28, **Le P'tit Troquet** is popular with locals and ideal for a last night splurge—allow 150F per person for dinner (closed Sunday and Monday, tel. 01 47 05 80 39). The quieter **La Maison de Cosima** at #20 offers a refined, creative French cuisine and excellent 100F and 150F menus that include a vegetarian option (closed Sunday, tel. 01 45 51 37 71, run by friendly Helene). The softly-lit tables and red velvet chairs of **Auberge du Champ de Mars** at #18 draw a romantic crowd in search of a good value (100F menu only, limited wine menu, closed Sunday, tel. 01 45 51 78 08). Around the corner, just off rue de Grenelle, the friendly and unpretentious **La Varanque** is a good budget bet with 60F *plats* and a 80F menu (27 rue Augereau, tel. 01 47 05 51 22).

Ambassade du Sud-Ouest, a wine and food boutique/ restaurant, specializes in French Southwest cuisine such as *daubes de canard*—duck meatballs (46 avenue de la Bourdonnais, tel. 01 45 55 59 59). **L'Ami de Jean** is a lively place to sample Basque cuisine (closed Sunday, 27 rue Malar, tel. 01 47 05 86 89).

Picnicking: The rue Cler is a moveable feast that gives "fast food" a good name. The entire street is clogged with connoisseurs of good eating. Only the health-food store goes unnoticed. A festival of food, the street is lined with people whose lives seem to be devoted to their specialty: stacking polished produce, rotisserie chicken, crêpes, or cheese squares.

For a magical picnic dinner at the Eiffel Tower, assemble it in no fewer than six shops on rue Cler and lounge on the best grass in Paris (the police don't mind after dark) with the dogs, Frisbees, a floodlit Tower, and a cool breeze in the Parc du Champs de Mars.

The **crêpe stand** next to Café du Marché does a wonderful top-end dinner crêpe for 25F. An Asian deli, **Traiteur Asie** (across from Hôtel Leveque, another across from the Hotel du Champs de Mars), has tasty low-stress, low-price take-out treats. Its two tables offer the cheapest place to sit, eat, and enjoy the rue Cler ambience. For quiche, cheese pie, or a pear/chocolate tart, try **Tarte Julie's** (take-out or stools, 28 rue Cler). The elegant **Flo Prestige** *charcuterie* (at École Militaire Métro stop) is open until 23:00 and offers mouth-watering meals to go. **Real McCoy** is a little shop selling American food and sandwiches (194 rue de Grenelle). There's a small late-night grocery on rue de Grenelle at rue de l'Exposition.

The bakery (*boulangerie*) on the corner of rue Cler and rue

de Champs de Mars is the place for a fresh baguette, sandwich,
tiny quiche, or *pain au chocolat*, but the almond croissants at the
boulangerie on rue de Grenelle at rue Cler make my day. The
bakery at 112 rue St. Dominique is in a league by itself and worth
the detour, with classic decor and tables to enjoy your *café au lait*
and croissant.

Cafés and Bars: If you want to linger over coffee or a drink
at a sidewalk café, try **Café du Marché** (see above), **Petite
Brasserie** (opposite #53 rue Cler), or the traditional **La Terasse**
café (at École Militaire Métro). **Café La Roussillon,** peopled and
decorated belle epoche, also offers a quintessential café experience.
Sip a 7F wine at the bar or enjoy the good bistro fare at a table
(hearty 50F *plats du jour* and salads, corner of Grenelle and Cler).
Le Sancerre wine bar/café is wood-beam warm and ideal for a
light lunch or dinner (great omlettes), or just for a glass of wine
after a long day of sightseeing—served by the owner whose cheeks
are the same color as his wine (open until 21:30, 22 avenue Rapp,
tel. 01 45 51 75 91). The almost no-name **Maison Altmayer** is a
hole-in-the-wall place for a drink quietly festooned with reality
(9:00–19:30, 6 rue du Gros Caillou, next to Hôtel Eiffel Rive
Gauche). Cafés like this originated (and this one still functions) as
a place where locals enjoyed a drink while their heating wood,
coal, or gas was prepared for delivery.

Nightlife: This sleepy neighborhood is not the place for
night-owls, but there are three notable exceptions: **Café du
Marché** (above) hops with a Franco-American crowd until about
midnight. **O'Brien's Pub** is an upscale and popular Parisian ren-
dition of an Irish pub (77 St. Dominique). **Café Thoumieux** is a
new hip, happening place with big screen sports and a young
international crowd (4 rue de la Comete, Mo: Latour Maubourg).

Eating in the Marais Neighborhood

The windows of the Marais are filled with munching sophisticates.
The place du Marche Ste. Catherine, a tiny square midway
between the St. Paul Métro stop and place des Vosges is home to
several good places. **Le Marais Ste. Catherine** is a good value
(100F menu, daily from 19:00, extra seating in their candle-lit cellar, 5 rue Caron, tel. 01 42 72 39 94), though many seem willing to
pay 30F more for the menu at **Le Marche** (2 place Marche Ste.
Catherine, tel. 01 4 77 34 88). Just off the square, **l'Auberge de
Jarente** offers a well-respected and traditional cuisine (117F menu,
closed Sunday and Monday, 7 rue Jarente, tel. 01 42 77 49 35).

Dinners splurging under the candle-lit arches of the place des
Vosges are *très* romantic: **Nectarine** at #16 serves fine salads,
quiches, and *plats du jour* day and night, while **Ma Bourgogne** is

where locals go for a splurge (open daily, at northwest corner, tel. 01 42 78 44 64).

For a fast, cheap change of pace, eat at (or take-out from) the Chinese/Japanese **Delice House**. Two can split 200 grams of chicken curry (or whatever, 26F) and a heaping helping of rice (20F). There's lots of seating, with pitchers of water at the ground-floor tables and a roomier upstairs (81 rue Saint Antoine, open until 21:00).

Near Hôtel Castex, the restaurant **La Poste** and the **Crêperie** across the street (13 rue Castex) offer inexpensive, light meals (both closed on Sunday). I like **La Bastoche**'s cozy ambience and good 100F menu (7 rue Saint Antoine, tel. 01 48 04 74 34). Across the street, **Le Paradis de Fruit** serves salads and organic foods to a young local crowd (on the small square at rues Tournelle and Saint Antoine). Several cafés on the Boulevard Henri IV (such as **Brasserie Le Reveil** at #29, near rue Castex) offer reasonable and good *plats du jour* and salads.

Wine lovers shouldn't miss the excellent Burgundy wines and exquisite, though limited, menu selection at the cozy **Au Bourguignon du Marais** (52 rue Francois Miron, call by 19:00 to reserve, tel. 01 48 87 15 40).

For a worthwhile splurge, try the romantic and traditional **L'Excuse** (185F menu, closed Sunday, 14 rue Charles V, call ahead, tel. 01 42 77 98 97). Across the street, **L'Énoteca** has lively and reasonable Italian cuisine in a relaxed, open setting (across from Hôtel du 7ème Art at 20 rue St. Paul, closed Sunday, tel. 01 42 78 91 44).

Vegetarians will appreciate the fine cuisine at **Picolo Teatro** (closed Monday, 6 rue des Ecouffes, tel. 01 42 72 17 79) and **l'As du Falafel**, serving the best falafel on the rue Rosier at #34.

Picnicking: Picnic at the peaceful place des Vosges (closes at dusk). Hobos stretch their francs at the supermarket in the basement of the Monoprix department store (close to place des Vosges on rue Saint Antoine) and connoisseurs prefer the gourmet take-out places all along rue Saint Antoine, such as **Flo Prestige** (open until 23:00, on the tiny square where rue Tournelle and rue Saint Antoine meet). A few small grocery shops are open until 23:00 on the rue Saint Antoine (near intersection with rue Castex). An open-air market, held Sunday morning, is just off place de la Bastille on boulevard Richard Lenoir.

For a cheap breakfast, try the tiny *boulangerie/pâtisserie* where the hotels buy their croissants (coffee machine, 3F; 10F baby quiches, 5F *pain au chocolat*, one block off place de la Bastille, corner of rue Saint Antoine and rue de Lesdiguieres).

Cafés and Bars: This hip area is overrun with atmospheric cafés and bars (open generally till 02:00). **Hamman** is an ethnically hip cyber-café (4 rue des Rosiers, on place du Marche Ste. Catherine.) The *très* local wine bar at **Au Temps des Cerises** is amiably run and a welcoming if smoky place (rue du Petit Musc and rue de Cerisaie, around the corner from Hôtel Castex).

Nightlife: Le Vieux Comptoir is tiny, lively, and not too hip (just off place des Vosges at 8 rue Biraque). **La Perla** is trendy with Parisian yuppies in search of the perfect margarita (26 rue Francois Miron). **Auld Alliance**, Paris' only Scottish pub, feels a bit like a frat house in Paris with Scottish barmen (80 rue Francois Miron).

Eating in the Contrescarpe Neighborhood

The rue Mouffetard and rue du Pot-de-Fer are lined with inexpensive, lively, and forgettable restaurants. Study the many menus, compare crowds, then dive in. **Le Jardin d'Artemis** is one of the better inexpensive values on rue Mouffetard at #34 (85F menu). **Restaurant l'Epoque**, a fine neighborhood restaurant, has excellent value menus at 68F and 118F (one block off place Contrescarpe at 81 rue Cardinal Lemoine, tel. 01 46 34 15 84). **Restaurant Le Vigneron** is well respected and serves traditional French cuisine (20 rue du Pot-de-Fer) and **Savannah Café**'s creative Mediterranean cuisine attracts a loyal, artsy crowd (27 rue Descartes, tel. 01 43 29 45 77). **Le Jardin des Pates** is popular with vegetarians, serving pastas and salads at fair prices (4 rue Lacepede, near Jardins des Plantes, tel. 01 43 31 50 71). **Café Tournebride** serves delicious salads (104 rue Mouffetard).

Cafés: Brasserie La Chope, a classic Parisian brasserie right on the place Contrescarpe, is popular until the wee hours. Indoor and outdoor sitting is people-watching good. **Café Le Mouffetard** is in the thick of the street market hustle and bustle (at the corner of rue Mouffetard and rue de l'Arbalete). At **Café de la Mosque**, you'll feel like you've been beamed to Morocco. In this purely Arab café, order a mint tea, pour in the sugar, and enjoy the authentic interior and peaceful outdoor terrace (2 rue Daubenton, behind the mosque).

Eating in the Latin Quarter

La Petite Bouclerie is a cozy place with classy family cooking (70F menu, closed Monday, 33 rue de la Harpe, center of touristy Latin Quarter, tel. 01 43 54 18 03). The popular **Restaurant Polidor** is an old turn-of-the-century-style place, with great *cuisine bourgeois*, a vigorous local crowd, and a historic toilet. Arrive at 19:00 to get a seat in the restaurant (65F *plat du jour*, 100F menus, 41 rue Monsieur le Prince, midway between Odéon and Luxembourg Métro stops, tel. 01 43 26 95 34).

Eating on the Île St. Louis

Cruise the island's main street for a variety of good options from cozy *crêperies* to romantic restaurants. Sample Paris' best sorbet and ice cream at any place advertising *les glaces Berthillon*; the original Berthillon shop is at 31 rue St. Louis en l'Île.

All listings below are on the rue St. Louis en l'Île. **Café Med** at #53 serves inexpensive salads and crêpes in a delightful setting. My romantic splurge is **Le Tastevin** (150F and 220F menus, #46, tel. 01 43 54 17 31). **La Castafiore** at #51–53 serves fine Italian dishes in a cozy setting (160F menu). For crazy, touristy cellar atmosphere and hearty fun food, feast at **La Taverne du Sergeant Recruiter**. The "Sergeant Recruiter" used to get young Parisians drunk and stuffed here, then sign them into the army. It's all-you-can-eat, including wine and service, for 190F (daily from 19:00, #41, tel. 01 43 54 75 42). There's a near-food-fight clone next door at **Nos Ancêtres Les Gaulois** ("Our Ancestors the Gauls," 190F, daily at 19:00, tel. 01 46 33 66 07).

Eating near the Pompidou Center

The **Mélodine** self-service is right at the Rambuteau Métro stop. **Dame Tartine** overlooks the Homage to Stravinsky fountain, serves a young clientele, and offers excellent, cheap, lively meals. The popular **Café de la Cité** fills one long line of tables with locals enjoying their 44F lunches and 65F dinner specials (22 rue Rambuteau, tel. 01 48 04 30 74).

Elegant Dining on the Seine

La Plage Parisienne is a nearly dress-up riverfront place popular with locals, serving elegant, healthy meals at good prices (Port de Javel-Haut, Mo: Javel, tel. 01 40 59 41 00).

LES GRANDS CAFÉS DE PARIS

Please see Café Culture in this book's introduction for help in approaching Parisian cafés.

History of Cafés in Paris

The first café in the Western world was in Paris—established in 1686 at Le Procope (still a restaurant today). Coffee had just been discovered by the French. And at about the same time, La Comedie Française theater was inaugurated, creating the necessary artsy, coffee-sipping crowds. France's robust economy was growing a population of pleasure seekers and thinkers looking for places to be seen, to exchange ideas and plot revolutions—political and philosophical. By the year 1700, over 300 cafés had opened their doors and at the time of the Revolution there were over 1800 cafés in Paris. Revolutionaries from Marat to Napoleon to Dali enjoyed the spirit of free-thinking the cafés engendered.

Café society took off in the early 1900s. Life was changing rapidly with the Industrial Revolution and wars on a global scale. Many retreated to Parisian cafés to try to make sense out of the confusion. Vladimir Lenin, Leon Trotsky, Igor Stravinsky, Ernest Hemingway, Scott Fitzgerald, James Joyce, Albert Einstein, Jean Paul Sartre, Gene Openshaw, and Albert Camus were among the devoted café society. Some virtually lived at their favorite café, keeping their business calendars, entertaining friends, and having every meal. Parisian apartments were small and walls thin (still often the case), and heating (particularly during war times) was minimal, making the warmth of cafés all the harder to leave.

There are over 12,000 cafés in Paris today. They're still used for business meetings, encounter sessions, and political discussions. Most Parisians are loyal to their favorites and know their waiter's children's names. And with the recently approved 35-hour work week, most will have even more time to linger longer over their *café creme*.

Here's a short list of grand Parisian cafés, worth the detour only if you're not in a hurry and don't mind paying outrageous prices for a shot of espresso. Think of these cafés as museums. Try to understand why they matter today as much as yesterday.

Grand Cafés by Neighborhood

St. Germain
Where the boulevard St. Germain meets rue Bonaparte (Mo: St. Germain-des-Prés), you'll find two famous cafés. **Les Deux Magots** offers great outdoor seating and a warm, wood-paneled interior. Once a favorite of Ernest Hemingway (in the *Sun Also Rises*, Jake met Brett here) and of Jean Paul Sartre (he and Simone de Beauvoir met here), today's café is filled with tourists. **Le Café de Flore**, right next door, feels more local, hip and literary—wear your black turtleneck. Picasso was a regular here while painting Guernica. The smoky interior is European popular.

For great outdoor seating at almost half the price, skip these places and set up at **Café Bonaparte**, one block down rue Bonaparte toward the river from Les Deux Magots. You're farther from the large boulevards and exhaust fumes here, but still in the thick of this pleasant café sitting area. Skip the inside tables.

Boulevard Montparnasse
Along the boulevard Montparnasse, just a few blocks from Luxem-

bourg Gardens at the intersection with boulevard Raspail (Mo: Vavin), gather an eclectic assortment of historic cafés.

La Coupole, built in the 1920s, was decorated by aspiring artists (Leger, Brancusi, Chagall among others) in return for free meals. This cavernous place feels like a classy train station, with grand chandeliers, red velvet booths, brass decor, and waiters by the dozen. Bring your friends and make noise. The food is fine, but not the reason you came (102 boulevard Montparnasse, tel. 01 43 26 70 50).

Le Dome sits right at the intersection of Raspail and Montparnasse and forms a dramatic contrast to the party atmosphere of La Coupole. Smaller, more elegant and refined in every way, this place makes me want to dress up and look better than I do. The sumptuous decor is pure 1920s, and the best tables are just inside, facing the sidewalk. While La Coupole is not known for its cuisine, le Dome is. Come here for a splurge dinner (figure 250F per person, tel. 01 43 35 25 81).

Le Select was popular with the more rebellious types—Leon Trotsky, Jean Cocteau, and Pablo Picasso loved it. It feels more conformist today, with good salads from 50–60F, outdoor seating, and pleasant tables just inside the door (99 boulevard Montparnasse, across from La Coupole).

Champs-Élysées
Le Fouquet's, which opened in 1899, served as James Joyce's dining room. Today it's known as the film stars' place to go (99 Champs-Élysées, Mo: George V). Those golden plaques at the entry are from winners of France's version of our Oscar awards, the Cesars. Fouquet's was recently saved from foreign purchase and eventual destruction when the government declared it a historic monument. Fouquet's serves the most expensive shot of expresso I found in Paris (27F), but the outdoor setting is Champs-Élysées great.

Near the Louvre
Within a short walk of the Louvre, you'll find two "melt in your chair" cafés (Mo: Palais Royal/Musée du Louvre).

The staunchly Parisian **Café Le Nemours** is tucked into the corner of Palais Royal adjacent to Comedie Francaise (2 place Colette). Brass and art deco elegant with outdoor tables under an arcade two minutes from the pyramid, this place makes a great post-Louvre retreat.

Café de l'Epoque, inside a classy pedestrian mini-mall, is softly lit, elegantly appointed, and a tranquil escape from city street noise (2 rue du Bouloi).

On Place de la Concorde

Hotel de Crillon's four-star elegance can be yours for an afternoon. Considered the most exclusive hotel in Paris (and the last of the great hotels to be French-owned), come here to experience château life. Wear the best clothes you packed, arrive after 15:00, let the bellhop spin the door, and settle into the royal blue chairs in the *salon du thè* (45F for a pot of tea or double *café au lait*, 155F for high tea). You'll be serenaded by a harpist and surrounded by famous people you won't recognize.

PARIS WITH
CHILDREN

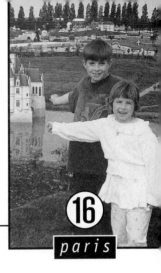

This city of 3 million is actually kid-friendly. With so much space devoted to parks, squares, and pedestrians, and such a variety of kid-friendly sights, your children can leave Paris wanting to return. While you can take your child to play at the French funplex, you can visit a funplex at home. The art to a successful family trip to Paris is making everyone happy, including the parents. Our family-tested recommendations have this objective in mind. Consider these tips:

- Hotel selection is critical. Stay in a kid-friendly area near a park. The rue Cler neighborhood is ideal. If you're staying a week or more, rent an apartment; you'll appreciate the extra space and kitchen (see Sleeping: For Longer Stays).

- Eat dinner early (19:30 at restaurants, earlier at cafés) and you'll miss the romantic crowd. Skip the famous places. Look instead for more relaxed cafés and bistros (or even fast-food restaurants) where kids can move around without bothering others. Picnic lunches and dinners work well.

- Follow this book's crowd-beating tips to a tee. With kids, standing in a long line for a museum (that they probably don't even want to see) adds insult to injury.

- Get your kids in the spirit before you go (e.g., rent or read *The Hunchback of Notre-Dame* or *The Man in the Iron Mask*).

- The best toy selection is in the large department stores, such as Galleries Lafayette, Printemps, and Le Bon Marche (see Shopping).

- French marionette shows, called *guignols*, are fun for the entire family. They take place in several locations in Paris, mostly in the big parks. See *Pariscope* or *l'Officiel des Spectacles* under "Marionettes" for times and places. The plots, while in French, are easy to follow. Arrive 20 minutes early for good seats.

TEN TOP KIDS' SPOTS IN PARIS

1. Luxembourg Gardens: This has the most extensive big-toys play area in Paris with imaginative slides, swings, and jungle gyms (kids-14F, adults-7.5F, open daily). Kids enjoy the pedal go-karts, merry-go-round, pony rides, toy sailboats in the main pond, and big open areas perfect for kicking a ball. Adults and kids enjoy the terrific puppet shows (*guignols*) held in the afternoons (tel. 01 43 26 46 47, Mo: St. Sulpice, Odéon, or Notre-Dame-des-Champs; RER: Luxembourg).

2. Jardin des Plantes: These pleasant, colorful botanical gardens are short on grass, but have a small zoo, a children's maze made of plants, and several kid-friendly natural science museums. Kids go bug-eyed at the Insect Museum (Galerie d'Entomologie, kids-10F, adults-15F, Wednesday–Monday 13:00–17:00) and love the dinosaur exhibit (Galerie d'Anatomie Comparée et de Paléontologie, kids-20F, adults-30F, Wednesday–Monday 10:00–17:00; includes Musée de Mineralogie, featuring precious stones). From the main riverside entrance on place Valhubert, the museums line the left side of the park (Mo: Gare d'Austerlitz or Jussieu).

3. Eiffel Tower, Trocadero, and Champs-de-Mars Park: All ages enjoy the view from Trocadero across the river to the Eiffel Tower, especially after dark (Mo: Trocadero). Rollerbladers and skateboarders make Trocadero a Parisian teenage scene, particularly in afternoons and evenings. A ride up the tower is a hit day or night. See the video on the tower's first floor. The vast Champs-de-Mars park at the tower offers grassy play areas (bring your own ball), childrens' big-toys, pony rides, and picnic-perfect benches (Mo: École Militaire). For more information, see Eiffel Tower under Sights.

4. Notre-Dame, Towers, and Crypt: Paris' famous Gothic cathedral doesn't have to be dry and dull. Replay Quasimodo's stunt and climb the tower. Kids love being on such a lofty perch with an up-close look at a gargoyle. The crypt on the square in front of Notre-Dame is manageable and fun. Kids can push buttons to highlight remains of Roman Paris and leave with a better understanding of how different civilizations build on top of each other. The small but beautiful park along the river and behind Notre-Dame has sandboxes, picnic benches, and space to run (Mo: Cité). ✪ See Historic Paris Walk on page 39.

5. Seine River Boat Rides: The Bateaux-Mouches offer one-hour cruises on huge glass boats with departures (every 30 minutes from 10:00–23:00) from the pont de l'Alma, the centrally-located pont Neuf, and from right in front of the Eiffel Tower (20F–under age 14, 40F–adult, tel. 01 42 25 96 10). The Bateau-Bus is a river bus that runs June through September connecting five stops along the river: Eiffel Tower, Orsay, Louvre, Notre-Dame, and place de la Concorde (30F–youth, 60F–adult, departures every 45 minutes from about 10:00–19:00; pick up a brochure at any TI). Use the Bateau-Bus by day and take a twilight cruise on a Bateau-Mouche.

6. Arc de Triomphe, Champs-Élysées, and Palais de la Découverte: Watching the crazy traffic rush around the Arc de Triomphe provides endless entertainment. Then stroll the Champs-Élysées with its car dealerships (particularly Renault's with its antique car museum), Virgin Megastore, Disney Store, and the river of humanity that flows along its broad sidewalks. You can end this walk at the Grand Palais' Palais de la Découverte, a hands-on science musuem for kids (15F–under age 18, 25F–adult, Tuesday–Saturday 9:30–19:00, Sunday 10:00–19:00). ✪ See Champs-Élysées Walk on page 57.

7. Versailles: This huge complex of palaces, gardens, fountains, and forest is a great Parisian family getaway. Kids even enjoy the 30-minute train ride to Versailles. Rent a bike for the gardens or a rowboat for the canal. Come on Sunday when the fountains are flowing. The Hameau has barnyard animals nearby. Visit the palace at the end of the day and you can do cartwheels in an empty Hall of Mirrors. ✪ See Versailles Tour on page 137.

8. The Pompidou Center: The Pompidou Center is closed until 2000, but kids love the wild fountains (*Homage to Stravinsky*) next door. The big square in front is filled with crazy entertainers (Mo: Rambuteau).

9. The Cité des Sciences in the Parc de la Vilette: Paris' sprawling hands-on Explora science museum has an aquarium, sound and light shows, a flight simulator, and a childrens's playground (25F, Tuesday–Sunday 12:00–20:00, closed Monday). La Geode is a giant spherical movie screen with films (Mo: Port de la Vilette).

10. La Butte Chaumont Park: Rather than manicured gardens, this is a big park where your kids can explore the hills, lakes, trails, and waterfall. Baron Haussmann designed this converted city dump into a remarkable mix of cafés and outdoor fun (Mo: Buttes-Chaumont).

MORE SUGGESTIONS FOR CHILDREN

• Place des Vosges, with sandboxes and some playground toys, is good for younger children (Mo: Bastille or St. Paul, in Marais neighborhood).

• Palais Royal, with sandboxes, provides an ideal break from the Louvre, across rue du Rivoli. Picnic here in the peaceful gardens (Mo: Palais Royal/Musée du Louvre).

• Take a Sewer Tour (Les Egouts de Paris; see page 32).

• Go to a movie on the Champs-Élysées.

• Bois de Boulogne, Paris' largest park, has lakes, boat rental, and paths ideal for bike riding. Inside this huge park you'll find a variety of activities for kids, including the Jardins d'Acclimatation with a mini-zoo, mini-golf, pony rides, and bumper cars (12F, Mo: Sablons).

LE SHOPPING
IN PARIS

paris

Consider three ways to shop in Paris:

1) If all you need are souvenirs, a surgical strike at a souvenir shop will do.

2) For more elaborate purchasing plans, the city's large department stores offer relatively painless one-stop shopping in elegant surroundings.

3) Neighborhood boutiques offer the greatest reward at the highest risk. While clerks and prices can be intimidating, the selection is generally more original and the experience totally Parisian.

Tips

Before you enter a Parisian store, remember:

• The customer is not always right. In fact, figure the clerk is doing you a favor by waiting on you.

• Except for department stores, it's not normal for the customer to handle clothing. Ask first if you can look at an item.

• Forget returns (and don't count on exchanges).

• Saturdays are busiest.

• Observe French shoppers. Then imitate.

Souvenir Shops

Avoid souvenir carts in front of famous monuments. Prices and selection are better in shops. Look under the arcades of the rue de Rivoli (across from Tuileries Gardens), around the Pompidou Center, on the streets of Montmartre, and in department stores (see below). The riverfront stalls near Notre-Dame sell a variety of used books, magazines, and tourist paraphernalia in the most romantic setting.

Key Phrases

Just looking. - *Je regards.* (zhuh ruh-gar)
How much is it? - *Combien?* (kohm-bee-en)
Too big/small/expensive. - *Trop grand/petit/cher.* (troh
  grahn/puh-tee/sher)
May I try it on? - *Je peut l'essayer?* (zhuh puh luh-say-yay)
Can I see more? - *Puis-je en voir d'autres?* (pweezh en vwahr
  doh-truh)
I'll think about it. - *Je vais y penser.* (zhuh vay ee pahn-say)
I'd like this. - *Je voudrais ça.* (zhuh voo-dray sah)

Department Stores (*Les Grandes Surfaces*)

Like cafés, department stores were invented here (surprisingly, not
in America). While the stores seem overwhelming at first, they
generally work like ours, and those listed here are accustomed to
foreign shoppers. These stores are not only beautiful monuments
to more elegant times, but a great lesson on how others live. Most
have spectacular perfume sections, a good selection of souvenirs at
fair prices, great view terraces, reasonably-priced restaurants, and
helpful information desks (near the front door). Choose from
these four great Parisian department stores:

Galleries Lafayette and Printemps

You'll find both Galleries Lafayette and Printemps *(pran-tom)*
department stores in many Parisian neighborhoods. The most
convenient and busiest are side by side behind the old Opéra (Mo:
Opéra). Both Galleries Lafayette and Printemps sprawl over three
buildings and consume entire city blocks. Selection is huge. Continue your shopping by walking from this area to the place
Vendôme (see Boutiques, below).

Samaritaine

Samaritaine (sah-mah-ree-ten) is Paris' most central department
store (on the Seine at Pont Neuf, Mo: Pont Neuf, see Historic
Paris Walk). Polished, yet not high priced, this is a handy place
to take care of business and enjoy one of the best views over
Paris. Review the history of the store in dioramas at the top of
the elevator. Then climb to the panorama terrace on the ninth
floor.

Le Bon Marche

Combine this classy department store with a great neighborhood
shopping experience. The Bon Marche, quieter and more upscale

than the others, is surrounded by pleasant shopping streets (see Boutiques, below). Graze through the gourmet grocery store in the basement. (Mo: Sevres-Babylone.)

Boutiques

I enjoy window shopping on city streets, pausing at cafés, and observing the rhythm of neighborhood life. While the shops are more intimate, sales clerks can be in-your-face intimidating. Here are three very different areas to try:

Sevres-Babylone to St. Sulpice

Start at the elegant Bon Marche department store, described above (Mo: Sevres-Babylone), then shop the smart boutiques that line the streets between the Bon Marche and St. Sulpice church. The rue de Sevres (turns into rue du Four) is the spine of this upscale area. Explore the rues du Dragon, Cherche Midi, Bonaparte, and Vieux Colombier. End your shopping stroll in the Luxembourg Gardens or at a grand café on the boulevard St. Germain (see Les Grands Cafés de Paris on page 181).

Le Marais

For more eclectic, avant-garde stores, peruse the shops between the Pompidou Center and place des Vosges. Stick to the east-west axis formed by rue des Francs Bourgeois, rue des Rosiers, and rue Ste. Croix de la Bretonniere. (These streets are part of the Marais Walk, on page 64.) On Sunday afternoons this trendy area thrives with shoppers and café crowds.

Place Vendôme

The ritzy streets connecting the Galleries Lafayette with place de la Concorde are a miracle mile of jewelry stores, four-star hotels, perfumeries, and exclusive clothing boutiques.

From place de l'Opéra (Mo: Opéra), walk down rue de la Paix to place Vendôme. The *très* elegant place Vendôme is home to the Ritz hotel (Hemingway liberated the bar in WWII) and equally exclusive boutiques. The square was created by Louis XIV in the 17th century as a setting for a statue of himself. One hundred and fifty years later, Louis was replaced by a statue of Napoleon.

Continue on rue Castiglione, window-shopping the arcades, to rue de Rivoli. Turn right on Rivoli, passing Paris' largest English bookstore, W.H. Smith, at #248, to reach place de la Concorde.

PARIS AT
NIGHT

Paris is most beautiful after dark. Save energy from your day's sightseeing and get out at night. Whether it's a concert at Sainte Chapelle, a boat ride on the Seine, an elevator up the Arc de Triomphe, or a late-night café, experience the city of light lit. The *Pariscope* magazine (3F at any newsstand) offers a complete weekly listing of music, cinema, theater, opera, and other special events—we decipher this useful periodical for you below. The *Free Voice* newspaper, in English, has a monthly review of Paris entertainment (available at any English-language bookstore, French-American establishments, or the American Church).

A TOUR OF PARISCOPE

The weekly *Pariscope* (3F) or *L'Officiel des Spectacles* (2F) are both cheap and essential if you want to know what's happening. Pick one up and page through it. For a headstart, *Pariscope* has a Web site: www.pariscope.fr.

Each begins with culture news. Skip the bulky *Theatres* and *Diners/Spectacles* sections and anything listed as *des environs* (outside of Paris). *Musique* or *Concerts Classiques* follow, listing each day's events (program, location, time, and price). Venues with phone numbers and addresses are listed in an *Adresses des Salles de Concerts* sidebar. Touristic venues (such as Sainte-Chapelle and Église de la Madeleine) are often featured in display ads. *Opéras*, *Musique Tra-ditionelle*, *Ballet/Danse*, and *Jazz/Rock* listings follow.

Half of these magazines are devoted to Cinema—a Paris forte. After the *Films Nouveaux* section trumpets new releases, the *Films en Exclusivite* pages list all the films playing in town. While a code marks films as *Historique*, *Karate*, *Erotisme*, and so on, the key mark for tourists is "v.o." which means *version original* (American films have their English soundtracks and French subtitles). Films are listed alphabetically, with theaters and their *arrondissements* at the end of each entry. Later films are listed by neighborhood (*Salles Paris*) and by genre. To find a showing near your hotel, simply match the *arrondissement*. (But don't hesitate to hop on the Métro for the film you want.) *Salles Périphérie* is out in the suburbs. Film festivals are also listed.

Pariscope has a small English "Time Out" section listing the week's events. The *Musées* sections (*Monuments, Jardins, Autres Curiosites, Promenades, Activites Sportives, Piscines*) give the latest hours of the sights, gardens, curiosities, boat tours, sports, swimming pools, and so on. *Clubs de Loisirs* are various athletic and social clubs. *Pour les Jeunes* is for young people (kids' films, animations/cartoons, marionettes, circuses, and amusement parks such as Asterix and Disney). *Conferences* are mostly lectures. For cancan mischief, look under *Paris la nuit*, cabarets, or the busty *spectacles erotiques*.

Finally, you'll find a TV listing. Paris has four country-wide stations: TF1, France 2, France 3, and the new Arte station (a German/French cultural channel). M6 is filled with American series. Canal Plus (channel 4) is a cable channel that airs an American news show at 7:00 in the morning and an American sports event on Sunday evening.

MUSIC

Jazz Clubs

With a lively mix of American, French, and international musicians, Paris has been an internationally acclaimed jazz capital since World War II. You'll pay from 30–130F to enter a jazz club (one drink may be included; if not, expect to pay 30–60F per drink; beer is cheapest). See *Pariscope* magazine under *Musique* for listings, and the American Church's *Free Voice* paper for a good monthly review (in English). Music starts after 22:00 in most clubs. Here are good bets:

Caveau de la Huchette, the handiest characteristic old jazz club for visitors, fills an ancient Latin Quarter cellar with live jazz and frenzied dancing every night (60F weekday, 70F weekend admission, 30F drinks, open 21:30–2:30 or later, closed Monday, 5 rue de la Huchette, tel. 01 43 26 65 05).

Au Duc des Lombards is one of the most popular and respected jazz clubs in Paris (42 rue des Lombards, Mo: Chatelet, 20-minute walk from place des Vosges).

At **Le Cave du Franc Pinot**, enjoy a glass of chardonnay at the main floor wine bar, then drop downstairs for a cool jazz scene. (1 quai de Bourbon, centrally located on Île St. Louis, Mo: Pont Marie, tel. 01 46 33 60 64).

The **American Church** regularly plays host to fine jazz musicians for the best price in Paris (65 quai d'Orsay, Mo: Invalides, RER-C: Pont de l'Alma, tel. 01 47 05 07 99).

Come to **Le Sunset** for more traditional jazz—Dixieland, Big Band—and fewer crowds (near Au Duc des Lombards, 60 rue des Lombards, Mo: Chatelet, tel. 01 40 26 46 60).

All Jazz Club, more expensive than the rest, is a hot club in the heart of the St. Germain area, attracting a more mature crowd in search of recognizable names (7 rue St. Benoit, Mo: St. Germain-des-Près, tel. 01 42 61 53 53).

Classical Concerts

For classical music on any night, consult *Pariscope* magazine; the *Musique* section under *Concerts Classique* lists concerts (free and fee). Look for posters at the churches. Churches that regularly host concerts include St. Sulpice, St. Germain-des-Près, Basilique de Madeleine, St. Eustache, and Sainte Chapelle. It's worth the 90–130F entry for the pleasure of hearing Mozart surrounded by the stained glass of the tiny Sainte Chapelle. Even the Galleries Lafayette department store offer concerts. Many are free (*entrée libre*), such as the Sunday *Atelier* concert sponsored by the American Church (18:00, 65 quai d'Orsay, Mo: Invalides, RER: Pont de l'Alma, tel. 01 47 05 07 99).

Opera

Paris is home to two fine operas. The **Opéra Garnier**, Paris' first opera house, hosts opera and ballet performances. Come here for less expensive tickets and grand belle epoque decor (Mo: Opéra, tel. 01 44 73 13 99). The **Opéra de la Bastille** is the massive modern opera house that dominates place de la Bastille. Come here for state-of-the-art special effects and modern interpretations of classic ballets and operas (Mo: Bastille, tel. 01 43 43 96 96). For tickets, either write ahead, call 01 44 73 13 00, or go to the opera ticket offices, open 11:00–18:00.

BUS TOURS

Paris Illumination Tours, run by Paris Vision, connect all the great illuminated sights of Paris with a 100-minute bus tour in 12 languages. Double-decker buses have huge windows, but Moulin Rouge customers get the most desirable front seats. You'll stampede on with a United Nations of tourists, get a hand-held audio stick, and listen to a tape-recorded spiel (interesting but occasionally hard to hear). Uninspired as it is, this provides a fine first-night overview of the city at its floodlit scenic best. Left seats are marginally better. Visibility is fine in the rain. You're entirely on

the bus except for one five-minute cigarette break at the Eiffel
Tower viewpoint (150F-adult, 75F-ages 4 to 11, free-under 3, second adult pays only 100f on 20:30 tours, departures at 20:30
nightly all year, and 22:00 April–October only, departs from Paris
Vision office at 214 rue de Rivoli, across the street from Mo: Tuileries). These trips are sold through your hotel (brochures in
lobby) or direct at the address listed above (tel. 01 42 60 30 01, fax
01 42 86 95 36, Web site: www.parisvision.com).

SEINE RIVER CRUISES
The **Bateaux-Mouches** offer one-hour cruises on huge glass boats
with departures (every 30 minutes from 10:00–23:00) from the pont
de l'Alma, the centrally-located pont Neuf, and from right in front
of the Eiffel Tower (40F, 20F-under age 14, tel. 01 42 25 96 10).

WALKS
Go for a walk to best appreciate the city of light. Break for ice
cream, pause at a café, and enjoy the sidewalk entertainers as you
join the post-dinner Parisian parade.

Champs-Élysées and the Arc de Triomphe
● See Champs-Élysées Walk, on page 57.
    The Champs-Élysées and the Arc de Triomphe are brilliant
after dark. Start at the Arc de Triomphe, taking the elevator to the
top (35F, covered by museum pass, open until 22:00 weekdays,
23:00 weekends). Then stroll down the lively Champs-Élysées. A
right turn on avenue George V leads to the Bateaux-Mouches river
cruises. A movie on the Champs-Élysées is a fun experience
(weekly listings in Pariscope under Cinema).

Trocadero and Eiffel Tower
These monuments glimmer at night. Take the Métro to the Trocadero stop, follow *Sortie Tour Eiffel* signs, and join the party on
place de la Trocadero for a magnificent view of the glowing Eiffel
Tower. It's a festival of gawkers, drummers, street acrobats, and
entertainers. Pass the fountains and cross the river to the base of
the tower, worth the effort even if you don't go up. If you spring
for the elevator, go to the first floor (20F) where the view is best
at night and pause for a break at the Altitude 95 restaurant/bar.
For more info, see Eiffel Tower, page 31.

Notre-Dame, Île St. Louis, and the Latin Quarter
From the elegant Île St. Louis to the fire-breathing Latin Quarter,
this evening stroll covers 1.5 miles. Start by strolling the main
street of the tiny island, Île St. Louis. Have dinner at a classy café

(see Eating in Paris) or at least an ice-cream cone at Berthillon. Cross the footbridge to the neighboring island (Île de la Cite) and take an immediate left across the bridge (pont de l'Archeveque) to the left bank. Turn right (for great views of Notre-Dame) and drop down to the riverbank. After walking the length of the Notre-Dame along the riverbank, climb back up to street level and venture into Left Bank. Here (opposite the cathedral), the tangle of small people-filled lanes lead eventually to the big busy boulevard St. Germain (if lost, ask for that street). At boulevard St. Germain, turn right and head toward St. Germain-des-Près church. You'll pass mimes, fire-breathers, musicians, and expensive cafés (see Les Grands Cafés de Paris on page 181). From St. Germain-des-Près, the Métro or city bus (bus 86 to Marais, 63 to rue Cler) takes you home.

TRANSPORTATION
CONNECTIONS ⑲

This chapter covers Paris' two airports, six train stations, and main bus station.

CHARLES DE GAULLE AIRPORT

Charles de Gaulle Airport is Paris' primary airport. It has three main terminals (T-1, T-2, and T-9). Those flying to or from the U.S.A. will probably use T-1. (Air France uses T-2; charters dominate T-9.) Terminals are connected every few minutes by a free *navette* (bus).

At T-1 you'll find an American Express cash machine, an automatic bill changer (at baggage claim 30), and an exchange window (at baggage claim 18). A bank (with barely acceptable rates) and an ATM machine are near gate 16. At the Meeting Point, you'll find the TI, which has free Paris maps and information (open until 23:00), and Relais H, where you can buy a *télécarte* (phone card). Car rental offices are on the arrival level from gates 10–22; the SNCF (train) office is at gate 22. For flight information, call 01 48 62 22 80.

Transportation between Charles De Gaulle Airport and Paris: There are plenty of choices. Three efficient public-transportation routes, taxis, and a couple of airport shuttle services link the airport's T-1 terminal and central Paris. The free *navette* (bus) runs between gate 28 and the **RER Roissy Rail** station, where a train zips you into Paris' subway system in 30 minutes (48F, stops at Gare du Nord, Chatelet, St. Michel, and Luxembourg Gardens). The **Roissy Bus** runs every 15 minutes between gate 30 and the old Paris Opéra (stop is on rue Scribe, in front of American Express), costs 45F (use the automatic ticket machine), and takes 40 minutes, but can be jammed. The **Air France Bus** leaves every 15 minutes from gate 34 and serves the Arc de Triomphe and the Porte Maillot in about 40 minutes for 60F, and the Montparnasse Tower in 60 minutes for 75F (from any of these stops you can reach your hotel by taxi). For most people the RER Roissy Rail works best. A **taxi** ride with luggage costs about 230F; there is a taxi stand, often with long waits, at gate 16. (The RER Roissy Rail, Roissy Bus, and Air France bus described above serve the T-2 terminal as efficiently and economically as T-1.) The Disneyland Express bus departs from gate 32.

For a stress-free trip between either of Paris' airports and downtown, consider an **airport shuttle minivan**, ideal for single travelers or families of four or more. Reserve from home and they'll meet you at the airport. Consider Airport Shuttle (120F for one person, 90F per person for two, cheaper for larger groups and kids, tel. 01 45 38 55 72, fax 01 43 21 35 67, Web site: www.paris-anglo .com/clients/ashuttle.html, e-mail: ashuttle@club-internet.fr) or the generally more expensive Paris Shuttle Services (tel. 01 49 62 78 78, fax 01 49 62 78 79, Web site: www.magic.fr/pas, émail: pas @magic.fr).

Sleeping at or near Charles de Gaulle Airport: Those with early flights can sleep in T-1 at Cocoon (60 "cabins," Sb-250F, Db-300F, CC:VM, tel. 01 48 62 06 16, fax 01 48 62 56 97). Take the elevator down to "boutique level" or walk down from the departure level; it's near the Burger King. You get 16 hours of silence buried under the check-in level with TV and toilet. Hôtel IBIS, at the Roissy Rail station, offers more normal accommodations (Db-420F, CC:VMA, free shuttle bus to either terminal takes two minutes, tel. 01 49 19 19 19, fax 01 49 19 19 21).

ORLY AIRPORT

This airport feels small. Orly has two terminals: Sud and Ouest. International flights arrive at Sud. After exiting baggage claim (near gate H) you'll be greeted by signs directing you to city transportation, car rental, and so on. Turn left to enter the main terminal area and you'll find exchange offices with barely acceptable rates, an ATM machine, the ADP (a quasi–tourist office that offers free city maps and basic sightseeing information), and an SNCF French rail desk (sells train tickets and even Eurailpasses). Downstairs is a sandwich bar, bank (lousy rates), newsstand (buy *télécarte* phone card), and post office (great rates for cash or American Express traveler's checks). For flight info on any airline serving Orly, call 01 49 75 15 15.

Transportation Between Paris and Orly Airport: There are three efficient public-transportation routes, taxis, and a couple of airport shuttle services linking Orly and central Paris. The **Air France bus** (outside gate F) runs to Paris' Invalides Métro stop (40F, 4/hrly,

30 min), and is best for those staying in or near the rue Cler neighborhood (from the Invalides terminal, take the Métro two stops to École Militaire to reach recommended hotels). The **Jetbus #285** (outside gate F, 24F, 4/hrly) is the quickest way to the Paris subway, and the best way to the recommended hotels in the Marais and Contrescarpe neighborhoods (take Jetbus to Villejuif Métro stop, buy a carnet of 10 Métro tickets, then take the Métro to the Sully Morland stop for the Marais area or the Cardinal Lemoine stop for the Contrescarpe area). The **Orlybus** (outside gate H, 30F, 4/hrly) takes you to the Denfert-Rochereau RER-B line and the Métro, offering subway access to central Paris. The Orlyval trains are overpriced (57F). Allow 150F for a **taxi** into central Paris.

An **airport shuttle minivan** is ideal for single travelers or families of four or more. Reserve from home and they'll meet you at the airport. Consider Airport Shuttle (120F for one person, 90F per person for two, cheaper for larger groups and kids, tel. 01 45 38 55 72, fax 01 43 21 35 67, Web site: www.paris-anglo.com/clients/ashuttle.html, e-mail: ashuttle@club-internet.fr) or the generally more expensive Paris Shuttle Services (tel. 01 49 62 78 78, fax 01 49 62 78 79, Web site: www.magic.fr/pas, e-mail: pas@magic.fr).

Sleeping near Orly Airport: The only reasonable airport hotel is the IBIS (Db-400F, CC:VMA, tel. 01 46 87 33 50, fax 01 46 87 29 92). The Hilton offers more comfort for a price (Db-660F, tel. 01 45 12 45 12, fax 01 45 12 45 00). Both offer free shuttle service to the terminal.

PARIS' TRAIN STATIONS

Paris is Europe's rail hub with six major train stations, each serving different regions: Gare de l'Est (east-bound trains), Gare du Nord (northern Europe), and Gare St. Lazare (northwestern France), Gare d'Austerlitz (southwest Europe), and Gare du Lyon (northern Europe), and Gare Montparnasse (western France and TGV service to France's southwest). Any train station can give you schedule information, make reservations, and sell tickets for any destination. Buying tickets is handier from an SNCF neighborhood office (e.g., Louvre, Orsay, Versailles, airports) or at your neighborhood travel agency—worth their small fee (SNCF signs in their window indicate they sell train tickets). For schedule information, call 08 36 35 35 35 (3F/minute).

All six train stations are connected by Métro, bus, and taxi. All have banks or change offices, train information desks, telephones, cafés, luggage lockers (*consigne automatique*), newsstands, and pickpockets. Each station offers two types of rail service: long distance to other cities, called *Grandes Lignes* (major lines); and suburban service to outlying areas, either called *Banlieue* or RER.

Both *Banlieue* and RER serve outlying areas like Versailles and the airports; the only difference is that Banlieue lines are operated by SNCF (France's train system), and RER is operated by RATP (Paris' Métro and bus system). Paris train stations can be intimidating—but if you slow down, take a deep breath, and ask for help, you'll find them helpful and efficient. Bring a pad of paper for clear communication at ticket/info windows.

Key Train Phrases

acceuil = information assistance
billets = tickets
aller simple = one way
aller-retour = round-trip
voyageurs munis de billets = travelers with tickets
Grandes Lignes = major domestic and international lines
RER = suburban lines
Banlieue = suburban lines
quai = platform
voie = track
retard = delay
salle d'attente = waiting room
consigne automatique = storage lockers

Station Overview

Here's an overview of each major train station in Paris.

Gare du Nord: Serves cities in northern France and international destinations to the north of Paris. This is one of Paris' largest stations, offering the most services and confusion. You'll find a handy train information booth and Paris tourist information office near track 18. There are also information booths for Eurostar and Thalys trains in the center of the arrival area. Passengers departing on the Eurostar (London via the Chunnel) must check in on the second level, opposite track 4. (Note: Britain's time zone is one hour earlier than the Continent's; times listed on ticket are local times). You'll find Métro, RER, local buses (BUS), and taxis well signed. A peaceful waiting area is provided on the second level overlooking the tracks.

Key destinations served by the Gare du Nord Grandes Lignes: To **Brussels** (10/day, 3.5 hrs), **Amsterdam** (10/day, 5.5 hrs), **Copenhagen** (3/day, 16 hrs), **Koblenz** (3/day, 7 hrs), **London** via Eurostar Chunnel (12/day, 3 hrs); by Banlieue/RER lines to: **Chantilly**-Gouvieux (1/hrly, less frequently on weekends, 35 min), **Charles de Gaulle airport** (2/hrly, 30 min, from 5:30-23:00).

Gare de l'Est: Serves eastern France and European points to the east of Paris. Much smaller than the Gare du Nord, this single-floor station (with underground Métro) is a snap. A train information booth is at track 1; the main exit to buses and Paris is opposite track 8; luggage lockers are opposite track 12; and the Métro (well indicated as always) down the stairs.

Key destinations served by Gare de l'Est: To **Colmar** (6/day, 5.5 hrs, transfer in Strasbourg or Mulhouse), **Strasbourg** (10/day, 4.5 hrs), **Reims** (8/day, 2 hrs), **Verdun** (5/day, 3 hrs), **Munich** (4/day, 8.5 hrs), **Vienna** (3/day, 13 hrs), **Zurich** (4/day, 6 hrs).

Gare Montparnasse: This big modern station, which covers three floors, serves Lower Normandy and Brittany and offers TGV service to the Loire Valley and southwestern France. At street level you'll find a bank and *Banlieue* trains (serving Chartres); ticket windows are just to the right of the turnstiles in the center on this floor. (You can also reach the *Banlieue* trains from the second level). Lockers (*consigne automatique*) are on the mezzanine level. Most services are provided on the second level, where the *Grandes Lignes* arrive and depart. The ticket windows are to your left as you exit the escalators. The information office for the suburban trains (*Banlieue acceuil*) is near track 10; *banlieue* trains depart from tracks 10-17. The main rail information office is opposite track 15. The Métro and BUS are well-signed (RER does not serve this station).

Key destinations served by Gare Montparnasse: To **Chartres** (10/day, 1 hr), **Mont St. Michel** (2/day, 4.5 hrs, via Rennes), **Dinan** (7/day, 3 hrs, via Rennes and Dol), **Bordeaux** (14/day, 3.5 hrs), **Toulouse** (7/day, 5 hrs, possible transfer in Bordeaux), **Albi** (6.5 hrs, via Toulouse), **Carcassonne** (6.5 hrs, via Toulouse), **Tours** (14/day, 1 hr).

Gare du Lyon: This huge and confusing station offers TGV and regular service to southeastern France, Italy, and other international destinations. *Banlieue* trains serve Melun (near Vaux-le-Vicomte) and Fontainebleau. All trains arrive and depart from one level, but are divided into two areas (tracks A-N and 5-23); they are connected by the platform along track A and track 5 and by the hallway adjacent to track A and opposite track 9. This hallway has all the services, ticket windows, banks and shops. *Banlieue* ticket windows are adjacent to track A. Grandes Lignes (main lines) and *banlieue* (suburban) lines share the same tracks. A Paris tourist information office and the main train information office are at track L. From the RER or Métro, follow signs for *Grandes Lignes Arivées* to reach the platforms. Train information offices (*accueil*) are opposite track 13. Métro, RER, BUS, and taxis are all well signed.

Key destinations served by the Gare de Lyon: To **Melun** (hourly/30 min), **Fontainebleau** (nearly hourly, 45 min), **Beaune** (8/day, 2–3 hrs), **Dijon** (13/day, 1.5 hrs), **Chamonix** (3/day, 9 hrs, transfer in Lyon and St. Gervais, one direct night train), **Annecy** (8/day, 4–7 hrs), **Lyon** (12/day, 2.5 hrs), **Avignon** (10/day, 4 hrs), **Arles** (10/day, 5 hrs), **Nice** (8/day, 7 hrs), **Venice** (5/day, 11 hrs), **Rome** (3/day, 15 hrs), **Bern** (5/day, 5 hrs).

Gare St. Lazare: This relatively small station serves Upper Normandy, including Rouen and Giverny. All trains arrive and depart one floor above street level. Follow signs to *Grandes Lignes* from the Métro to reach the tracks. You'll pass a mini-mall of shops. Ticket windows and a Thomas Cook exchange are in the first hall you encounter on the second floor. The tracks are through the small hallways (lined with storage lockers that may be closed). *Grandes Lignes* (main lines) depart from tracks 17-27; *banlieue* suburban trains depart from 1-16. The train information office (*acceuil*) is opposite track 15; the reservation office is opposite track 16. Baggage consignment and the post office are along track 27, and WCs are opposite track 19. The Métro, buses, and taxis are well signed and downstairs (no RER available).

Key destinations served by Gare St. Lazare: To **Giverny** (train to Vernon, 5/day, 45 min; then bus or taxi 10 minutes to Giverny), **Rouen** (15/day, 75 min), **Honfleur** (6/day, 3 hrs, via Lisieux, then bus), **Bayeux** (9/day, 2.5 hrs), **Caen** (12/day, 2 hrs).

Gare d'Austerlitz: Provides non-TGV service to the Loire Valley, southwestern France, and Spain. This small station's tracks are at street level; follow signs to *Grandes Lignes* from the Métro or RER. Train information (*acceuil*) and Thomas Cook exchange are through the hall opposite track 10; baggage consignment is at Porte 27 (along the side of the station, opposite track 21).

Key destinations served by the Gare d'Austerlitz: To **Amboise** (8/day, 2.5 hrs), **Sarlat** (5/day, 5.5 hrs), **Cahors** (5/day, 7 hrs), **Barcelona** (3/day, 13 hrs), **Madrid** (5/day, 16 hrs), **Lisbon** (1/day, 24 hrs).

BUSES

Buses provide cheaper, if less comfortable and less flexible, transportation to major European cities. The main bus station is Gare Routière du Paris-Gallieni (avenue du General de Gaulle, in suburb of Bagnolet, Mo: Gallieni, tel. 01 49 72 51 51). Eurolines buses depart from here.

APPENDIX
PARIS

French (and Parisian) History

Celts and Romans (52 B.C.–A.D. 500)
Julius Caesar conquered the Parisii, turning Paris from a tribal fishing village into a European city. The mix of Latin (southern) and Celtic (northern) cultures—with Paris right in the middle—defined the French character.

Paris Sites: Cluny Museum (Roman baths), Louvre (Roman antiquities), and Archeological Crypt near Notre-Dame.

Dark Ages (500–1000)
Roman Paris fell to German pirates (the "Franks" = France), and later to the Vikings ("Norsemen" = Normans). During this turbulent time, Paris was just another island state ("Île de France") in the midst of many warring kingdoms. The lone bright spot was the reign of Charlemagne (800 A.D.) who briefly united the Franks, giving a glimpse of the modern nation-state of France.

Paris Sites: Cluny Museum artifacts and statue of Charlemagne near Notre-Dame.

Border Wars with England (1066–1500)
In 1066, the Norman king William (the Conqueror) invaded and conquered England. This united England, Normandy, and much of what is today western France, sparking centuries of border wars and French-speaking kings of England. In 1328, a Norman-English king declared war on the king of France, leading to more than 100 years of Franco-Anglo wars (called the Hundred Years' War). Rallied by the teenage visionary Joan of Arc, the French finally united north and south, driving the English across the Channel in 1453. Modern France was born, with Paris as its capital.

Paris Sites: Notre-Dame, Sainte-Chapelle, Cluny Museum tapestries, Carnavalet Museum, Sorbonne and the Latin Quarter.

Renaissance and Religious Wars (1500s)

A strong centralized France emerged, with French kings setting Europe's standard. Francois I made Paris a cultural capital, inviting Leonardo and Mona Lisa to visit. Catholics and Protestants fought openly, with 2000 Parisians slaughtered in the St. Bartholomew's Day Massacre.

Paris Sites: Louvre (palace and Renaissance art), Pont Neuf, place des Vosges, and Fontainebleau.

Louis XIV, the Absolute Monarch (1600s)

Louis XIV centralized power in himself, neutered the nobility and moved the capital to Versailles, which also became the center of European culture. France's wealth sparked new Enlightened ideas. With these came the seeds of democracy.

Paris Sites: Versailles, Vaux-le-Vicomte, Les Invalides, paintings by Poussin and Lorraine.

Decadence and Revolution (1700s)

A financial crunch from wars and royal excess drove the French people to revolt. On July 14, 1789 they stormed the Bastille. Later, they kidnapped and beheaded the king and queen. Thousands lost their heads—guillotined if suspected of hindering progress. A charismatic commoner rose amid the chaos, promising stability— Napoleon Bonaparte. Along with Napoleon, this was the age of Louis XV, Louis XVI, Marie Antoinette, Voltaire, Rousseau, and Robespierre.

Paris Sites: Versailles, place de la Concorde, place de la Bastille, Conciergerie, and paintings by Watteau, Boucher, Fragonard, and David.

Elected Emperors and Constitutional Kings (1800s)

Napoleon conquered Europe, crowned himself emperor, invaded Russia, and ended up defeated on the battlefields of Waterloo. The monarchy was restored, but a series of popular uprisings (1830, 1848, 1870) forced rulers to toe the democratic line. Napoleon's nephew, "Napoleon III," presided over a wealthy, middle-class nation with a colonial empire in slow decline. France's political clout was fading even as Paris remained the world's cultural center during the "belle epoque," or beautiful age.

Paris Sites: Arc de Triomphe, Haussman's wide boulevards, Eiffel Tower, Les Invalides, Pont Alexandre, Grand and Petit Palais, Montmartre, Opéra Garnier, paintings of Ingres and

Delacroix at the Louvre, and Impressionist and Post-Impressionist paintings (Manet, Monet, Renoir, Degas, Toulouse-Lautrec, Cézanne, and so on) at the Orsay, L'Orangerie, and Marmottan.

War and Depression (1900–1950)

France began the turn of the century as top dog, but two World Wars with Germany (and the earlier Franco-Prussian War of 1870) wasted the country. France lost millions of men in WWI, sank into a Depression, and was easily overrun by Hitler in WWII. Paris, now dirt cheap, attracted foreign writers and artists.

This was the age of Picasso, Ravel, Debussy, Satie, Stravinsky, Nijinsky, Hemingway, Fitzgerald, Stein, Pound, Sartre, Edith Piaf, and Maurice Chevalier.

Paris Sites: Picasso Museum, Deportation Memorial, Pompidou Center (closed until 2000).

Post-War France (1950–Present)

Wartime hero Charles de Gaulle reestablished a democratic Republic. France's colonial empire dissolved after bitter wars in Algeria and Vietnam. Immigrants from former colonies flooded Paris. The turbulent 60s, progressive 70s, socialist-turned-conservative 80s bring us to another *fin de siécle* (end of century) culture.

Paris Sites: Montparnasse Tower, La Defense, Louvre's Pyramid, and Pompidou Center (closed until 2000).

Contemporary Politics in France

The key political issues in France today are the high level of unemployment (about 12 percent), a steadily increasing percentage of ethnic minorities, and a recognized need to compete in a global marketplace. The challenge is to address these issues while maintaining the comfortable social benefits French people expect their government to provide. As an interesting result, national policies seem to conflict with each other (e.g., France supports the lean and mean economic policies of the European Union while recently reducing the French work week to 35 hours).

The unification of Europe has been powered by France and Germany. The 15-member European Union—which is well on its way to becoming a "United States of Europe"—is dissolving borders, freeing up trade, and establishing an all-European currency called the Euro. Some stores already have prices marked in francs and Euros.

French national politics are fascinating. While only two parties dominate American politics, France has five major parties. From left to right, these include the reformed Communists (*PCF-Parti Communiste Francaise*), the moderate Socialists

(*PS-Parti Socialiste*), the aristocratically conservative UDF (*Union pour la Democratie Francaise*), the center-right RPR (*Rassemblement pour la République*), and the racist *Front National*. In general the UDF and RPR split the conservative middle ground and the Socialists dominate the liberal middle ground. But in France (unlike the USA) coalitions are generally necessary for any party to "rule." At the fringes you'll read about the racist *Front National* party, led by Jean-Marie Le Pen. Le Pen's "France for the French" platform calls for the expulsion of ethnic minorities and broader police powers. As unemployment has gone up so has the popularity of this far right party. Garnering 15 percent of a recent national vote, Le Pen has been able to force center-right parties farther in his direction. On the far left the reformed Communists, still recovering from the fall of the Soviet Union, have had to work more flexibly with the less radical Socialist and the environmental parties.

While the French president is elected by popular vote every seven years, he is more of a figurehead than his American counterpart. The more powerful Prime Minister is elected by the parliament (every three years). With five major parties, a single majority is rare—it takes a coalition to elect a Prime Minister. Currently the left is working together better than the right and France has a liberal Prime Minister (socialist Lionel Jospin) with a conservative president (Jacques Chirac). This "cohabitation," as it's called in French, is similar to an American president having to deal with a Congress controlled by an opposing party.

Let's Talk Telephones

Dialing Direct
Here are general instructions for making phone calls. International access codes and country codes are listed below. Most European countries use area codes, but France is one of the exceptions (see Europe's Exceptions, below).

Calling Between Countries: Dial the international access code (of the country you're calling from), the country code (of the country you're calling), the area code (if it it starts with zero, drop the zero), and the local number.

Calling Long Distance Within a Country: First dial the area code (including its zero), then the local number.

Europe's Exceptions: Some countries do not use area codes, such as France, Italy, Spain, Norway, and Denmark. To make an international call to these countries, dial the international access code (usually 00 in Europe, 011 for America), the country code (see chart below), then the local number in its entirety (okay, so there's one exception; for France, drop the initial zero of the local number). To make long-distance calls within any of these countries, simply dial the local number in its entirety.

International Access Codes

When dialing direct, first dial the international access code of the country you're calling from. For most countries, it's "00." Only the exceptions are noted below.

Estonia—800	Lithuania—810	Sweden—009
Finland—990	Russia—810	U.S.A./Canada—011
Latvia—800		

Country Codes

After you've dialed the international access code, then dial the code of the country you're calling.

Austria—43	Germany—49	Portugal—351
Belgium—32	Greece—30	Russia—7
Britain—44	Ireland—353	Spain—34
Czech Rep.—420	Italy—39	Sweden—46
Denmark—45	Latvia—371	Switzerland—41
Estonia—372	Lithuania—370	U.S.A./Canada—1
Finland—358	Netherlands—31	
France—33	Norway—47	

Handy Phone Numbers

Directory assistance for Paris and France: 12
Police: 17
Emergency medical assistance: 15

Calling Card Operators

AT&T: 0800 99 00 11
MCI: 0800 99 00 19
Sprint: 0800 99 00 87

Medical Needs

American Hospital (63 boulevard Victor Hugo, in suburb of Neuilly, Mo: Porte Maillot, then bus 82, tel. 01 46 41 25 25).
American Pharmacy: tel. 01 47 42 49 40 (Mo: Opéra).
Chiropratic Centers: tel. 01 43 54 26 25 or tel. 01 43 87 81 62.

Consulates/Embassies

U.S.A.: Consulate (2 rue St. Florentin, tel. 01 43 12 48 45), Embassy (2 avenue Gabriel, tel. 01 43 12 22 22). Same Métro stop, Concorde, for both.
Canada: Consulate and Embassy (35 avenue Montaigne, Mo: Franklin-Roosevelt, tel. 01 44 43 29 00).

Tourist and Transportation Information

Paris Tourist Information: tel. 01 45 26 94 82, tel. 01 43 43 33 24, or tel. 01 49 52 53 54; recorded information for events: tel. 01 49 52 53 56

Île de France Tourist Information (Paris area): tel. 01 42 60 28 62
Train (SNCF) information: tel. 08 36 35 35 35
Bus and Métro (RATP) information: tel. 08 36 68 77 14

Travel Companies

The American Express Travel Company (11 rue Scribe, Mo: Opéra, tel. 01 47 77 77 07) is a popular hangout for American travelers, but you'll find cheaper flights at:
- Cash and Go (34 avenue Champs-Élysées, Mo: Franklin-Roosevelt, tel. 01 53 93 63 63).
- Voyageurs en Amerique du Nord (55 rue Sainte Anne, Mo: Pyramides, tel. 01 42 86 17 30).
- CTS Voyages (20 rue des Carmes, Mo: Maubert Mutualité, tel. 01 43 25 00 76).

Airports

Charles de Gaulle: tel. 01 48 62 22 80
Orly: tel. 01 49 75 15 15

Airlines

Air France: tel. 0802 802 802 (fee call)
Air Canada: tel. 01 44 50 20 20
Air Lingus: tel. 01 47 42 95 00
Alitalia: tel. 01 44 94 44 00
American Airlines: tel. 0801 872 872 (fee call)
British Airways: tel. 0802 802 902 (fee call)
British Midlands: tel. 01 48 62 55 65
Continental: tel. 01 42 99 09 09
Delta: tel. 01 47 68 92 92

Iberia: tel. 01 40 47 80 90
KLM: tel. 01 44 56 18 18
Lufthansa: tel. 01 55 60 43 43
Northwest: tel. 01 42 66 90 00
Olympic: tel. 01 42 65 92 42
Sabena: tel. 08 36 67 88 00
SAS: tel. 01 53 43 25 25
Swissair: tel. 0802 30 04 00 (fee call)
TWA: tel. 01 49 19 20 00
United: tel. 0801 72 72 72 (fee call)
US Air: tel. 01 49 10 29 00

Classes

French-Language Classes

- American University of Paris (tel. 01 40 62 07 20, fax 01 40 62 07 17, Web site: www.aup.fr).
- France Ecole Langue (tel. 01 45 00 40 15, fax 01 45 00 53 41, Web site: www.france-langue.fr).

Cooking Schools

These have demonstration courses:
- Le Cordon Bleu (tel. 01 53 68 22 50, fax 01 48 56 03 96).
- Ritz Escoffier Ecole de Gastronomie Francaise (tel. 01 43 16 30 50).
- La Cuisine de Marie Blanche (tel. 01 45 51 36 34, fax 01 45 51 90 19).

Wine Classes
- Maison de la Vigne (tel. 01 47 20 20 76).

Climate Chart for Paris

First line is average daily low; second line is average daily high; third line, days of no rain.

J	F	M	A	M	J	J	A	S	O	N	D
34°	34°	39°	43°	49°	55°	58°	58°	53°	46°	40°	36°
43°	45°	54°	60°	68°	73°	76°	75°	70°	60°	50°	44°
16	15	16	16	18	19	19	19	19	17	15	14

Best Three-Week Trip of France

France's surprising range of sights includes the Alps, beaches, Germanic Alsace, prehistoric caves (Dordogne), D-Day memorials (Normandy), wine country (Burgundy), elegant châteaux (Loire), and sleepy hill towns (Provence). For our best three-week trip through this diverse country, see *Rick Steves' France, Belgium & the Netherlands.*

Basic French Survival Phrases

Hello (good day).	**Bonjour.**	bohn-zhoor
Do you speak English?	**Parlez-vous anglais?**	par-lay-voo ahn-glay
Yes. / No.	**Oui. / Non.**	wee / nohn
I'm sorry.	**Désolé.**	day-zoh-lay
Please.	**S'il vous plaît.**	see voo play
Thank you.	**Merci.**	mehr-see
Goodbye.	**Au revoir.**	oh vwahr
Where is...?	**Où est...?**	oo ay
...a hotel	**...un hôtel**	uhn oh-tehl
...a youth hostel	**...une auberge**	ewn oh-behrzh
	de jeunesse	duh zhuh-nehs
...a restaurant	**...un restaurant**	uhn rehs-toh-rahn
...a grocery store	**...une épicerie**	ewn ay-pee-suh-ree
...the train station	**...la gare**	lah gar
...the tourist info office	**...l'office du tourisme**	loh-fees dew too-reez-muh
Where are the toilets?	**Où sont les toilettes?**	oo sohn lay twah-leht
men / women	**hommes / dames**	ohm / dahm
How much is it?	**Combien?**	kohn-bee-an
Cheaper.	**Moins cher.**	mwan shehr
Included?	**Inclus?**	an-klew
Do you have...?	**Avez-vous...?**	ah-vay-voo
I would like...	**Je voudrais...**	zhuh voo-dray
...a ticket.	**...un billet.**	uhn bee-yay
...a room.	**...une chambre.**	ewn shahn-bruh
...the bill.	**...l'addition.**	lah-dee-see-ohn
one	**un**	uhn
two	**deux**	duh
three	**trois**	twah
four	**quatre**	kah-truh
five	**cinq**	sank
six	**six**	sees
seven	**sept**	seht
eight	**huit**	weet
nine	**neuf**	nuhf
ten	**dix**	dees
At what time?	**À quelle heure?**	ah kehl ur
Just a moment.	**Un moment.**	uhn moh-mahn
Now.	**Maintenant.**	man-tuh-nahn
today / tomorrow	**aujourd'hui / demain**	oh-zhoor-dwee / duh-man

For more user-friendly French phrases, check out *Rick Steves'
French Phrase Book and Dictionary* or *Rick Steves' French, Italian &
German Phrase Book and Dictionary*.

American Cathedral.

The mission of the Cathedral, properly known as the Cathedral Church of the Holy Trinity, is to share the good news of God in Christ by worship, word and example, as a parish church in the city of Paris and as a cathedral in Europe, using the richness of our American and Anglican heritage to serve the common good. We pursue this mission through fellowship, education, stewardship and outreach for both our parish family and the greater Paris community.

Address: 23, avenue George V, Paris 75008
Telephone: 01 53 23 84 00
Metro: George V or Alma Marceau
Services – Sunday: 9:00 a.m. Holy Eucharist, Rite I; 11:00 a.m. Holy Eucharist, Rite II
Third Sunday: 5:00 p.m. Solemn Evensong
Monday-Friday: 9.15 a.m. Morning Prayer; 12:30 p.m. Wednesday, Holy Eucharist and Healing Service in English (Sept. - June)
The Cathedral and the office are open Monday-Friday 9:00 AM to 5:00 PM
The church is also open Saturday morning.

Barnes&Noble, Inc.
500 16th Street
Denver, CO 80202
303-825-9166 03-02-00 S02854 R005

CUSTOMER RECEIPT COPY

| Rick Steves' Paris | 12.95 |
| 1562614681 | |

| SUB TOTAL | 12.95 |
| SALES TAX | .95 |

TOTAL 13.90

AMOUNT TENDERED

VISA 13.90

CARD #:	4495739000352713
EXP DATE	0401
AMOUNT	13.90
AUTH CODE	065101

TOTAL PAYMENT   13.90
Thanks for shopping at Barnes & Noble!
#37485 03-02-00 12:39P BC

Booksellers Since 1873

If you are not satisfied with your purchase for any reason you may return it in salable condition accompanied by this receipt within 30 days.

If you are not satisfied with your purchase for any reason you may return it in salable condition accompanied by this receipt within 30 days.

Road Scholar Feedback for Paris 1999

*We're all in the same travelers' school of hard knocks. Your feedback
helps us improve this guidebook for future travelers. Please fill this out
(attach more info or any tips/favorite discoveries if you like) and send it
to us. As thanks for your help, we'll send you our quarterly travel
newsletter free for one year. Thanks! Rick*

**Of the recommended accommodations/restaurants used,
which was:**

Best _____

    Why? _____

Worst _____

    Why? _____

**Of the sights/experiences/destinations recommended by this
book, which was:**

Most overrated _____

    Why? _____

Most underrated _____

    Why? _____

Best ways to improve this book:

_____

I'd like a free newsletter subscription:

___ Yes   ___ No   ___ Already on list

Name

_____

Address

_____

City, State, Zip

_____

E-mail Address

    Please send to: ETBD, Box 2009, Edmonds, WA 98020

Jubilee 2000—Let's Celebrate the Millennium by Forgiving Third World Debt

Let's ring in the millennium by convincing our government to forgive the debt owed to us by the world's poorest countries. Imagine spending over half your income on interest payments alone. You and I are creditors and poor countries owe us more than they can pay.

Jubilee 2000 is a worldwide movement of concerned people and groups—religious and secular—working to cancel the international debts of the poorest countries by the year 2000.

Debt ruins people: In the poorest countries, money needed for health care, education, and other vital services is diverted to interest payments.

Mozambique, with a per capita income of $90 and life expectancy of 40, spends over half its national income on interest. This poverty brings social unrest, civil war, and often costly humanitarian intervention by the U.S.A. To chase export dollars, desperate countries ruin their environment. As deserts grow and rain forests shrink, the world suffers. Of course, the real suffering is among local people born long after some dictator borrowed (and squandered) that money. As interest is paid, entire populations go hungry.

Who owes what and why? Mozambique is one of 41 countries defined by the World Bank as "Heavily Indebted Poor Countries." In total, they owe $200 billion. Because these debts are unlikely to be paid, their market value is only a tenth of the face value (about $20 billion). The U.S.A.'s share is under $2 billion.

How can debt be canceled? This debt is owed mostly to the U.S.A., Japan, Germany, Britain, and France either directly or through the World Bank. We can forgive the debt owed directly to us and pay the market value (usually 10 percent) of the debts owed to the World Bank. We have the resources. (Norway, another wealthy creditor nation, just unilaterally forgave its Third World debt.) All America needs is the political will . . . people power.

While many of these poor nations are now democratic, corruption is still a concern. A key to Jubilee 2000 is making certain that debt relief reduces poverty in a way that benefits ordinary people: women, farmers, children, and so on.

Let's celebrate the new millennium by giving poor countries a break. For the sake of peace, fragile young democracies, the environment, and countless real people, forgiving this debt is the right thing for us in the rich world to do.

Tell Washington, DC.: If our government knows this is what we want, it can happen. Learn more, write letters, lobby legislators, or even start a local Jubilee 2000 campaign. For details, contact Jubilee 2000 (tel. 202/783-3566, www.j2000usa.org). For information on lobbying Congress on J2000, contact Bread for the World (tel. 800/82-BREAD, www.bread.org).

Faxing Your Hotel Reservation

Most hotel managers know basic "hotel English." Faxing is the preferred method for reserving a room. It's more accurate and cheaper than telephoning and much faster than writing a letter. Use this handy form for your fax. Photocopy and fax away.

One-Page Fax

To: _____ @ _____
            hotel   fax

From: _____ @ _____
            name   fax

Today's date: ____ /_____ /____
                       day   month   year

Dear Hotel _____,

Please make this reservation for me:

Name: _____

Total # of people: _____   # of rooms: _____   # of nights: _____

Arriving: ____ /_____ /____ My time of arrival (24-hr clock): _____
                 day   month   year   (I will telephone if I will be late)

Departing: ____ /_____ /____
                    day   month   year

Room(s):   Single___   Double___   Twin___   Triple___   Quad___

With: Toilet___   Shower___   Bath___   Sink only___

Special needs: View___   Quiet___   Cheapest Room___

Credit card: Visa___   MasterCard___   American Express___

Card #: _____

Expiration Date:_____

Name on card: _____

You may charge me for the first night as a deposit. Please fax or mail me confirmation of my reservation, along with the type of room reserved, the price, and whether the price includes breakfast. Thank you.

_____
Signature

_____
Name

_____
Address

_____
City   State   Zip Code   Country

_____
E-mail Address

INDEX